Powers of the Real

Harvard East Asian Monographs 424

Powers of the Real

Cinema, Gender, and Emotion in Interwar Japan

Diane Wei Lewis

Published by the Harvard University Asia Center
Distributed by Harvard University Press
Cambridge (Massachusetts) and London 2019

Printed in the United States of America

The Harvard University Asia Center publishes a monograph series and, in coordination with the Fairbank Center for Chinese Studies, the Korea Institute, the Reischauer Institute of Japanese Studies, and other facilities and institutes, administers research projects designed to further scholarly understanding of China, Japan, Vietnam, Korea, and other Asian countries. The Center also sponsors projects addressing multidisciplinary and regional issues in Asia.

Library of Congress Cataloging-in-Publication Data

Names: Lewis, Diane Wei, 1979- author.
Title: Powers of the real : cinema, gender, and emotion in interwar Japan / Diane Wei Lewis.
Other titles: Harvard East Asian monographs ; 424.
Description: Cambridge, Massachusetts : Published by the Harvard University Asia Center, 2019. | Series: Harvard East Asian monographs ; 424 | Includes bibliographical references and index.
Identifiers: LCCN 2018057676| ISBN 9780674241152 (hardcover : alk. paper) | ISBN 9780674241169 (pbk. : alk. paper)
Subjects: LCSH: Kanto Earthquake, Japan, 1923, in motion pictures. | Motion Pictures—Japan—History—20th century. | Emotions in motion pictures. | Sex differences in mass media. | Japan—Civilization—1912–1926. | Japan—Civilization—1926–1945.
Classification: LCC PN1993.5.J3 L48 2019 | DDC 791.430952—dc23
LC record available at https://lccn.loc.gov/2018057676

Index by Arc Indexing, Inc.

♾ Printed on acid-free paper

Last figure below indicates year of this printing
28 27 26 25 24 23 22 21 20 19

For my teachers

Contents

Illustrations

Acknowledgments

The research and writing for this book took shape over many years and several stages. I am indebted to many for the incredible support and suggestions I received along the way. This project began at the University of Chicago, where my fascination with the connections among cinema, mass culture, and modernity was indelibly shaped by my advisers, Michael Raine, Tom Gunning, and Michael Bourdaghs, and courses with Miriam Hansen, Loren Kruger, Jim Lastra, and Yuri Tsivian. Julia Gibbs was a mentor and invaluable resource, as well as a friend. Fellow students were my sounding board, in Chicago and beyond—especially Doron Galili, Alan Goodrich, Laura Lee, Katharina Loew, Dan Morgan, Christina Petersen, Scott Richmond, Ariel Rogers, Adrienne Seely, and Junko Yamazaki.

My colleagues at Washington University in St. Louis have been an amazing source of support and motivation. It has been a true joy to work in their company. Gaylyn Studlar, Bill Paul, Colin Burnett, Philip Sewell, Rebecca Copeland, Marvin Marcus, Bob Hegel, Lori Watt, Zhao Ma, Rebecca Wanzo, Amber Musser, John Powers, and Caroline Kita were among many who animated my thinking with their ideas and advice. Early versions of chapter 6 were presented at the East Asian Studies Colloquium and the Women, Gender, and Sexuality Studies Colloquium. I especially thank Amber Musser and Rebecca Copeland for their generous feedback on this research. I am also grateful to the College of Arts & Sciences, Washington University in St. Louis, for a much appreciated book subvention.

This project would not have been possible without access to valuable resources and collections at many institutions. In particular, I thank the Waseda University Tsubouchi Memorial Theatre Museum; the National Film Archive of Japan; Shōchiku Ōtani Library; Kawakita Memorial Film Institute; National Diet Library; Harvard University Yenching Library; the Makino Collection, C. V. Starr East Asian Library, Columbia University; Tokyo Metropolitan Library; and the libraries at the University of Chicago and Washington University in St. Louis.

Grants and fellowships made it possible for me to acquire necessary training and focus on my research and writing at key junctures. Heartfelt thanks to Imai Hisae, Hayashi Toshio, and Hamaguchi Miyuki at the Japan Foundation Japanese-Language Institute, Kansai. During my language training there, the Japan Foundation supported the valuable mentoring I received from Tomita Mika at Ritsumeikan University as well as several research trips to Osaka and Tokyo.

The bulk of my research at the dissertation stage was conducted on a Fulbright-Hays Dissertation Research Abroad grant in Tokyo, where I was fortunate to attend courses by the brilliant scholars Saitō Ayako and Yomota Inuhiko at Meiji Gakuin University and Komatsu Hiroshi at Waseda University. My thanks to Aaron Gerow, Jonathan Hall, Pat Noonan, Paul Roquet, Ken Shima, Naoki Yamamoto, Alex Zahlten, and others with whom I overlapped in Tokyo. You asked questions, shared resources, and clarified my thinking about emotion and the Great Kanto Earthquake.

I was able to complete the dissertation with the support of a Center for East Asian Studies, University of Chicago, Japanese Studies Dissertation Writing Fellowship and immediately began reexamining my assumptions about what exactly this book was about as a postdoctoral fellow at the Reischauer Institute of Japanese Studies at Harvard University. Eric Rentschler, Tomiko Yoda, Aaron Gerow, and William Gardner read chapters and pushed me to rethink the stakes of the project in a book workshop organized by the amazing Stacie Matsumoto. Roy Chan enlivened long days in a shared office at the Harvard Asia Center with daily conversations over cups of tea, devastating insights, and advice that stuck with me for years and years of research and writing to come.

A Japan Society for the Promotion of Science postdoctoral fellowship allowed me to return to Meiji Gakuin University in 2012 and continue researching under the guidance of Saitō Ayako. Her study screenings at the National Film Archive of Japan made it possible for me to view rare film prints, and her research has provided an incomparable model for viewing Japanese film history through the lenses of gender, identification, and the body. Roland Domenig pointed me to invaluable resources (some of which I borrowed from his library). Thanks too to Takasaki Ikuko, Abe Kurumi, and Matsukawa Yuma for your warm friendship and help with my research. Once again, Komatsu Hiroshi humbled me with his incredible kindness and advice. Thanks to Johan Nordstrom, Chie Niita, Taniguchi Norie, and many others who graciously offered suggestions and shared materials, time after time.

Revising and finalizing the manuscript was a collaborative effort. At the Harvard University Asia Center Publications Program, Bob Graham expertly and efficiently guided me through the publication process. My readers, Daisuke Miyao and an anonymous reviewer, provided penetrating critical feedback that allowed me to understand my core investments in this project better than ever before. Markus Nornes offered pages of notes and hours of advice as I began revisions, and Lori Watt shared extensive comments on my updated chapters with a magical sense for language, style, and argumentation. Thanks to Tyler Gahrs for cross-checking the translation and original text of *Der Meister*, Kaoru Tamura for helping me prepare requests for images, and Torrie Hester and Andie Divelbiss for helping me check the typeset pages and proofreading. I also thank Omuka Toshiharu; Nishizawa Harumi at the Museum of Modern Art, Kamakura & Hayama; Okada Hidenori and Kamiya Makiko at the National Film Archive of Japan; and the Tokyo Metropolitan Library for its help in acquiring images.

Portions of chapter 5 previously appeared in the proceedings of the 2013 Association for Japanese Literary Studies annual conference on Performance and Japanese Literature.

Love and thanks to all my friends who shared in this journey. You kept me going with advice, perspective, and support. My gratitude especially to Michael Cronin, Phil Kaffen, Luis Rego, Hiroko and Shūji Tachibanazono, Michael Papish and the Papish family, Colin Burnett, Rebecca Wanzo, and Renee Thompson. I am also grateful to my parents, Jim Lewis and Anne Kuan, for supporting me through this long and mysterious process with optimism, patience, encouragement, and curiosity. Finally, to my longtime interlocutor and my partner, Michael, thank you for dreaming and believing. And to our son, who arrived just as this book was being finished: I look forward to learning so much from you.

Note on Japanese Names and Translations

Japanese names for individuals primarily working and writing in Japan are written family name first, as is customary in Japanese. All translations from Japanese to English are mine, unless otherwise indicated.

INTRODUCTION

In the spring of 1921, the *Tokyo asahi shinbun* reported on the strange case of Kuma Toshi, a maid employed in the Nishi-sugamo home of a Tokyo Imperial University law student. The beautiful fifteen-year-old girl from Hokkaido was adored by her employers and so prized by her mistress that she frequently joined the lady of the house at the theater and the movies. On March 14, Kuma visited the Koyamakan movie theater in the nearby neighborhood of Ōtsuka and watched a European film in which the protagonist, a servant her own age, set fire to her employer's estate, became a vagabond, and achieved fame as a successful French actress. Seemingly "possessed" by the actress in the film, Kuma returned home and set fire to her employer's storehouse. Her employer extinguished the blaze, explained the danger involved, and delicately expressed concern for the girl, but Kuma repeated the arson on March 19, 20, 21, and 23, leaving the family no choice but to turn her in to authorities.[1]

Over the next few years, such tales of "movie madness" became a veritable genre of crime reporting in Japan. Sensational newspaper and magazine articles warned of an epidemic of delusional aspiring actresses sweeping the country. The article "Miserable Aspiring Actresses Lured by the Hell of Vanity!" ("Kyoei jigoku ni akogareru, kanashiki joyū shigansha!"), published in Nikkatsu (Nippon Katsudō Shashin) film company–affiliated magazine *Nikkatsu gahō* (Nikkatsu illustrated) in 1926 included cases of girls stricken with movie fever from all over Japan. Stories described young girls from rural areas running away in hopes of becoming stars, only to be robbed, kidnapped, raped, or sold into prostitution. The reports reflect widespread concerns regarding the relationship between cinema, women's sexual agency, and geographic mobility as well as more generally a growing awareness of cinema's expanding address to and power over spectators.

These stories frame cinema as facilitating new (forbidden) forms of identity and self-expression. Tales of movie madness depicted aspiring actresses as rebels. Reports describe studios and police stations as being utterly overwhelmed by crowds of applicants. Consider headlines such as "Dreaming of Being Famous Actresses, Women Leave Home and Sweep Kamata" ("Meijoyū o yumemite, Kamata e oshiyoseru iede onna") and "To the Depths of Hell: Details of Crimes That Accompany Descending Throng of Actresses" ("Naraku no dontei e, mizukara shizumu joyū shigansha no mure, sore ni shitagau hanzai no iro iro").[2] These reports characterized aspiring actresses as ordinary women who refused socially and economically subordinate positions and were determined to revolt, no matter what the physical and psychological cost.

Numerous examples of aspiring actresses' exploits were compiled in the article "Isn't It Tragic, the Corpses of Aspiring Actresses!" ("Itamashiki kana, joyū shigansha no mukuro") by Matsumoto Yoshirō, an *Asahi* newspaper reporter, as part of a series on aspiring actress crimes in *Nikkatsu gahō* magazine. Matsumoto describes silk factory workers in Toyohashi in Aichi prefecture, aged seventeen and eighteen, who left their jobs declaring, "If we can't become actresses, we won't return home." They were eventually apprehended by police and forced to go back to their jobs.[3] A fifteen-year-old girl from Fukui prefecture occupied a studio, saying, "I won't work unless you make me an actress." She was ultimately driven away, and the police picked her up wandering around Kyoto while contemplating suicide.[4] Another story centers on a fifty-year-old Tokyo man whose job was installing *fusuma* (sliding paper doors) in Honjo homes before the Great Kanto Earthquake. After losing his wife in the disaster, he became the sole caretaker of their two children and struggled to keep them in school. His sixteen-year-old daughter grew up to be "movie crazy" (*katsudōkyō to nari*) and hellbent on becoming a film actress. The father attempted to punish her and even tried to keep her home by cutting off her hair while she slept. When the girl awoke to discover her father's deed, she became tearful and enraged and ran away. Her eleven-year-old brother left home to find her, and neither was ever heard from again.[5] A bright young woman from Tōyama, Fukuoka prefecture, aged eighteen, ran away to Kyoto after graduating from high school with honors. She was picked up from lodgings opposite Kyoto Station in the act of writing this note: "If I don't attain my goal [of becoming a film actress], I'll kill myself." The police took her into protective custody, called her father, and sent her home.[6]

In the first decades of cinema in Japan, discussions of cinema and delinquency generally focused on the movie theater and entertainment district as dangerous spaces. Public discourse concerned the thefts and assaults that took place in darkened venues and in the midst of large crowds. By the mid-1920s, however, concern had shifted toward cinema's influence over audiences, and journalists examined the role films played in manufacturing copycat behavior and spreading urban culture across Japan. The focus of moral concern moved away from the local effects of urban amusement centers to take up a new issue: cinema's ability to act at a distance. This shift can be linked to the expansion of the Japanese film industry, the rise of the mass audience for cinema, and changes in cinema's spectatorial address. In new popular representations of cinema's influence, the bodies and behaviors that best exemplified cinema's reach and power over spectators belonged to women.

Why was cinema's address to a mass audience and its influence over spectators represented in the cultural imaginary by images of women? In stark contrast to the top-down modernization project initiated by Japan's political and economic leaders during the Meiji period (1868–1912), the modernity of mass culture was generated from below and widely perceived as democratic.[7] A popular culture of magazines, films, and consumer products sought broad appeal and targeted new audiences, spreading rapidly by reaching out to untapped female consumers.[8] This led leftist critic Hirabayashi Hatsunosuke (1892–1931) to describe the spread of consumer capitalism as a "feminization of culture."[9] More recently, scholars such as Miriam Silverberg have described mass culture of the late Taishō period (1912–26) and early Shōwa period (1926–89) as a site of popular mobilization that created "consumer-subjects" and revealed tensions between official discourse and commercial culture.[10] As Silverberg points out, the powerful ability of mass media to solicit the public could challenge or reinforce the mechanisms through which Japanese officialdom interpellated imperial subjects. In this context, images of women enthralled by mass media not only reflected alarm regarding reconfigured families, sexual mores, and gender roles, but also provided a metaphor for broader concerns about internationalization and national sovereignty, the corrosive effects of materialism, and the changing nature of citizenship and the public sphere—all of which can be traced to the spreading influence of media and consumer culture.

The 1920s are said to have inaugurated the "age of the mass society" in Japan.[11] This decade witnessed exponential growth in mass media and commercial industries. Transformations in the Japanese film industry—including the use of actresses rather than female impersonators, the emergence of the star system, and the shift to and centralization of the film industry in Kyoto (which became known as the "Hollywood of Japan")—contributed to the commodification of Japanese cinema and its increasing imbrication with a burgeoning consumer culture that was widely perceived as feminizing. As a result of these transformations, emotion in cinema and film culture was often linked to women's culture and frequently described in disparaging terms reserved for "feminine" weaknesses, such as sentimentality, narcissism, materialism, frivolousness, and overidentification. The growth of mass media took off after a devastating national disaster, the Great Kanto Earthquake of 1923, and coincided with ongoing social and political upheaval caused by rapid modernization. In the 1920s, a surge in populist movements, labor disputes, and radical leftist activism, along with changing lifestyles influenced by Western film and fashion, raised challenges to entrenched political and cultural hierarchies. Together with the catastrophic earthquake, ongoing political struggles heightened the stakes for thinking about cinema as a powerful experiential medium able to connect large segments of the public and shape popular sentiment. Although many scholars have examined the role that mass media and consumer culture played in disseminating images of Western modernity in Japan, shaping new identities and cultural practices, less attention has been paid to how the rise of commercial media culture in a time of national crisis drew intense scrutiny to the affects and emotions associated with these changes. These transformations drew special scrutiny because they took place against the background of the Great Kanto Earthquake, a shocking national tragedy that imbued emotion with new importance in the public sphere, boosted newspaper sales, and stimulated hunger for entertainment and escapism.

Mass culture and technological media enabled new forms of intimacy and emotional intensity. The 1920s provides fascinating insights into how the commodification and technological manipulation of imagination, emotion, and desire were perceived as "new." What is distinct about 1920s media culture is not simply a matter of volume or scale, even though the growing ubiquity of modern media and their unprecedented reach are crucial to how cinema's effects were imagined in this period. What is more important was the shared sense that the affective connections forged by modern media in the postearthquake context were qualitatively different than anything that had come before. In other words, what had transformed was not simply the variety or amount of information and images, nor the increased speed and distance of media circulation—there was something new about the *feeling* of modernity. As representations of the Great Kanto Earthquake make clear, public feeling was now mediated by mass-produced representations that relied on machine technology for their realism, immediacy, and scale. Cinema participated in a transformation of the texture of everyday experience and what could be known and sensed through media. Just as the rise of internet-based social media has changed our current sense of publics, privacy, intimacy, and the social, in 1920s Japan new technologically enabled and commodified forms of intimacy and emotion became increasingly visible in conjunction with the rise of cinema as a mass medium. This is why it can be argued that the controversy regarding the feminization of culture relates to a far broader shift in the meaning and importance attributed to emotion—and not simply to women's identities and their participation in public life. This book investigates how filmmakers, activists, policy makers, intellectuals, and artists reacted to this shift, focusing in particular on public discourses that figured cinema's persuasive realism in terms of the emotional and affective dimensions of film-going. These discourses produced new vernacular understandings of the medium and new concerns with "feminine" (though not necessarily women's) desires and subjectivity.

To this end, I offer a historically situated consideration of film realism that foregrounds emotion as integral to the experience of cinema and to the perception of cinema as meaningfully interwoven with everyday life. In cinema studies, "realism" is a debated term with many definitions. It is generally understood in terms of verisimilitude or the semblance of reality, its creation by means of technological and material properties of the cinematic image, and certain narrative and expressive strategies that may or may not be unique to film. Realism may be defined variously as a set of stylistic practices that define the work of a particular director, film genre, or film movement. The realism of *Avatar* (dir. James Cameron, 2009) is not the realism of French filmmaker Robert Bresson, nor that of 1930s and 1940s British documentary film. Therefore, realism must be carefully defined for specific critical purposes and historical contexts, though it may also be examined more broadly and theoretically, not simply in terms of individual texts or a single body of work but in terms of the medium's physical, technological, ideological, or perceptual properties.[12]

My work here insists on the emotional and identificatory structures that produce "realism" as a form of relation between viewer and viewed. In addition, I argue that realism is not exclusively a question of what can be seen and sensed (the question of verisimilitude) but often involves desire, imagination, and even unreasonable and impractical forms of attachment. Finally, I treat realism as a form of power that can be used to captivate and persuade. These several aspects of film realism in 1920s Japan—the powers of the real—are explored from a variety of perspectives in this book.

This approach returns us to the concept of identification, which has long been associated with the question of realism in film studies, particularly since the 1970s, when apparatus theory and feminist film theory attributed the seeming coherence and plentitude of the cinematic diegesis to the careful management of spectatorial identification and desire in narrative film. Much 1970s ideology critique regarded cinema as a *dispositif* (formation or apparatus) that reproduced pleasurable structures of infantile self-recognition and gratification. For these theorists, identification and desire were the twin pillars of cinema's illusory realism. They argued that classical Hollywood cinema allowed (male) spectators the narcissistic pleasure of identifying with an idealized proxy, the voyeuristic-sadistic pleasure of peering at beautiful (female) bodies as sexual objects, and the transcendental pleasure of identification with a mobile, invisible camera.[13] Even theorists who contested the notion that the pleasures of classical Hollywood cinema were always empowering and self-affirming, always sadistic and never masochistic, always for men at the expense of women, and who abandoned the Freudian Oedipal stage or Lacanian mirror stage as the basis for their readings, did not reject the central tenet that identification and desire are what gird the powerfully seductive fantasy of narrative cinema and its illusory realism.[14] Later cultural historians extended these arguments to how films cater to fantasies of recognition and social mobility as well as gratify consumerist desires, thereby intensifying spectatorial involvement and projection.[15] Recent scholarly attention to questions of affect and emotion has led to a reappreciation of historical film criticism and film theory that foregrounds questions of identification and desire. A deeper understanding of emotion further contributes to this appraisal.[16] Emotion is often implied in these discussions but undertheorized.

How does a cultural historian deal with emotion and sensation? This book proposes to examine cinema and the politics of emotion in interwar Japan, but what does that politics consist of? Emotion and sensation seem to resist such an examination, in part because of what Lauren Berlant has described as the political incoherence and ambivalence of "the intimate," which dwells "in *proximity* to the political" but cannot always easily be enlisted in political projects.[17]

Rather than conceiving of emotions as issuing from inside individuals or relating to the properties of things, I generally follow scholars such as Sara Ahmed in thinking about emotion in terms of orientations and effects that arise from the circulation of objects and signs.[18] Ahmed introduces the concept of "affective economies" to describe the sociopolitical production and management of emotions in terms of differences and alignments rather than inherent values. To analyze emotion as an economy means to recognize "relationships of difference and displacement without positive value. That is, emotions work as a form of capital: affect does not reside positively in the sign of commodity, but is produced as an effect of its circulation."[19] In Japan, commentators grappling with the rise of cinema as a mass medium conceived of its power and influence in these very terms, recognizing cinema's ability to produce, reinforce, exploit, or derail social and governmental mechanisms whose operations were essential for the production of identity and value. This ability was identified as the source of cinema's importance and its dangers. Although I cannot fully retrieve the emotions, feelings, sensations, or affects of interwar Japanese, I will examine how those feelings were nominated, evaluated, and positioned within larger discourses and assigned to particular film narratives and representations. Throughout the book, I continually ask: what does it mean to write a cultural history of emotion and sensation? What does a politics of emotion consist of?

To pursue these questions, it is of the utmost importance to address the specific historical, cultural, and geopolitical conditions of Japanese modernity and modernization. This allows us to understand how these contexts gave rise to particular constructions of film spectatorship in the interwar period—a project in some ways initiated by Aaron Gerow but which resonates with other cultural histories of the "modern gaze" from Yoshimi Shun'ya (1987), Takashi Fujitani (1998), Noriko Aso (2013), and others.

In the 1970s, French film theorist Christian Metz argued that the film spectator is a canny viewer who takes fetishistic pleasure in cinema's substitution of imaginary presence for real lack. Metz posited that what makes cinema unique in comparison to live performance is that in narrative films the unreality of the signifier *enhances* the cinematic illusion.[20] We find a similar idea—that cinema is a paradoxically realistic fantasy that derives its potency from its contradictory qualities—in popular discourses on cinema in 1920s Japan. Only now, that phantasmatic realism is given a geopolitical turn of the screw. As Miriam Hansen has argued, in the 1920s and 1930s, classical Hollywood cinema "offered a sensory-reflexive horizon for the contradictory experience of modernity" around the world—contradictory because American cinema "meant different things to different people and publics, both at home and abroad," and Hollywood films and their local versions "not only had a leveling impact on indigenous cultures but also challenged prevailing social and sexual arrangements and advanced new possibilities of identity and cultural styles."[21] This vexed relationship of Japanese spectators to spectral images of modernity—in other words, images of modernity that had yet to become a reality in Japan—is a powerful current in 1920s film discourse that must be examined more closely.

In particular, I explore the resonances that cinematic identification took on when imagined on a mass scale in modernizing Japan, during a period in which cinema offered attractive images of a consumerist cultural modernity that many commentators criticized as lacking in substance or authenticity. My approach makes visible the bodies, subjectivities, and desires that were used to define and evaluate cinema's illusions, which otherwise might go missing from more narrow film historical or film theoretical accounts that focus on specific studios, film texts, auteurs, or film theorists and critics. This research makes legible a broader, vernacular understanding of cinematic realism that linked cinema to women's purportedly vacuous but overwhelming desires, experiences, and identities.

I seek out the cinematic imagination through popular representations, political discourses, aesthetic practices, and media technologies that lie beyond film practice and film theory narrowly defined. By shifting attention away from film proper, I am better able to foreground a new modality of experience and sensation that was associated with cinema as well as, more broadly, technological media and consumer culture. As Weihong Bao has argued, affect is key for understanding the modern condition, its institutions, and especially "the consolidation and authentication of mass media as platforms of the public sphere and engines of social experience."[22] Bao usefully introduces a critical notion of cinema as an "affective medium," arguing that by conceiving of cinema in terms of its emotional, perceptual, and bodily interplay with the spectator, we can better grasp the shifting boundaries of what defines the cinematic medium in periods of dynamic industrial, aesthetic, cultural, and technological change. As I argue, careful attention to the cinematic imagination, as well as to the technological mediation of emotion, ideation, and behavior, is also crucial for understanding sociocultural transformations in Japan in the 1920s.

To be clear then, this will not be a history of film practices or film theories per se. I do not intend to define realism strictly in terms of film-specific (or even visually specific) stylistic practices. Nor is this book an intellectual history, even though it deals with the cinematic imagination writ large. Instead, these pages offer an examination of diverse and overlapping engagements with cinema as a mass medium and a form of popular culture, focusing in particular on the identification of cinematic realism with the medium's powerful sensory-affective address to a mass audience. My main argument is that the rise of the mass audience for cinema during a period of cultural instability and rapid social transformations created an urgent context for thinking about cinematic realism in terms of audience identification, imitation, and emotional response. This widespread fascination with cinema's persuasive sensory realism—and its representation as feminine or feminizing—is my primary concern. Discourses pertaining to cinema's reality status (its ontology) and its reality effects (its illusions) posed broader questions about the new lifestyles and experiences, new forms of identity and affiliation, and new fantasies and desires that consumer capitalism trafficked in.

I analyze numerous instances of this strain of thinking about cinema as expressed in and through a variety of forms: film productions, studio publicity, fan magazines, daily newspapers, artworks, film theory, moral panics, literature, cultural criticism, and political activism. Together, these examples suggest a pervasive understanding of film realism in terms of the medium's sensual and emotional persuasiveness, as well as its capacity to shape the values, identity, behavior, and reality of the beholder. This vernacular understanding is often only implicit to the discourses and practices I analyze, and thus could not properly be called a "theory" of film realism, however it does attest to a widely shared imaginary of the medium, which, as I will demonstrate, inspired positive, negative, and ambivalent reactions to cinema. Ideas about how films solicited identifications and produced mimetic responses were not simply attributed to the film medium or film form alone, but were also strongly linked to the rise of the mass audience for cinema. By focusing on cinema's extensive reach and its socially transformative aspects, this strain of thinking about cinematic realism identified cinema's most important attributes with modernity and mass culture. Mass culture produced new forms of identification and alienation, and cinema was just one arena for these new affective experiences.

The following three chapters focus on the Great Kanto Earthquake as a crucial event within the history of mass media in Japan. Chapters 1 and 2 examine how demand for images and information about the disaster stimulated the production of a wide variety of representations of the earthquake in different media forms. Chapter 1 focuses on earthquake documentary films and their use of montage to impose order and draw meaning from an event that staggered the imagination. I use the term *montage* loosely in this context to designate the strategy of assembling many partial views to create something greater than the sum of its parts.

Montage tactics created aesthetic interplay between the part and the whole, closeness and distance, the concrete and the abstract, distanced contemplation and sensory engagement. The strategy was not unique to earthquake documentary films, for public exhibitions, anthologies, photo collections, and special magazine issues also used sampling and juxtaposition to make sense of the catastrophe. I am interested in how montage allowed earthquake media producers to make productive use of practical, official, and ethical constraints on representation by mobilizing gaps, omissions, abstraction, and distance to suggest what could not be directly said or shown. In these representations, it is difficult not to see an emotional dialectic between overwhelming intimacy and incredible scale, between immediacy and distance. I argue that montage produces a strange relation between estrangement and sensory intensity, whereby alienation is not distancing but becomes the basis for more radical forms of relationality. Chapter 1 examines the dialectic between intimacy and alienation through the documentary films' use of space, particularly in how the films creatively exploit dissonance between spatial cues and tactile cues in their photography of Tokyo's ruins. Moving camera shots facilitate the viewer's ability to place themselves within the scene. At the same time, the disturbingly rummaged quality of unrecognizably transformed landscapes activates a haptic relation to the image, stymying the viewer's ability to project their body into a recessive illusionistic space. Filmmakers' choices in these films suggest their awareness of the contradictory qualities of the cinematic image at a time when cinematic conventions tended increasingly toward the creation of a stable, illusionistic, transparent, and fully dimensional diegetic space.

Chapter 2 focuses on fictional films about the Great Kanto Earthquake made by Tokyo film workers who survived the disaster and whose real-life experiences were publicized in conjunction with the films. What makes these fictional earthquake films unique is that they exemplify a new marshaling of film publicity and paratexts to intensify audience involvement, model spectatorial engagement, and authenticate the realism of cinema. I examine how the body of the actor was imagined as an indexical link to traumatic experiences that could not easily be expressed in images and words alone. As with the documentary films, the strategies used to enhance the earthquake melodrama films' realism reflect a shift in narrative and publicity strategies similar to what occurred in

American cinema in the 1910s. In Japan, as in the United States, an emerging star discourse provided access to actors' private lives, taught appreciation for the filmmaking craft, and contributed to deeper immersion in the cinematic image. At this moment in the development of the narrative film in Japan, such immersion could not rely on the film diegesis alone because of the insufficient realism and unstable representational practices of transitional-era Japanese films. What is at issue here, as with the earthquake documentaries, is the question of how filmmakers responded to the demand for realism at a time when Japanese films had not yet accomplished "narrative integration" or the "complete internalization of narrative enunciation within the text."[23] Chapter 1 frames this question with respect to the problem of emplacement: how might spectators have oriented themselves within or in relation to the space of films and meshed with a film's perceptual apparatus? Chapter 2 examines how film realism was bolstered by press discourse that encouraged spectators to "read in." This analysis provides an opportunity to reflect on the possibilities and limitations of using paratextual materials to imagine historical spectators and reconstruct their experiences. "Reading in," I argue, requires us to reflect on the heuristics of reading historical emotions and spectators' experiences.

The last chapter in the first section, chapter 3, attends to the rise of mass media after the Great Kanto Earthquake. The earthquake drew attention to cinema's ability to produce emotionally affecting images and harness public sentiment. At the same time, cinema's connections with commercial culture raised concerns about the authenticity and allure of cinematic images. Any consideration of film realism in this period must take into account this cultural politics.

This politics becomes the main focus of the second half of the book, which addresses how the rise of the mass audience for cinema in 1920s Japan produced new models for understanding cinematic absorption, pleasure, and identification that in their most general and extreme forms were imagined as "feminine" and "feminizing."

Chapter 4 examines how the persuasive sensory address of cinema was taken up in press articles that fueled moral panics about cinema's ability to blur the lines between fantasy and real life. In many ways, the aspiring actress panic of the mid-1920s epitomizes how the rise of the mass audience for cinema created new popular understandings of cinematic realism. Tellingly, commentators were especially preoccupied with the problem of rural women leaving their homes for the studios, hoping to imitate women they had seen on screen. My reading focuses on how this panic foregrounded "the liberating impulses and pathologies" that mass culture was imagined to unleash, and the role that cinema was believed to play in the production of exorbitant bodily, psychological, and emotional states.

This use of women's bodies and subjectivities as a site for imagining the transformations wrought by mass culture was not limited to the aspiring actress panic. In chapter 5, I examine two film-inspired works by interwar avant-garde artist Murayama Tomoyoshi (1901–77), who could very well be called the quintessential artist of Japan's media age. Murayama paid close attention to the emergence of new forms of stardom and consumer desire, and he was one of the first Japanese artists to use modern media celebrity and commercial culture as artistic inspirations. He dabbled in different media forms while maintaining a strong personal brand across his diverse works. This chapter examines Murayama's fascination with forms of affect and celebrity that operated within commercial mass culture. His works plumbed the shocking forms of intimacy and estrangement engendered by modernity, which he viewed as the result of new strategies to sell sex and celebrity, stimulate consumption, and gratify desire. Murayama used female bodies and feminizing experiences to reflect on tangled relationships between art and commerce, sexual liberation and sexual commodification, and self-expressive and sexually exploitative presentations of the body in modern media culture.

Finally, chapter 6 turns to the so-called feminization of culture and to the representation of women within the interwar proletarian arts movement. The movement strategically deployed markers of femininity and representations of women in sensational depictions of the victimization of the proletariat and the decadence of the bourgeoisie. I analyze this rhetorical use of female bodies and femininity through close analysis of two texts—one authorized by the movement and one unauthorized, one literary and one cinematic—that feature representations of women's bodies in extremis. In both cases, these representations were intended to create identification with capitalism's victims and thus foster proletarian consciousness. The works, Hayama Yoshiki's short story "Inbaifu" ("The Prostitute," 1925) and Suzuki Shigeyoshi's film *Nani ga kanojo o sō saseta ka* (*What Made Her Do It?*, 1930), demonstrate the "stickiness" of women's bodies within interwar media culture. Ahmed uses the concept of stickiness to refer to the capacity of certain objects to accrue associations and produce strong emotional reactions.[24] In 1920s Japan, women were imagined to be particularly susceptible to cinematic images and consumerist fantasies, and representations of women and signifiers of femininity were frequently used to produce strong textual effects and political sentiments. I analyze the political mobilization of excessive female bodies to attract, repel, and create radical forms of empathy premised on women's status as somehow both more than and less than men. This shows how sensational images of female suffering could be used to legitimate certain forms of media engagement while delegitimizing others. Of course, we cannot hope to understand how these texts work by simply reading such images "positively" or "negatively." Instead, we must think about the form of media engagement authorized by the text. This involves considering genre and medium as well as subject matter.

What I ultimately seek to explore through the readings in this book is the cultural politics of film realism in the age of mass media in Japan. A new concern with identification and mimesis in the 1920s discourse on realism can be linked to three factors. First, it emerges in part from the foregrounding of female behaviors in relation to mass culture, which often involved a problematization of fans' imitative behavior and emotional responses to media. This discourse gained traction through public conversations regarding the introduction of the film actress, cinema's undue influence over women, and notions of consumer culture as decadent, frivolous, and "feminizing." Second, the rise of the mass audience for cinema fostered greater awareness of film's ability to shape public sentiment. Third, the Great Kanto Earthquake created demand for "realism" and contributed to industrial and cultural shifts that hastened the emergence of Hollywood-style classical film narration in Japan. The catastrophe simultaneously raised the stakes for understanding and wielding cinema's power over spectators.

Attention to these issues allows us to understand how film was experienced and imagined in 1920s Japan. It draws our attention to new forms of fantasy and pleasure that propelled media consumption. It allows us to analyze the expanded sensorium of the decade and see how perception and emotion were shaped by new forms of media and technology.

My approach is influenced by modernity studies, early film histories, and cultural histories of Meiji, Taishō, and early Shōwa Japan—but also (and at times especially) media studies, with its emphasis on media ecologies, connectivity, and the mobilization of affect. The unreasonable affective investments solicited by media are now more than ever at issue with the increasing "feminization" of labor and consumption within the global economy. This study contributes to how we understand and historicize the emotionally invested consumer of commercial media, demonstrating the importance of gender to histories of technology and media transformation.

PART I

Backgrounds: The Great Kanto Earthquake and Mass Media

CHAPTER 1

Great Kanto Earthquake Documentary Films and the State

> We lost everything at once. Nothing but ruins in the distance as far as the eye can see . . . nothing but incomprehension and a total state of shock.
>
> So that, even now, we can't unsee the havoc we have seen . . . As long as the rumbling aftershocks continue every day . . . impulses of dread in our hearts, like an electric current, make it so we can't relax, we nervously rise to our feet.
>
> —Naturally, our artistic inspiration, the books we read, people saying something like words—none of it sticks inside our heads.
>
> In fact, we have truly become weaklings and cry babies.
>
> —Suzuki Kensaku, "Taishō buruburuki" [Record of the Taishō quake], *Nikkatsu gahō* (November 1923), 9

The Great Kanto Earthquake marks the beginning of a new appraisal of cinema as an important mass medium. The catastrophe was not only a powerful catalyst for the reorganization of the Japanese film industry; in its violence and immensity, the earthquake was instrumental in inspiring new aesthetic practices and crucial in reframing what was at stake in cinema's persuasive sensory representations and its address to a mass audience. Media producers achieved unprecedented realism in their representations of the earthquake through the use of technologically produced forms of immediacy, sensory intensity, and scale. New critical engagement with the material, technological, social, and sensory specificity of cinema generated a wide range of opinion on the significance of the medium. As this book demonstrates, commentators with very different social perspectives were invested in describing film's realism, power of persuasion, and somatic effects. As Miriam Hansen has argued, in the 1920s cinema was widely apprehended as a sensory-affective medium that shaped new ways of thinking and behaving and therefore could be regarded as an instrument for the "mass production of the senses." She writes,

> While the spread of urban-industrial technology, the large-scale disembedding of social (and gender) relations, and the shift to mass consumption entailed processes of real destruction and loss, there also emerged new modes of organizing vision and sensory perception, a new relationship with "things," different forms of mimetic experience and expression, of affectivity, temporality, and reflexivity, a changing fabric of everyday life, sociability, and leisure.[1]

We cannot ignore cinema's important role in this radical dislocation of habitual ways of seeing and rendering time and space. Great Kanto Earthquake documentary films allow us to reflect on cinema's capacity to produce profoundly compelling yet thrillingly disorienting representations of events.

In what follows, I pay close attention to how earthquake documentary films positioned viewers vis-à-vis the disaster. I am particularly interested in how these films informed viewers and solicited emotional and moral responses to the tragedy, as well as staged perceptual encounters with the Great Kanto Earthquake. Earthquake films feature a range of formal strategies to intensify affective engagement, which include manipulating the viewer's sense of space and place through the use of editing, framing, camera movement, and spatial and tactile cues. These films exemplify the aesthetic interplay between closeness and distance, part and whole, that characterizes many representations of the earthquake. This interplay foregrounds relations between signifier and signified and viewer and viewed, drawing attention to the production of affect through relationality. Cinematic techniques are used to create vivid impressions of immersive spaces and tactile effects that elicit strong bodily and affective responses. This produces conflicting impressions of recessive space and messy, bursting textures. Although many earthquake representations drew on established visual genres and familiar narrative formulas to clarify the meaning of the disaster and mobilize public sentiment in socially and culturally authorized ways, it is also necessary to pay attention to how earthquake films produced new forms of emotional and perceptual engagement.[2] Technologically produced images of the Great Kanto Earthquake contributed to the ongoing disembedding of habitual ways of viewing the world, and thus the emergence of new idioms of representing time, space, and experience. Moreover, media producers who used film and photography did not simply claim to represent the disaster with unrivaled realism but also boasted of the capacity of mass-produced images to reach a massive audience and used new technologies, new strategies of representation, and a new aesthetics of defamiliarization to enhance the novelty of their products.

In addition to close analysis of Great Kanto Earthquake documentary films, I examine the Japanese government's involvement in the film industry and its role in encouraging some film activities while censuring and censoring others. Modern, mass-produced "emotive" media such as Great Kanto Earthquake documentary films were instrumental in constructing the regional disaster as a national tragedy, due to their patriotic and emotional address to the nation and their grandiose, synoptic rendering of the disaster's events.[3] By the time of the earthquake, the Ministry of Education and the Imperial Household Ministry had already begun exploring the influence of motion pictures on audiences and made early efforts to publicize the imperial family using film. The Great Kanto Earthquake marks the Japanese government's first serious foray into film production. Earthquake documentary films were shown all over the country, in civic halls and schools as well as commercial cinemas, at fundraisers, and accompanied by lectures. As these films swept the country, Ōsawa Jō writes, they provided a startling revelation of "the potential power of documentary film as a mass medium."[4] Analyzing earthquake mass media, J. Charles Schencking underscores the moral tone of many earthquake representations, which were instrumental in building support for reconstruction, memorializing the tragedy, and encouraging charitable giving. Not all earthquake representations, however, were intended to "instill hope and compel recognition."[5] Media producers also commodified the sights and experiences of the earthquake-ravaged capital, translating its physical and psychological shocks into sensational consumer experiences. Many images of the dead, such as postcards displaying prostitutes' corpses in Yoshiwara, were violent, voyeuristic, and unsettling.[6] Earthquake documentary films were temporarily banned in Tokyo, and the government forced filmmakers and distributors to remove potentially incendiary images from their films. The government's interactions with the film industry at this time provide a fascinating lens through which to examine the state's complex attitudes toward cinema and its ability to educate, arouse strong emotions, and forge affiliations.

Part of this discussion will revolve around close analysis of earthquake documentary films, but it should be noted that for a variety of reasons, it is difficult to know to what extent surviving film prints represent what audiences actually saw. Earthquake films were frequently reedited and re-screened. Even if we examine existing film prints, historical publicity, and censorship records, we still have little sense whether surviving films are "complete" or accurately reflect what was exhibited in 1923. Regular film censorship and recordkeeping did not begin until 1925, and the content and length of earthquake footage shown could vary from screening to screening. It is impossible to know exactly how many earthquake documentary films were made, how often they were altered, and whether the versions we have are what most audiences saw. Nevertheless, research suggests that the most widely circulated film footage of the earthquake is included in most of the films that survive.[7] This provides some basis for making claims regarding historical audiences' viewings.[8]

Emerging Film Policy before the Earthquake

Until the Great Kanto Earthquake, there was no regular news film or documentary production in Japan. Regular documentary film production began with the development of mass communications in the 1920s and 1930s, when authorities became interested in using cinema for educational purposes and documenting transformations in Japanese society.[9] In the early 1910s, the Ministry of Education began monitoring the film industry and its impact on society, particularly youth, but did not actively begin producing films until after the earthquake. Until a designated film production budget was established in 1923, the Ministry of Education and the Imperial Household Agency conducted film activities on an ad hoc basis. Notably, much of this activity revolved around the crown prince and future Shōwa emperor Hirohito (1901–89). In the early 1920s, the government experimented with ways of achieving the nearly simultaneous mass dissemination of the prince's film image. This suggests a new appreciation of cinema's ability to consolidate and communicate the state's power.

The first films made of Hirohito were commissioned by the government on the occasion of his departure for a six-month trip to Europe in March 1921. Until this trip it was strictly forbidden to film any member of the imperial family.[10] Hirohito's journey was unprecedented and highly controversial when plans were first hatched in 1919, for no Japanese prince had ever traveled to the West. One of the main goals of the journey was to introduce Hirohito to the British royal family, allowing him to learn about modern rule directly from the monarchy on British soil. By 1918, Hirohito's father's health was rapidly deteriorating, and his grave illness was announced to the public in 1919. When Hirohito returned to Japan, the twenty-year-old prince formally assumed powers as regent until the Taishō emperor passed away in 1926. The European tour was intended to groom the prince for his future duties, particularly by encouraging the reclusive young man to adopt a more outgoing personality.[11] This also provided an opportunity to modernize the Japanese emperor system by adopting a more dynamic media policy. Nikkatsu (Nippon Katsudō Shashin Kabushiki Kaisha, est. 1912) and Shōchiku (est. 1920) were asked to film the prince's departure. After submitting petitions to the Imperial Household Ministry, the *Osaka mainichi shinbun* (with *Tokyo nichi nichi shinbun*) and the *Osaka asahi shinbun* were granted permission to film Hirohito in Europe. Hirohito left Japan March 3 and arrived in England May 9. The newspapers sent requests to affiliates in Europe (Evans/Gaumont and Williamson Film) to film footage that they fashioned into newsreels. The *Osaka mainichi shinbun* footage was first screened in film theaters in London in May, and the prince viewed the footage at the Japanese embassy in London on May 29. The film was then sent to Japan and released to the public after the emperor and empress had the opportunity to view the film privately at the Numazu Imperial Villa on June 6, 1921. Two days later, *Actuality of His Highness the Crown Prince on His Trip Abroad* (*Kotaishi Denka gogaiyū jikkyō*, Osaka Mainichi Shinbunsha and Tokyo Nichinichi Shinbunsha, 1921) became the very first film of the crown prince to be viewed by ordinary Japanese people at a special screening in Hibiya Park on June 8.[12] In the following months, films of Hirohito's travels were screened widely throughout Japan, distributed by film and newspaper companies, as well as sent on a nationwide tour sponsored by the Home Ministry that sent footage as far south as Kagoshima in Kyushu and as far north as Asahikawa in Hokkaido.[13]

Kamiya Makiko suggests that these events show the government's concerted effort to a create a single image of the prince to be viewed as the same content and via the same medium by many people simultaneously. A welcoming event was filmed upon Hirohito's return, and the footage was flown to Osaka the following day and disseminated quickly to other cities, allowing the same cinematic images to be seen across the country within a short time frame.[14] Whereas only select film companies and newspapers were granted limited filming permission on the prince's departure, many organizations were allowed to film his return. To Kamiya this indicates a rapidly developing media policy and concerted effort "to amplify public response" using new technology.[15]

Films documenting Hirohito's trip to Europe were primarily aimed at promoting the future emperor's public visibility; in contrast, once Hirohito returned to Japan, his film activities were used to promote the medium of cinema itself. On November 20, 1921, one day before Hirohito's formal investiture as regent, the Ministry of Education opened a three-week Motion Picture Exhibit (Katsudō Shashin Tenrankai) at the Yushima Seidō, a Confucian temple near Ueno Park. Yushima Seidō had been used as an exposition site since the Edo period (1603–1868) and was the original site of the Japanese national museum.[16] The prince regent was given a personal tour from museum director Tanahashi Gentarō on December 8. As part of his inspection, Hirohito watched several reels of the *Osaka mainichi shinbun* and *Tokyo nichi nichi shinbun* film *Actuality of His Highness the Crown Prince on His Trip Abroad* in a separate projection room. His visit to the exhibit was captured in two films commissioned by the Ministry of Education and filmed by cameramen from Nikkatsu, Shōchiku, Taishō Katsudō Shashin (Taikatsu), and Kokusai Katsudō Shashin (Kokkatsu): *Actuality of His Highness the Prince Regent's Inspection of the Motion Picture Exhibition* (*Sesshōnomiya Denka Katsudō Shashin Tenrankai gotairan jikkyō*) and *The Farewell Scenes of Kusunoki Masahige and His Son* (*Shigeki Nankō ketsubetsu*).[17] The first film shows the prince arriving at the exhibition hall by car and, having viewed the exhibition, inspecting a miniature set from the Shōchiku Kamata film *Nightmare* (*Akumu*, dir. Tamura Uichirō, 1921) about the Great Fire of Meireki (1657).

FIGURE 1.1 Hirohito (background right), in a military uniform with folded hands in white gloves, looks on during the performance of *The Farewell Scenes of Kusunoki Masahige and His Son*. Courtesy of the National Film Archive of Japan.

It ends with him about to view an open-air performance featuring film star Onoe Matsunosuke.[18] *The Farewell Scenes of Kusunoki Masahige and His Son* begins at this point, showing Onoe arriving at the outdoor set and portraying Lord Kusunoki parting from his son, Kusunoki Masatsura, at Sakurai (fig. 1.1).[19] The film concludes with the prince passing through the gate of the museum and leaving in a car. These actualities of Hirohito at the Motion Picture Exhibit were screened together at major film theaters just four days after the footage was shot.

It seems likely that the Ministry of Education and Imperial Household Ministry intended the Motion Picture Exhibit to enhance cinema's credibility before continuing with a more expansive film policy. Hirohito's visit conferred film with legitimacy and sanctioned the state's use of cinema. The Motion Picture Exhibit attracted more than 130,000 visitors before closing December 10. Thereafter the Ministry of Education planned its move into film distribution and production. In late August 1923, the Ministry of Education received orders from the Imperial Household Ministry to disseminate films pertaining to the imperial family.[20] Around the same time, the Ministry of Education established a designated budget for film production with roughly 100,000 yen from its budget for the Committee for Social Education (Shakai Kyōiku Iinkai).[21]

Then the Great Kanto Earthquake struck.

The Great Kanto Earthquake and Popular Entertainment

The Great Kanto Earthquake began two minutes before noon on September 1, 1923, measuring between 7.9 and 8.3 on the Richter scale.[22] The epicenter of the quake was located approximately ten to fifteen kilometers under the earth's surface and sixty kilometers south-southwest of Tokyo, off the coast of Odawara below the Sagami Bay. It shook the Kanto plain for approximately ten minutes, affecting a total of seventeen prefectures around the coastal cities of Tokyo and Yokohama. The tremors were felt as far south down the coastline as Shizuoka prefecture and extended north and east up the shore into Ibaraki prefecture. The violent shaking alone was enough to destroy 90 percent of the buildings in Yokohama. In Tokyo, the shaking toppled structures and set off a raging conflagration. Fires leapt from cooking hearths, and chemical fires sprang up in factories and spread out of control, creating firestorms that wiped out 43 percent of the city within three days.[23] By mid-afternoon September 1, the sun was blotted out by black smoke as neighborhoods of tightly packed wooden row houses were engulfed in flames. The fires burned hot enough to melt iron girders, causing even the sturdiest brick and reinforced concrete buildings to topple well after the first impact. Winds spread the fires, which burned unabated until September 3. In the final reckoning, the earthquake, fires, and flooding left approximately 100,000 dead, 100,000 wounded, and 44,000 missing.[24] Seventy percent of the buildings in Tokyo were destroyed, leaving 1.5 million homeless and 250,000 without jobs.[25] The earthquake displaced 48 percent of the population in Tokyo prefecture and an astonishing 65 percent of the population in the Tokyo metropolitan area as a result of homes being destroyed or becoming uninhabitable.[26] A total 362 of Tokyo's bridges were decimated, including 82 bridges in Fukagawa, Honjo, and Nihonbashi that supported piping for the city's water supply. Another seventy were heavily damaged, slowing the delivery of food, fresh water, and other crucial supplies.[27] The total financial cost of the disaster exceeded 6.5 billion yen, more than four times Japan's national budget for 1923.[28] This enormous blow created lasting consequences, contributing to later economic shocks and the financial crisis of 1927. In the short term, the disaster produced a humanitarian crisis that deprived survivors of their basic needs, with food, water, and shelter in short supply. Emergency rice rations in army supply depots in Fukagawa and Etchūjima were destroyed by fires, causing massive food shortages that alarmed officials who feared a repeat of the 1918 rice riots.[29]

Tragically, not all of the disaster's casualties could be blamed on nature. The earthquake was also used as an excuse for violence against ethnic minorities and leftist activists. In the Kameido and Amakasu incidents, Japanese police assassinated twelve high-profile radical political organizers. Anti-Korean violence began the evening of the earthquake and intensified in the following days as rumors spread of Koreans planting bombs and poisoning wells. In the Korean massacres, vigilantes attacked thousands of men, women, and children in Tokyo and neighboring prefectures. Street mobs tortured and killed their victims with swords, bats, tools, and other improvised weapons. Suspected Koreans were singled out and forced off trains or stopped at checkpoints where they were screened for nonnative accents.[30] More than 6,000 Koreans and 700 Chinese were killed in Tokyo alone.[31] Members of Japan's police and army played an instrumental role in the violence and assassinations, as if to convey the message that in this chaos, threats to national security would not be tolerated.[32] With the declaration of martial law on September 2, Tokyo was treated like a war zone, ground zero for an empire under siege. From September 2 until November 16, the army took control over areas affected by the quake.[33] Approximately 35,000 army personnel were actively stationed in Tokyo, and an estimated 52,000 military personnel total were stationed in Yokohama and Tokyo—equivalent to nearly 20 percent of Japan's entire standing army.[34] Martial law had been imposed on Tokyo only once before, to suppress the Hibiya riots of 1905. Martial law allowed the army to maintain order by dispersing large gatherings, censoring publications, seizing property, and entering buildings, including private residences.

The devastation and violence of the Great Kanto Earthquake highlighted ethnic, socioeconomic, and cultural divisions in modernizing

Tokyo. The newest cultures of modernity were blamed for inviting heaven's wrath, and the empire's most marginalized populations, who lived in Tokyo's poorest communities, suffered disproportionately. In Tokyo in particular, the earthquake's horrific impact on the urban poor, the working class, and ethnic minorities from the colonies provided shocking evidence of socioeconomic inequality and the violence of imperialism within modernizing Japan. When it came time to assign blame for the destruction, many commentators pointed the finger at a decadent and Westernized nouveau riche, an influx of colonial subjects who sought to undermine imperial authority, a flourishing consumer culture, and a bawdy working-class culture that thrived in movie theaters, musical revues, and vaudeville halls. All were scapegoated for the disaster. Since the abolition of the feudal system in 1868, Japan had undergone a rapid program of industrialization that was carefully managed by the upper-echelon political elite. Industrialization produced a new middle class, an increasingly large wage labor force, and stark divisions between the poor and the prosperous. These divisions were especially evident in the aftermath of the quake. The disaster spared the Imperial Palace in the center of Tokyo and only lightly damaged the hilly, more wealthy Yamanote region to the west, but the densely populated neighborhoods of the Shitamachi (the "low city") east of the palace were reduced to scorched earth and rubble. Lower-class neighborhoods were far more vulnerable to earthquake damage. Industrial slums such as Honjo and Fukagawa were home to crowded wooden constructions that were erected on an unstable floodplain. The packed mud below these buildings essentially liquefied during the violent quaking. Older aristocratic estates and newer middle-class homes in Yamanote neighborhoods were of sturdier construction than Shitamachi row houses. They had large gardens and were widely spaced throughout the western hills, which provided protection against spreading fires. As a result, about 95 percent of Tokyo's earthquake casualties were Shitamachi residents, whereas less than 5 percent of the dead were from the Yamanote.[35] The Honjo ward in Shitamachi alone accounted for approximately 64 percent of earthquake deaths in Tokyo.[36] Alex Bates has mapped the deadly fires to show how the extent of the damage reached nearly exactly to the virtual boundary between the Yamanote and Shitamachi neighborhoods. As he argues, socioeconomic differences and the natural geography of the city prevented the earthquake from taking a higher toll in the capital's physically and socially more elevated neighborhoods.[37]

The Shitamachi neighborhoods were also the heart of Japan's burgeoning mass culture. This was the center of the nation's publishing industry, home to the booksellers, publishers, and printing presses of Kanda, Nihonbashi, Kyōbashi, Honjo, and Fukagawa, as well as to the bustling entertainment centers of Ginza's "brick town" and Asakusa's movie theaters and *misemono* (visual attraction) halls. According to theories of the earthquake as *tenbatsu* (divine punishment), these lively urban leisure cultures were to blame for the terrible wrath of the earthquake. Many believed the earthquake was sent to wipe out entertainment districts and expunge modern decadence and crass materialism from Tokyo. In a 1923 article "In What Ways Was the Great Kanto Disaster God's Will?" ("Kantō no daisaiga wa ikanaru shin'i ka"), Okutani Fumitomo, a Tenrikyō priest and one of the leading proponents of *tenbatsu* theory, wrote:

> If you peruse a map of the devastated areas of Tokyo, those places completely burnt to the ground include Nihonbashi, Kyōbashi, Kanda, Fukagawa, Honjo, and Asakusa. In other words, the amusement districts. Generally speaking, these areas were extremely prosperous in business and industry, and, on 1, 2, and 3 September, they were burnt to ash. Even the main road of Ginza, which prided itself on being the jewel of the urban, has been reduced to a dreamscape. Mitsukoshi, the number one department store in Japan where crowds flocked to satisfy their vanity, has even become a miserable wreck. On the other hand, the residential areas of Koishigawa [*sic*], Ushigome, Kōjimachi, Akasaka, and Azabu mostly escaped the earthquake and fires. . . . That the entertainment districts were completely destroyed must be an expression of divine will.[38]

Keio University economics professor Horie Kiichi opined that the destruction of Mitsukoshi department store and luxury stores in the Ginza modern shopping district gave "truth to the theory that this earthquake is heaven's punishment for the evil deeds the people of Tokyo conducted over the years."[39] Writing on *tenbatsu* discourse, Schencking notes, "According to Horie, heaven had done what the people of Tokyo and its leaders had failed to do: eliminate the centers of hedonist consumer culture.

In this light, the disaster was a blessing."[40] Although Tokyo's culture industries soon recovered and *tenbatsu* theories quickly faded, the new urban cultures and their challenge to official culture continued to be a subject of intense debate.[41]

Across the nation, the earthquake had an immediate impact on public recreation, including film and theater attendance. In Kansai, the red-light districts of Osaka observed the tragedy with solemnity, suppressing loud laughter and songs. Audiences rushed to theaters to see footage of Tokyo, but attendance fell off at plays, restaurants, and other entertainments. According an article in *Osaka asahi shinbun* on September 7, theater attendance had been unusually high just before the earthquake, but news of the disaster led to cancelled performances on September 2 and 3. The paper reported a general sense that "going out is impermissible." It claimed that those who did attend the theater went home midway through the performances and that weekday pedestrian traffic in Dotonbori and Sennichimae was one-third the usual volume, while Shōchiku playhouses were forced to resort to charity performances to attract customers. The article observed that low ticket prices and charity events were being used to encourage consumption at a time when entertainment was otherwise regarded as unseemly. According to the *Osaka asahi shinbun*, it seemed that films about the earthquake were the only thriving form of entertainment, for the movie theaters playing earthquake actualities were all full.[42]

As Schencking points out, larger newspapers such as the *Tokyo nichi nichi shinbun*, *Osaka mainichi shinbun*, and *Osaka asahi shinbun* heavily marketed in-house-produced photographs and films as what he calls "emotive media" that smaller newspapers could not afford to produce.[43] These larger papers' cutting-edge imaging technology, superior printing and distribution capacities, and highly emotional rhetoric helped fashion the Great Kanto Earthquake into a national tragedy for mass consumption. Schencking suggests that competition among newspapers, although primarily intended to increase circulations, also probably increased charitable donations in the first few weeks after the disaster.[44] Newspaper company film screenings bestowed the medium with new prominence and purpose while drumming up publicity for the papers. The *Tokyo nichi nichi shinbun* boasted that its documentary footage of the earthquake offered the best coverage of the disaster.[45] *Osaka mainichi shinbun* screenings of earthquake actualities took place in Osaka, Kobe, and other locations in western Japan beginning September 3, and the newspaper's footage was later shipped to Shanghai for a screening sponsored by the Chinese Young Men's Association and the Chinese Students Federation.[46] According to the newspaper, more than 20,000 attended its Nakashino Park screening in Osaka on September 10. The *Osaka asahi shinbun* sponsored charity screenings of earthquake film footage as early as September 3. The first screenings took place in Osaka at Tennōji Park and at an elementary school in the Ichioka neighborhood.[47] Subsequent screenings took place in the cities of Sakai, Kobe, Wakayama, Maruyama Park and Uzumasa in Kyoto, the Hirano neighborhood of Osaka, and Okayama, all by September 8. They continued throughout the month in Kansai, and on September 20, the newspaper announced plans for itinerant exhibition in Manchuria.[48] In September (when film exhibition in Tokyo was still banned), commercial film studios' newsreel footage received an enthusiastic reception in Kansai. Just one week after the earthquake, Teikine (Teikoku Kinema) film company's earthquake documentary was released at eight different theaters. Nikkatsu's documentary opened September 9 on a whopping twelve screens in western Japan.[49] Smaller production companies that are generally unfamiliar to historians today—such as Konishi, Masa Shōkai, Hayakawa Art Film Production (Hayakawa Geijutsu Eiga Seisakujo, also known as Hayakawa Gakujutsu Eiga Satsueijo or Hayakawa Academic Film Production), Yokohama Shinema Shōkai, Hyōsaka Shinbunsha (a newspaper company), and Osaka Kinema—also shot newsreels.[50]

Whereas newspapers and film studios shot earthquake footage as early as September 1 and screened these films outside of the disaster zone as early as September 3, the military did not begin shooting film footage until September 9, and the Ministry of Education did not begin production on its documentary film until September 16. The government's earliest photographic documentation of the Great Kanto Earthquake was produced by the Japanese Army Fifth Air Squadron, the Japanese Army Air Academy, the Navy Air Squadron, and the Army Balloon Corps, which were charged with producing aerial surveillance photographs of the devastation after verifying the safety of the emperor and empress at their imperial villa in Nikkō as well as the survival of the Imperial Palace and other government buildings. From September 2 through October 4, the Fifth Air Squadron flew as many as nine missions a day for a total of 123 flights and 807 hours, 10 minutes of flight time.[51] The army's Balloon Corps ascents began September 6 and continued multiple times daily until September 13, for a total of forty-six ascents that each lasted on average just over an hour.[52] Photographs taken by the Japanese army were among the most widely circulated and reproduced images of the quake (fig. 1.2).[53]

Despite the relatively late onset of the Ministry of Education's documentary film production plans, the disaster marked an important step forward for government film production, with state involvement in the industry increasing markedly over the next few months. During the temporary ban on entertainment in Tokyo, government officials provided support and encouragement to the film industry in other ways. As early as September 27, 1923, Home Minister Gotō Shinpei gathered the leaders of the film world to encourage their relief efforts, recommend free public screenings of "comfort films" (*ian eiga*), and praise fundraising screenings that collected money and supplies for relief. The Ministry of Foreign Affairs purchased earthquake films for the purpose of educating the international community about the Great Kanto Earthquake, shipping these out from Yokohama on December 15. By the end of January 1924, the Imperial Household Ministry was importing Bell and Howell cameras. In April 1924, the government lowered the entertainment tax to provide additional support to struggling Japanese film companies.[54]

When regular film screenings resumed in Tokyo on October 1, 1923, audiences were reported to "smack their lips at earthquake films" (*shinsai eiga ni shitatsuzumi o utta*) and foreign comedies.[55] Police warned exhibitors to refrain from frivolity or musical accompaniment that would prove too stimulating to the postearthquake public and cautioned the industry not to show films that could have a bad influence.[56] When earthquake documentaries were briefly banned, *Tokyo asahi shinbun* suggested that the cause for concern was not the content of the films so much as audience comportment. According to an October 5 *Tokyo asahi shinbun* article reporting the ban, theaters showing earthquake documentaries amassed crowds more than three times their seating capacity. Patrons who couldn't get into packed shows swarmed the ticket sellers, raising a huge uproar.[57] The head of Tokyo law enforcement told reporters that these films were sensitive because of the timing and location of the screenings, although he expressed confidence that the ban would be lifted in time.

FIGURE I.2 Aerial photograph of the ruins around Kanda and Jinbōchō taken by the Japanese Army Air Academy, September 4, 1923. Reprinted in *Taishō Shinsaishi shashinchō* (Home Ministry, Bureau of Social Affairs, 1926). Courtesy of the Tokyo Metropolitan Library.

The *Tokyo asahi shinbun* interpreted this to mean that the ban would be removed after the Tokyo populace had settled down.[58] On October 6, 1923, the *Yomiuri shinbun* reported that the police had moved quickly to ban screenings of earthquake films because of the incendiary nature of images of dead bodies, for such content was inimical to the goals of the Martial Law Headquarters, which wanted to promote the influence of the army and the prince regent through the use of film.[59] Subsequent ads for earthquake films in Tokyo played up the controversy, with Nikkatsu fanning interest in the "controversial Great Earthquake actuality screenings" (*mondai no Daishinsai jissha jōei*).[60] Despite officials' recommendations that entertainment be respectful and subdued, Nikkatsu made a spectacular presentation of a 3,000-foot earthquake documentary *Great Earthquake Actuality* (*Daishinsai jissha*) at the Meguro Kinema in Tokyo beginning October 15. The film combined the footage of more than ten cameramen, was billed with four *benshi* (including renowned foreign film narrator Tokugawa Musei), and featured a conducted orchestra.[61]

Against all obstacles, postearthquake construction of film theaters boomed. Once the entertainment ban imposed by martial law was lifted on October 1, Tokyo audiences demonstrated an astounding appetite for cinema and escapist entertainments. The *Tokyo asahi shinbun* linked enthusiasm for the movies to large numbers of "people starved of entertainment" (*goraku ni ueteita minshū*) and "people robbed of entertainment" (*goraku o ubawareta minshū*) since the earthquake.[62] As it looked back at 1924, *Nihon eiga nenkan* (Japanese film yearbook) attributed the industry's startling growth to the impact of the disaster, suggesting that the flourishing film and entertainment industries were rooted in postearthquake "audience psychology" (*kankyaku shinri*): "People who lapped up all kinds of tragedies before these extraordinary events have been starving for amusement [*goraku*] in general, not just film." According to *Nihon eiga nenkan*, it was understandable that audiences who had experienced the agony of life in the "barracks," temporary constructions housing the displaced, now craved entertaining movies (*"goraku" to shite no eiga*) and escapist films (*"kibarashi" no tame no eiga*).[63] October 2, just one month after the quake, was not too soon for comic relief: for the first postearthquake program at the Tokyo Ushigomekan, Nikkatsu's earthquake documentary was paired with a Snub Pollard short called *Shake 'Em Up* (1921, Hal Roach-Pathé), a one-reel American romantic comedy about an

American in disguise dodging earthquakes and firing squads in Mexico. The film was given the title *Jishinkoku* or "earthquake nation" in Japanese.[64] In the wake of the disaster, foreign film imports rose dramatically to cover shortages caused by destroyed film stores and the interruption of domestic film production. However, the strong vertical integration of production, distribution, and exhibition in Japan made it difficult for US film companies (and small independent Japanese companies) to undercut large Japanese studios, even after the earthquake.[65]

After the disaster, the major Tokyo-based film companies moved their production facilities west to the cities of Kyoto, Osaka, and Kobe in the Kansai region. The Tokyo-area studios of Shōchiku and Nikkatsu survived the earthquake relatively unscathed, but both deemed it more prudent to move film personnel to Kyoto temporarily. The Kansai region's rapid rise to prominence as the new center of Japanese motion picture production was widely commented on in the postearthquake film press.[66] After the earthquake, for the first time, all four major production companies—Shōchiku, Nikkatsu, Teikine, and Makino—operated out of the same region. This breakaway from the crowded, eastern, cosmopolitan metropolis prompted comparisons with the US film industry in the early teens, when New York film companies began sending crews to a warm, sunny outcrop of Los Angeles where they could escape the litigious Motion Picture Patents Company and make films all year long. This California "film colony" was dubbed "Hollywood," and after the Great Kanto Earthquake, Kyoto became known as the "Hollywood of Japan." Comparisons between Hollywood and Kyoto began appearing in film magazines as early as spring 1924. From this year until the end of the 1920s, annual film production in Kansai surpassed Tokyo's output.[67]

The two largest film companies in Tokyo at the time of the earthquake were Nikkatsu and Shōchiku. Nikkatsu Mukōjima studio was located in the Mukōjima neighborhood near the east bank of the Sumida River in the Shitamachi, the "low city" of eastern Tokyo. Most of Mukōjima's buildings survived the shaking with minimal structural damage and narrowly escaped destruction by fire.[68] In the article "The Great Earthquake and Mukōjima Studio" ("Daishinsai to Mukōjima satsueijo"), studio vice chief Kozono Suenori vividly describes how Mukōjima was threatened by the firestorms that lay siege to adjacent Shitamachi neighborhoods on the night of September 1. Around midnight, winds began to drive the flames across the Sumida River toward Mukōjima studio. Fierce winds lifted burning blocks of wood and zinc plates off rooftops to pelt the waters. As the blaze approached, Mukōjima staff staved off the fire by dividing into groups that took turns pumping water.[69] Although the studio was saved, Nikkatsu lost its downtown office, eighteen of its twenty-nine directly managed Tokyo theaters, and approximately 200,000 feet of film for losses that totaled approximately 1.2 million yen.[70] However, as Nikkatsu head of distribution Negishi Kōichi observed, compared to what the rest of the city had endured, these damages were unthinkably light.[71]

Shōchiku film company was even more fortunate. Its Kamata studio was located in a thinly populated area outside the city, far to the west and separated from Mukōjima's location on the Sumida River by all of Tokyo. Kamata was safe from the firestorms and suffered only minor losses when shaking caused some damage to the studio: the foundation of the glass studio cracked, the film storage building collapsed, and the actresses' wardrobe and make-up building was destroyed. Most of the studio remained standing, and no employees were killed. Like Nikkatsu, Shōchiku lost its main Tokyo office and three of its directly managed theaters in the capital. Damaged and destroyed film prints included, Shōchiku's total losses came to an estimated 900,000 yen.[72] Nikkatsu stayed in Tokyo until November 14, after which Mukōjima ceased operations. By remaining in the capital for a few extra weeks, Nikkatsu was able to film melodramas about the disaster in Tokyo's actual ruins—films that I analyze in further detail in chapter 2. In contrast, Shōchiku only temporarily closed operations but began relocating its employees much earlier, in mid-September.[73] When Shōchiku Kamata reopened in early 1924, it was the only major studio operating in Tokyo until 1932.

Positioning the Spectator

These were the conditions in which the Ministry of Education inaugurated its film production program with *Actuality of the Great Kanto Earthquake and Conflagration* (*Kanto Daishin taika jikkyō*), a feature-length film believed to have been approximately 5,700 feet on five reels with a runtime of ninety-five minutes at sixteen frames per second.[74] Norisugi Kazu, a section chief in the General Education Bureau (Futsū Gakumukyoku), initiated planning of the film, a collaboration with Tokyo Shinema Shōkai and its cameraman, Shirai Shigeru.[75] This film was not shown at commercial cinemas but was sent on a tour with a traveling lecture given at public halls in major cities all over Japan.[76] It was first shown in Kyoto on October 10 and toured around Chugoku, Kyushu, Shikoku, Shizuoka, and other parts of western Japan, playing at a total of forty-nine cities between October 10 and December 1.[77]

Tokyo Shinema Shōkai was located in Kohinata near the Koishi River in Tokyo, founded in 1914 (or 1917 according to some accounts) by former M. Pathe employees who left Nikkatsu a few years after the merger of M. Pathe with other small firms in the creation of Nikkatsu in 1912. Tokyo Shinema Shōkai specialized in making, selling, and providing projection of educational films that generally ran two to five reels in length. It also produced film sequences on demand for theater troupes that performed *rensageki* (chain drama), contracted with government agencies, and provided raw film footage for the American newsreel company Selznick News. Shirai Shigeru began working as a cameraman at Tokyo Shinema Shōkai in 1921 after having worked at the Shōchiku Kinema Kenkyūjo and Shōchiku Kamata studio. On the day of the earthquake, he was shooting footage for a *rensageki* in Kumagaya in Saitama prefecture. After a day's journey back to the capital, he began filming the aftermath of the earthquake with assistant Ōta Yoshitarō using a box camera by Universal Camera that carried 400 feet of film.[78] It seems likely that Shirai's footage was later added to the Ministry of Education coproduction.[79]

Earthquake documentary films surveyed the damage and documented reconstruction in Tokyo and neighboring cities.[80] These films generally have a loose digest or compilation structure, with footage grouped by location and theme, framed by intertitles. Many include images of ravaged bodies, suggesting that filmmakers may have tried to evade the prohibition on images of the dead due to the documentaries' stated intention to inform. The Ministry of Education and Tokyo Shinema Shōkai film shows bones piled high at the former site of the Honjo factory. Footage shot by Kōsaka Toshimitsu and Isayama Saburō for Nikkatsu Mukōjima studio includes similarly gruesome scenes, such as bodies of ash in Honjo and corpses floating in the Sumida River. Ina Seiichi's

Great Kanto Earthquake (*Kantō Daishinsai*, 1923) is even more graphic, showing horrific images of blackened corpses interlaced in piles of still-recognizable human forms. Lurid blue, orange, and green tinting was used to further heighten the emotional impact of these sensational images. As Tsuneishi Fumiko observes, the fact that these films employed such aesthetic strategies suggests that earthquake documentary films were "not simply news about the real, but also experienced by the audience as a rich cinematic experience."[81]

Earthquake documentary films drew on a common repertoire of images. Most of the surviving films include footage of the wreckage of the famous Asakusa Jūnikai, images of human remains at the site of the Honjo army clothing depot, and images of messages left on statuary by survivors looking for loved ones. September 1923 advertisements for Shōchiku's and Nikkatsu's films listed scenes by location and emphasized shocking content, sensational spectacles, and famous landmarks. Terse descriptions from an ad for the Shōchiku film *Great Tokyo Earthquake Actuality* (*Tōkyō Daishinsai jissha*) suggest the paratactic construction of the film:

- the confusion in front of Tokyo station
- distant view of Tokyo from Ueno station
- the army marching in Manseibashi
- the police station and Teigoku-jō
- viewing the entire city from Ueno station
- the main intersection at Ueno
- the crowds at Nippori station
- Nijūbashi and the wireless telegraph station
- the collapsed Kanda bridge, refugees crossing the river
- viewing the palace from Babasakimon
- the area around Kyōbashi from Ginza Blvd
- refugees in Ueno Park
- the scene of great confusion at Shinobazu Pond
- dead bodies drifting under Azuma Bridge[82]

Such lengthy enumerations of scenes are unusual for newspaper ads from the period. Ads typically announced what was playing and where, the film director, principal stars, film company, and number of reels, with only a few words about genre and subject matter. Some ads included the name of the *benshi* or information about musical accompaniment, but rarely did newspaper ads provide descriptions of discrete scenes. The parataxis of these advertisements informs us what kind of footage was filmed and what sort of imagery was conventionally associated with the Great Kanto Earthquake. More important, as surviving films confirm, ads reflect the piecemeal construction of earthquake documentary films and their rhetorical address to the viewer.

For instance, this Nikkatsu ad (fig. 1.3) was used to publicize Kansai screenings of its earthquake documentary film—

> Misery upon misery! A world-class wonder / See! And know the reality of the Tokyo Great Earthquake! / Nikkatsu company Mukōjima studio technicians / Kōsaka Toshimitsu and Isayama Saburō / Began filming with sacrificial spirit as the quake started, and completed shooting in the face of death / Bringing us this superb work / As the great city of Tokyo goes up in flames: / The horror of September 1, 2, 3, 4 reported in detail

- the misery of Ginza Blvd and its surroundings
- the terrible sight of Nihonbashi
- the terrible sight of Kanda bridge in flames
- the terrible sight of Yūrakuchō
- a sea of corpses
- the instant of the Asakusa Jūnikai's collapse
- the police headquarters, Teigeki, and Maruzen building burning down
- Kuramae Technical High School
- misery upon misery
- a distant view of Tokyo

This is a perfect example of the unabashedly sensationalistic rhetoric of ads that emphasized scale, scope, intensity, and detailed visual description by using lengthy listings of scenes. As the copy suggests, earthquake documentaries were like travelogues that brought the viewer on a tour of Tokyo neighborhoods to behold the remains of famous buildings and landmarks, providing a glimpse of the new rhythms and unfamiliar lifestyles that characterized "earthquake culture" in the demolished city.

FIGURE 1.3 Ad for Nikkatsu's earthquake documentary: "Misery upon misery! A world-class wonder / See! And know the reality of the Tokyo Great Earthquake!" *Osaka asahi shinbun*, September 8, 1923, evening edition.

Several earthquake documentary films have a strong ethnographic character that is evident in their attempts to map the postearthquake city and its emergent social practices. The piecemeal construction of these films is not always orderly but often disorderly and disturbing. In sequences of the destruction, this digest format, together with the roving gaze of the moving camera, implies a horror that cannot be fully exhausted or grasped in its entirety.

In the remainder of this chapter, I pay special attention to the use of camera movement, space, and textures in Great Kanto Earthquake documentary films, focusing on the Ministry of Education and Tokyo Shinema Shōkai film *Actuality of the Great Kanto Earthquake and Conflagration*. In particular, three features of these films deserve attention. The first is camera movement. In earthquake documentary films, the motion of the camera automatically prompts the sense that one is traveling through the landscape—an important strategy for soliciting the viewer's engagement and suggesting the incomprehensible scale of the disaster. Moving shots in earthquake documentary films produce a disorienting feeling, for it is not always clear where we are or what we are looking at.

Motion solicits an embodied perceptual response by producing visual cues that suggest direction, depth, and velocity. At the same time, the space in which the camera travels is extremely difficult to decipher, so total is the surrounding obliteration. A sense of cinematically produced emplacement—orientation produced by identification with the camera that places the viewer "in" the scene—threatens to unravel as the camera sweeps across the destruction's unending expanse. Without consistent spatial cues, it is difficult to experience the image as immersive. Such disturbing unmoorings of perspective were not limited to representations of the earthquake. Even in real life, the leveling of so much of the city enabled the unaided human eye to traverse large expanses of space in ways that previously had been unthinkable. This technique recalls film actualities circa 1895–1906 that similarly exploited the tracking shot's ability to produce an uncanny sense of embodiment by soliciting the viewer's identification with the camera. In the early cinema period, such identification with the camera allowed viewers to enjoy a thrilling sensation of movement while remaining still in their seats. Wolfgang Schivelbusch, Lynne Kirby, and Tom Gunning connect this sensational use of moving camera shots in early cinema to the increasingly common experience of rail travel and the moving views afforded by this and other forms of modern conveyance. The modern technological visuality that emerged with the railroad was also explored by philosophical toys that exploited the embodied nature of human perception. Devices such as the stereoscope, the phenakistoscope, and the zoetrope depended on the corporeality of vision, undermined the notion of an ideal Cartesian observer, and suggested new modes of seeing that emphasized the body.[83]

Second, it is important to consider how space is presented to the spectator in documentary earthquake films. Filmmakers could choose among various techniques to situate and orient the viewer within the depicted landscape. They could invite distanced contemplation, or they could actively frustrate the viewer's desire to position themselves vis-à-vis the image in a spatial relation that involved fixed scale and recessive depth. This latter possibility relates to the third formal feature I consider: the tactile quality of images in earthquake documentary films. Together, these three features—motion, spatial cues, and tactility—can be used to analyze the positioning of the spectator in *Actuality of the Great Kanto Earthquake and Conflagration*.

Actuality of the Great Kanto Earthquake and Conflagration was one of the most important films made about the catastrophe. Few other documentaries were as lengthy or as comprehensive. The structure of the film can be divided into roughly three sections. The first creates an impression of the ferocity of the quake, the second is a visual ethnography of the city that maps the extent of the earthquake's destruction, and the third depicts the benevolence of the imperial family, shows provisions made by the Japanese government, and portrays relief organizations managing cleanup and disaster relief.

The film offers two different modes of experiencing the earthquake: one diegetic and immersive, and another more distanced and rhetorical. Imagery, shot scale and composition, editing, intertitles, and camera movement create two distinct orientations toward the landscape. The noticeable difference between these two modes suggests a deliberate attempt to use cinematic techniques to produce different kinds and degrees of closeness, distance, and embodied involvement in the represented world.

This difference is most marked in the last few shots of the first section of *Actuality of the Great Kanto Earthquake and Conflagration*, which place the viewer within scenes of destruction. Here, camera movement and framing convey a strong sense of "being there," even though a lack of well-known landmarks or expository intertitles creates an eerie, disorienting effect. In one shot, slender brick chimneys are all that remain of what appears to have been a grand Western-style building. We then see another burned-out building that is just a husk of bricks and stone. In subsequent shots, the camera is set up in empty rooms and scans wreckage strewn about deserted hallways. A slow tilt and pan over one building reveals nothing but iron girders where a roof used to be. Peering down corridors and into crumbling architectural interiors, what the camera shows in these shots is neither a spectacle nor a landscape, for the images lack organization from a distanced, commanding point of view. In one shot, the camera points out from within a blasted building, as if "peeping" out from a hiding place. The view opens onto an outdoor expanse and stretches across an open space toward the remnants of buildings on the far side of a street or courtyard. Architectural elements frame the image and emphasize the position of the camera as "inside," looking out. This framing of the view imbues the image with a reflexive register that sets it apart from all the preceding shots. Not only does this composition create a sense of actually being in the building, inhabiting the space and gazing on a scene from a determined position, but this bodily presence in the visual image presents an experience of looking that goes beyond merely presenting an image to be seen. This foregrounded "look," the look of the camera on the scene, brings the viewer into the space onscreen. Such a firmly situated or emplaced look can be contrasted with the postcard-like parade of views of famous places and horrible sights found in other sections of the film. One look situates the viewer within the image; the other tends to distance and aestheticize its object. The first look is diegetic and "realistic"; the second look is rhetorical, aesthetic, and presentational.

Noting the strong distinction between different modes of relating space to the spectator, film historian and theorist Noël Burch describes something akin to the postcard-like presentation of "distant" views with what he terms the Primitive Mode of Representation in early cinema. In contrast to this mode, classical narrative cinema and its Institutional Mode of Representation invest image and space with a narrative function by drawing spectators into the diegetic world.[84] Tom Gunning makes a similar distinction when he defines the cinema of narrative integration in contrast with the exhibitionist cinema of attractions. The concept of narrative integration describes how, from around 1908 onward, filmmakers such as American director D. W. Griffith pioneered strategies of creating spatial and temporal continuity in cinema that allowed for the development of more complicated stories. Gunning calls the cinema of narrative integration "highly spatialized and synthetic," because it "stich[es] together a larger spatial whole from separate shots. . . . No longer simply observing the action or directly addressed by an attraction, the spectator now [knits] together the space and time of the film following the logic of the narrative."[85] Although the links between shots in *Actuality of the Great Kanto Earthquake and Conflagration* are very weak, and therefore cannot be said to support "narrative causality and linearity extending over several shots and establish[ing] the continuity of space and time that subtend[s] narrative action," we can still see an attempt to situate the viewer within the image by the use of camera placement, camera movement, camera angle, editing, mise-en-scene, and (presumably) *benshi* narration.[86] The mixed address of the film, with its alternately distancing and emplacing use of image and space, can partly be explained by the transition between these two cinematic modes, which in Japan was still taking place at the beginning of the 1920s. This mix of modes is also common in documentary films that shift between different registers, such as demonstration, spectacle, reenactment, and audiovisual narration.

After the first section of *Actuality of the Great Kanto Earthquake and Conflagration*, the second and third sections seem markedly touristic in comparison. The second section is an overview of the damage that moves from place to place in a survey of the city, mapping the damage with footage of famous buildings, neighborhoods, and views. The camera lingers primarily on well-known streets and monuments, although some of the most affecting images are of neighborhoods in ruins and the unreadable debris where homes and businesses once stood.

The third and final section focuses on the reestablishment of order, providing glimpses of everyday life in the "barracks" (shanty towns), where basic shelters were improvised out of corrugated tin roofs and abandoned train cars. We see footage of Prime Minister Yamamoto Gonnohyōe and his cabinet, the temporary police headquarters, and shots of patrolling militia, followed by an overview of charitable activities and a progression of shots implying the government's important role in coordinating foreign relief and mobilizing ground volunteers.[87] A brief section commemorating the victims in Honjo is followed by a section on labor. Workers march two by two, use picks to demolish walls, and clear rubble with shovels and bare hands as soldiers stand watch. In a lengthy edited sequence, the army engineers detonate the ruins of the Asakusa Jūnikai. With hammer and stake, soldiers place explosives in its remaining walls. After the explosives are wired and checked, the men leave the site. The detonation and its aftermath are caught on film. When the smoke clears, all that remains of the tower is a single jagged shard. This sequence ends with a slow tilt from the rubble of the tower up toward the tip of what remains of the Jūnikai.

Notably, the film continues with a visual ethnography of everyday life in the devastated capital, showing that life goes on. A barber gives haircuts and a sake vendor sells alcohol on the street. Signs show where to line up for the trolley, and men work to clear wreckage and repair train lines. The film catalogs different types of temporary shelter, from simple wooden constructions to a large tent city, the expanse of which is revealed in a high-angle shot. A sequence on the earthquake damage in Yokohama includes several aestheticized shots of ruins in silhouette against the sky. Finally, in a segment that begins with a shot of a clock stopped at 11:58, we are offered glimpses of the imperial family and their activities. This imagery is followed by shots that clearly show the Imperial Palace safe with no visible damage. Dignitaries tour the hospital of Tokyo Imperial University and inspect sleeping patients. The prince regent goes about the city on horseback to survey the damage with a large party of soldiers who ride out in advance. He alone salutes the camera as the procession crosses a bridge (fig. 1.4). He looks out over the city from a high point in Ueno, where he is offered a covered table and chairs. A man points into the distance, directing the prince's gaze here and there; in the next shot, the camera seemingly adopts Hirohito's position, scanning the expanse from his point of view. Finally, women of the palace are shown sewing clothing for charity, and we see medical relief trucks dispatched by the Imperial Household Ministry. The film closes with a low-angle shot of the palace, which fades to black.

The three-part construction of *Actuality of the Great Kanto Earthquake and Conflagration* is crucial. It contains the charged imagery of death and destruction by foregrounding the authoritative presence of the imperial family and their important role in disaster relief. The final sections of the film emphasize charity, order, industry, and normalcy through the methodical and dispassionate presentation of cleanup efforts, social services, and daily activities. The spectator's identification with the camera, used in the first section to convey a thrilling sense of "being there," is later used to assert the prince's authority over the spectator and his authorization of what the spectator sees. This imprimatur is facilitated by the prince's direct gaze at the camera and the camera's adoption of his point of view as he surveys Tokyo from its heights.[88]

Despite Hirohito's importance in legitimizing the film's surveying gaze, the prince regent's appearance is also one of many uncanny moments in the film. If the construction of *Actuality of the Great Kanto Earthquake and Conflagration* gives rise to contradictory bodily sensations that produce dislocating affects, none is perhaps so strange as seeming to be seen by and then seeing as the future emperor. These are arguably the most startling shots in the film: one shows Hirohito directly acknowledging the camera as he inspects the damage, and later, a panoramic point-of-view shot of the city sutures the audience's look to the prince's

FIGURE 1.4 Hirohito acknowledges the camera in *Actuality of the Great Kanto Earthquake and Conflagration* (Ministry of Education and Tokyo Shinema Shōkai, 1923). Courtesy of the National Film Archive of Japan.

sweeping gaze. These shots represent a revolutionary attempt to fashion an intersubjective relationship between the future emperor and his subjects, using a medium whose inscription of the prince's living bodily presence defies what Hikari Hori has called the "non-viewing and non-listening policies of the emperor's media presentation."[89] As Hori argues, Hirohito's media presentation in films like this contradicted the typical viewing (or nonviewing) protocols involved in representing the imperial institution, which were designed to deny the emperor's corporeality to promote idealized, transcendental images of his sacred person for veneration (as opposed to public display). Hirohito's treatment as a media celebrity in the early 1920s was made possible by expanding modern media infrastructures, which paralleled Hirohito's rise to power as crown prince in 1916, prince regent in 1921, and emperor in 1926.

Other earthquake films do not evince this interest in elevating spectator response and channeling emotion toward appropriate ends. In the

Nikkatsu film shot by Kōsaka Toshimitsu and Isayama Saburō, *Actuality of the Great Kanto Earthquake*, camera movement and tinting are used throughout and give the imagery a disturbing charge (fig. 1.5). Red-tinted footage of the Shitamachi shows people fleeing as smoke and flames approach. The Jūnikai and Asakusa are shown engulfed in flames. Some footage overlaps with the Ministry of Education and Tokyo Shinema Shōkai film. Both show messages scrawled in chalk, views from within hollow ruins, and a shot of a burned-out train car slumped at the approach to a bridge, like a bizarre mechanical corpse. But the Nikkatsu film includes scenes of horror that the Ministry of Education and Tokyo Shinema Shōkai documentary does not. In the Nikkatsu film, a scene at the site of the Honjo clothing depot begins with wide shots of absolutely unreadable ruins that stretch toward the horizon with only a few scattered structures still standing here and there. The camera does not shrink from the carnage of the tragedy: we see piles of burned bodies, close-up shots of human-shaped ash, a horse's corpse, and more blackened cadavers. At the end of the film, moving shots taken from a boat on the Sumida River afford mobile, low-angle views of damaged bridges that are nothing but twisted metal girders and concrete remains. A man crossing a bridge above the canal, filmed from below, weaves his way through the warped metal until he cannot push on any further. At the river's level, the camera conveys the viewer swiftly through the water, providing fleeting glimpses of dead bodies in the river and of people huddled under a bridge. The only shot taken from the bank, at water level, is of a body floating up against the shore. Midstream, we see a corpse caught in some wreckage, washed up against the side of a stone retaining wall. The last shot of the film shows a black and bloated leg emerging from the water, partially obscured by debris. The film ends with this image as the camera creeps slightly to one side in a fluid, sliding movement. The conveyance of the viewer over the water, under bridges, and among the dead evokes an eerie sense of traversing subterranean space, and the roving gaze of the camera suggests what Giuliana Bruno has described as early cinema's morbid fascination with grotesquerie.[90]

Any discussion of the use of space in Great Kanto Earthquake documentary films must consider not only the content of the image and editing but also the position of the spectator. Viewers unfamiliar with early 1920s Tokyo undoubtedly feel stymied by a lack of familiarity with the

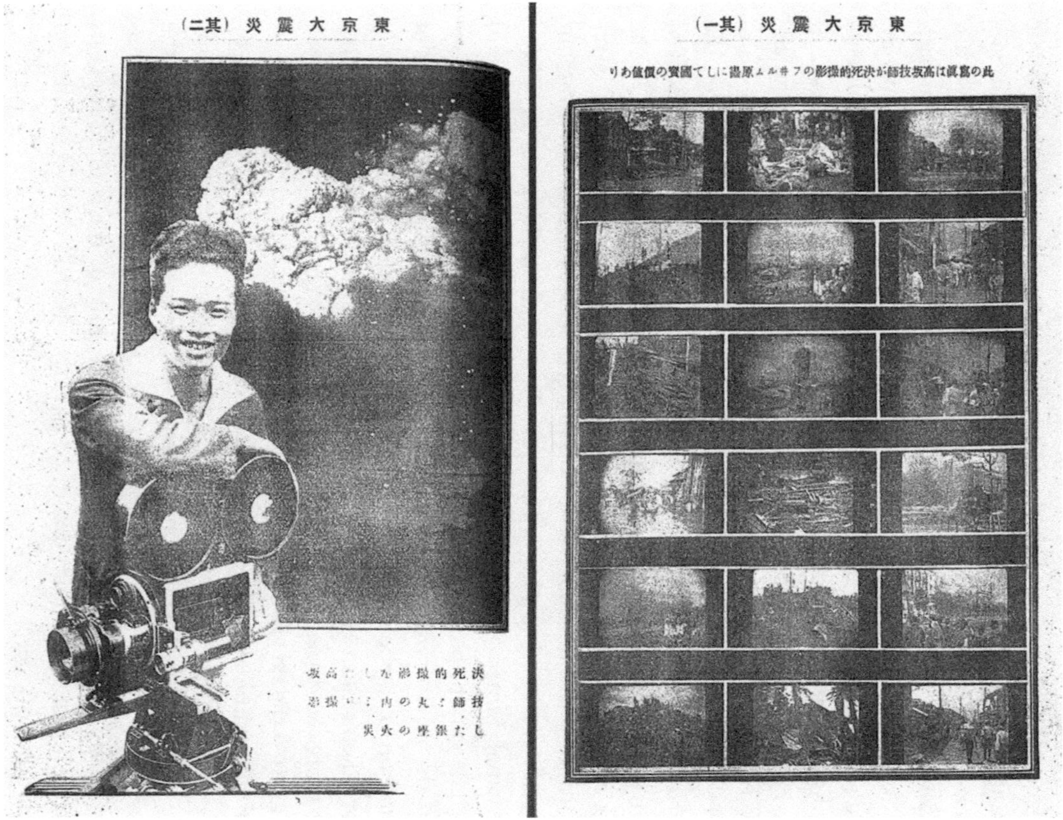

FIGURE 1.5 Nikkatsu Mukōjima's Kōsaka Toshimitsu, shown with his earthquake footage in a *Nikkatsu gahō* magazine spread, November 15, 1923.

built environment of the city. This lack of familiarity frustrates one's ability to project oneself into a landscape where few recognizable landmarks remain. It heightens the conflict between emplacement, the ability to insert oneself into the scene, and the tactile qualities of the image, which refuse the projection of the body into illusionistic space and instead engage a sense of texture and touch. The stymying textures of the earthquake documentaries suggest "crises and fissures of meaning," as Eve Kosofsky Sedgwick argues textures are wont to do, by refusing visual orientation and obvious meaning-making.[91] It is no wonder that the rummaged postearthquake landscape was often compared to expressionist images, for ruins have a powerfully plastic quality—all the more so when the jumble of destruction resists visual organization and when it is difficult to project oneself into the disorienting space.[92] When emplacement seems impossible, the texture of ruins takes over, engaging the haptic sense with a sickening plasticity of forms. Compared with familiar spaces then, which seem welcoming and habitable, ruins are much more available to our sense of touch than emplacement, and they invite a different experience of image and space. We see many examples of this in the Ministry of Education and Tokyo Shinema Shōkai earthquake documentary film: the melted girders of the Maruzen building droop this way and that, like the legs of a giant crushed spider, as if the building has been crumbled up by an enormous hand; steel pallets that used to carry train cars lie inert with the burned remains of those cars congealed on their backs; and burned-out train cars and bridges appear to have softly crumpled toward the ground. These industrial objects, whose hard, rigid, glossy exteriors once refused the suggestion that they had been shaped by a human touch, are now endowed with a disturbing human quality through the presence of messy textures.

Sedgwick notes that the terms "touching," "feeling," and "touchy-feely" bring the emotional and the haptic into intimate relation.[93] In earthquake films, texture interferes with our visual command over space, which allows us to hold the image at a distance and orient ourselves. Texture brings the two-dimensional surface of the image into competition with the illusion of depth. Texture arouses other perceptual registers, unseating vision's claim to clarity and knowledge, for texture "is not coextensive with any single sense, but . . . [i]ndeed, other senses beyond the visual and the haptic are involved in the perception of texture, as when we *hear* the brush-brush of corduroy trousers or the crunch of extra-crispy chicken."[94] Texture thus introduces perceptual and epistemological uncertainty, for "texture, in short, comprises an array of perceptual data that includes repetition, but whose degree of organization hovers just below the level of shape or structure."[95] To imagine this confusion, one need only imagine gazing out of an airplane at a mountain range that suddenly resembles a wrinkled bed sheet, or trudging down a winter city sidewalk that is lumpy with several-days-old snow that suddenly brings to mind stirred cookie dough.

The frustration of vision can produce a sense of historicity. The illegible ruins of the earthquake films are a reminder that no matter how dense the work of reconstructive history, we can never simply insert ourselves into the past in the same position as the subjects we write about. The dissonance between tactility and emplacement in earthquake images draws attention to the nonidentity of present-day and historical reception and the dizzying possibility of acts of identification across history via the film medium. This prompts us to think about affect and perception in terms of relationality. Our feelings and senses can be alienated and alienating, but this too is a form of relation. Earthquake documentary films push as well as pull.

Despite the radical perceptual encounter staged between viewer and devastation in *Actuality of the Great Kanto Earthquake and Conflagration*, it is important to remember that one of the major goals of its production was to publicize the benevolence and authority of the imperial family. As I have mentioned, this film, which is typically considered the Ministry of Education's first film production, was only made possible by the designation of special funds for the purposes of social education just prior to the earthquake. In many ways, *Actuality of the Great Kanto Earthquake and Conflagration* should be viewed as an extension of the Ministry of Education's and Imperial Household Ministry's rapidly developing media policy during the transition between the Taishō and Shōwa emperors' reigns—a transition that was planned for as early as 1919. In *Actuality of the Great Kanto Earthquake and Conflagration*, not only does the prince regent acknowledge the camera, but editing, camera angle, and camera movement make possible the technological binding of the spectator's gaze to his gaze. Here, too, we might imagine the viewer's dizzying and dislocating sense of identification with the prince as a force that acts in and beyond the space of the film. The alignment of our look to his look transports us into the diegetic world of the documentary, but this surprising moment is also extremely othering.

The explosion of mass media after the Great Kanto Earthquake—increased newspaper circulations, new magazine titles, and more film theaters than ever before—altered popular polemics on cinema's relationship to national identity and everyday life. The first discussions of cinema as a democratic medium appear after the earthquake. Despite widespread disapprobation of entertainment culture, even the Japanese government, including the Ministry of Education, embraced cinema's important role in reconstruction efforts. For instance, testifying to the Diet regarding measures being taken to educate the public and encourage spiritual reconstruction in the aftermath of the disaster, Minister of Education Okana Keijirō highlighted films and other visual materials among the various strategies being used to spread information about the catastrophe.[96] The ministry funded children's author Kurushima Takehiko's thirty-nine-city educational road show, which used films and visual exhibits—including postcards and actual objects taken from the rubble of the disaster—to inform the public of the enormity of the Great Kanto Earthquake.[97] Although authorities expressed concern regarding the impact that sensational earthquake films would have on unruly, distressed audiences, the Great Kanto Earthquake spurred government involvement in film exhibition and production, suggesting new appreciation for cinema as a potent medium.

Analysis of the earthquake documentary films enables new assessments of formal techniques that might otherwise be imagined as short-circuiting involvement. The imagery in earthquake documentary films is often startling, disorienting, and even repulsive. These effects do not necessarily contravene an intense sense of involvement, let alone a sense of realism, as we see in the case of the shocking experience of being seen by and then seeing as Hirohito. Thinking through these effects in terms of relationality (which includes carefully examining the spectator's position and spatial, haptic, and identificatory cues) fosters a more complex understanding of the affects they produce. These films engender vertiginous forms of perceptual dissonance. Camera movement creates a strong impression of immersive, recessive space; haptic textures frustrate spatial orientation and emphasize the surface of the image by engaging the sense of touch with messy, tactile, bursting textures. This frustration does not necessarily entail critical judgment or emotional disengagement, just as sharing the future emperor's gaze may seem self-alienating but should not necessarily break our connection with the film. In fact, I would argue, these feelings of disorientation and frustration work to foreground relationality. Sensitivity to this relationality can bring into relief connections between the personal, the public, and the historical.

CHAPTER 2

The Testimony of the Body

Nikkatsu's Earthquake Melodrama Films

In the November 15, 1923, article "The Great Earthquake and Mukōjima Studio" in *Nikkatsu gahō* (Nikkatsu illustrated) film magazine, Nikkatsu film studio executive Kozono Suenori defended the studio's fictional earthquake melodramas against charges of sensationalism. He argued that these *shinsai eiga* (earthquake films), which were filmed in Tokyo's ruins, should be valued for their unrivaled realism. In the studio's defense, Kozono envisioned a cinematic "moving history" that would capture the true terror and calamity of the quake, demonstrating the power of cinema and providing a realism commensurate with the audience's real-life experiences. Kozono asked,

> what kinds of films should we make in order to cater to today's audience? . . . our eyes and our ears have come to know calamity that surpasses the theater of the past. . . . Even though we would like to make serious works with a sense of realism, we are unable if we want to pass the censors. Just when we have an incentive that makes us want to make all-out dramatic pictures, officials warn that, at least for the time being and until public sentiment [*minshin*] dies down, we must do our best to refrain from sensationalism [*shigekisei no aru mono wa enryoshite kure*], and it is just not possible for us to do anything drastic with production . . . we've made [earthquake melodrama] films like *Daichi wa yuragu* [The earth shakes] and *Haikyo no naka* [In the ruins], but sure enough, now we wait to see what kind of response there will be. The Great Taishō Earthquake must be recorded,

> and these films were quick to capture it realistically [*shajitsuteki ni*], as a kind of moving history, which we would like to preserve for eternity [*hitotsu no katsudōshi to shite eikyū ni nokoshite okitai to omoimasu*].[1]

Protesting the authorities' indictment of incendiary cinema and the directive to refrain from sensationalism, Kozono argued that realistic earthquake films had historic significance as an important record of the unprecedented destruction. He went on to argue that *only* earthquake films could engender a powerful emotional response befitting the enormity of the Great Kanto Earthquake. Only *shinsai eiga* could provide representations tantamount to the actual experiences of those who had survived.

Kozono's choice of the phrase *katsudōshi* (moving history)—an evocative, abbreviated expression for "motion picture history" (*katsudō shashinshi*)—is notable in this context. In this period, it was not unusual to abbreviate *katsudō shashin* (motion pictures) as *katsudō* (movies) in longer compound phrases, but Kozono's elision of *shashin*, meaning "photos," is especially meaningful here. It allows for more imaginative readings of *katsudō* than usual, evoking the senses of *active*, *vital*, or *moving*, since the literal meaning of *katsudō* is "activity." His neologism *katsudōshi* or "moving history" emphasizes lifelike realism, implying the ongoing, active imagination of the Great Kanto Earthquake in the everyday lives of those who lived through it.

Moreover, Kozono's argument strategically references the Japanese government's ambivalence toward cinema's powerful realism. After the earthquake, officials enacted a temporary ban on film and entertainment and later instated a specific ban on earthquake films because of unruly audience behavior and objectionable content. At the same time, officials commended the industry for holding free "comfort screenings" that distracted audiences from the hardships of the quake and recovery, the Ministry of Education sponsored a feature-length earthquake documentary that promoted government relief efforts, and tax breaks and equipment were provided to film companies to facilitate the production and export of earthquake documentaries, which were used to raise foreign relief funds. With this passing reference to the government's heightened vigilance over film activities, Kozono invites curiosity about the supposed dangers of *shinsai eiga* even as he argues that cinema's powerful sensory address to a mass audience ought to be recognized as an important social and cultural asset. Using similar tactics to publicize new films in the same issue of *Nikkatsu gahō*, the studio's head of distribution, Negishi Kōichi, suggested that Nikkatsu would master the public's turbulent emotions with a policy to "lead today's masses—who easily lapse into savagery—to enlightenment" (*satsupatsu ni nagareyasui kyō no minshū o kyōka yūdōsuru*). Like Kozono, Negishi asserted that only a more serious, realistic cinema could accomplish this goal.[2]

This chapter focuses on Nikkatsu film workers' first-hand experiences of the earthquake and Nikkatsu Mukōjima studio's attempt to integrate actual Tokyo settings and film workers' emotions into earthquake films. Since none of these films survive today, I draw primarily on Nikkatsu-affiliated magazines and their presentation of earthquake *jitsuwa* ("true stories" or first-person testimony) and *shinsai eiga* publicity. This publicity shows very clearly that earthquake melodramas were not just intended to resonate with real-life experiences of the quake but to exhibit a heightened sense of realism. In *Nikkatsu gahō*, Nikkatsu Mukōjima actors, filmmakers, and staff wrote extensively about their own experiences of the disaster and their experiences making earthquake films. These paratexts—first-person narratives, behind-the-scenes reports, production diaries, and other forms of reportage—contextualized Nikkatsu's earthquake melodrama films in terms of what actors, filmmakers, and staff had lived through. Film actors' public accounts of their involvement in *shinsai eiga* productions emphasized the deeply troubling feelings and painful memories revived by their roles. Although the films are lost, *shinsai eiga* publicity suggests that the fascination of these melodramas lay in what could not actually be depicted on the screen. Kozono and Negishi allude to this taboo content while vigorously denying that such representations can be found in earthquake melodrama films. As I argue, although this content was not subject to visual representation, readers of *Nikkatsu gahō* were invited to imagine that the horrors of the earthquake were nevertheless put "in" the films via the participation of traumatized actors. Even in the actors' own first-person testimony, these horrors remained under erasure, signified by omissions in their stories and gaps in their memories.

Together, these films and their paratexts make possible what Jonathan Flatley calls "affective mapping." According to Flatley, "an affective map is essentially a mobile machine of self-estrangement" that holds up a particular emotion or experience for examination, allowing the reader/perceiver to better understand their own experiences in relation to others' histories.[3] Drawing on the description of a "revisable, rhizomatic affective map" in Gilles Deleuze and Felix Guattari's *A Thousand Plateaus*, Flatley emphasizes that

> the affective map is not a stable representation of a more or less unchanging landscape; it is a map less in the sense that it establishes a territory than that it is about providing a feeling of orientation and facilitating mobility. I mean the term to suggest something essentially revisable; when it works, it is a technology for the representation to oneself of one's own historically conditioned and changing affective life. . . . The revisable, rhizomatic affective map not only gives us a view of a terrain shared with others in the present but also traces the paths, resting places, dead ends, and detours we might share with those who came before us.[4]

Flatley's theory of affective mapping helps us understand how historical subjects may have linked earthquake melodrama films and paratexts to their own experiences. In addition, his concept usefully suggests how present-day historians may be able to read these affective links—even in the absence of extant films.

Earthquake melodrama films and paratexts—and the notion of "realism" circulating at the time of these films—can be linked to broader changes within the Japanese film industry and interwar society. Earthquake melodrama film publicity, which generally centered on actors' real-life experiences, gives us fascinating insight into the emergence of star discourse in Japan, which involved the increasing public disclosure of actors' private lives. As film historians such as Gaylyn Studlar and Jennifer Bean have shown, in the United States in the 1910s, star-centered film journalism elaborated on the relationship between real life and representation, allowing the industrializing film industry to shore up the film diegesis with supporting print and image media at a time when cinematic storytelling practices and representational conventions were rapidly changing and what constituted the filmic "world" was in a state of flux. Similarly, in Japan, earthquake melodrama film reviews, behind-the-scenes reports, and other paratexts helped Nikkatsu simultaneously authenticate the realism of earthquake melodrama films while promoting its actors as both public figures and ordinary, representative Japanese.

Conditions in the Film Industry after the Great Kanto Earthquake

Nikkatsu and Shōchiku film companies' Tokyo-area studios sustained light damage and suffered no casualties in the earthquake. At Shōchiku's Kamata studio, the wardrobe and makeup building was destroyed, the negative storage building collapsed, and the foundation of the glass studio cracked, but the main building remained intact. Nikkatsu's Mukōjima studio on the Sumida River also survived. However, damaged city infrastructure, harsh living conditions, and constant aftershocks prompted Nikkatsu and Shōchiku employees, as well as the offices of American companies Paramount, Fox, and United, to relocate to the Kansai region soon after the earthquake. Although postearthquake film theater construction boomed, local conditions were not favorable for film production.

In his article in *Nikkatsu gahō*, Mukōjima studio vice chief Kozono Suenori described confusion in the city, traffic congestion, and shortages of props and costumes as important practical concerns. He wrote,

> From now on, whatever we do, we'd like to try to make serious, realistic films [*shinkoku na, riarizumu no mono*]. However, as some among the public have kindly pointed out with concern, as key parts of Tokyo have burned down, we lack locations and it seems impossible to shoot. Yet regarding these matters I am extremely optimistic. Indeed, even if you look at films shot before the earthquake, I think you'll understand that locations have never been a concern.[5]

Still, Tokyo-based film companies faced serious obstacles to recovery. Studios were forced to import foreign pictures to have films ready for immediate release. In September, Nikkatsu and Shōchiku each imported twenty-seven foreign films.[6] Both studios sent representatives abroad to acquire raw film stock as soon as possible. By the end of September,

Nikkatsu was forced to dismiss 800 theater employees and 100 company workers. The studio planned fundraising screenings for October to raise money for over 1,000 earthquake victims with connections to the company. Before film theaters in Tokyo reopened October 1, the police issued a directive on September 25 warning theaters not to show films that would stir up audiences.[7] Fighting for the livelihood of the company as well as for its public, Nikkatsu's staff openly challenged the obstacles in the way of postearthquake filmmaking. But soon after the publication of Kozono's and Negishi's articles, Mukōjima studio closed its doors, and Tokyo personnel relocated to Kyoto on November 14, 1923, where they joined Nikkatsu's Kyoto studio operations as early as November 18.[8]

Shōchiku began relocating film workers to Kyoto as early as September 10, 1923, rushing the opening of its Kyoto Shimogamo studio. In early 1924, Shōchiku sent its former Kamata studio personnel on a publicity tour of Kyushu before bringing them back to Tokyo, where production resumed in February. Besides Shōchiku Kamata, no other major studio reopened in Tokyo until 1934. Not all commentators were enthusiastic about the relocation of filmmaking to Kyoto. As one griped in the May 1924 issue of *Nikkatsu gahō*, "I am worried that, as a result of coming to Kyoto, Mukōjima films will be somehow 'Kyoto-ified.'"[9]

In fact, the site of the first film screening in Japan in 1897, Kyoto had a long history of promoting local film production in conjunction with the city's modernization. Kyoto had lost cultural status with the transfer of the imperial capital to Tokyo after the Meiji Restoration of 1868. Unable to compete successfully with Osaka as the economic center of the Kansai region, the local government put large amounts of funding behind city renewal projects, which included widening and paving streets, modernizing waterways, installing electric street lighting, and laying city tram lines. Kyoto business organizations aggressively pursued railroad contracts to compete with other Kansai cities in creating rail lines between Kobe, Kyoto, Osaka, and Nara, as well as to major cities outside the region and into developing areas. By the time of the earthquake, Kyoto's image as a modern tourist's pleasure ground and cultural preserve was already in place.[10] It was also well established as a strong, secondary film industry. As early as April 1924, Kyoto became known as the "Los Angeles of Japan."[11]

The January 1, 1924, issue of *Kinema junpō* (Movie times) reported on the newly formed Japan Studio Film Directors Association (Nihon Satsuei Kantoku Kyōkai) in one of many articles assessing the state of the postearthquake industry:

> Following the Great Kanto Earthquake, the center of motion picture production has quite unexpectedly converged in Kansai. At the moment, Japan's production companies are Shōchiku, Nikkatsu, Teikine, and Makino—all together, four key players. With Shōchiku and Nikkatsu moving to Kansai, all four came together. After the New Year, Shōchiku returns to Kamata once more. Before this happens, the creation of the "Japan Studio Directors Association" this past mid-December is a logical and much called-for development.[12]

For the first time in Japanese film history, nearly the entire film world had been brought together in the same region of Japan.

On Location: Tokyo-Made Earthquake Melodrama Films

Several film companies made *shinsai eiga* that were filmed outside of Tokyo, including Shōchiku after its relocation to Kyoto. Shōchiku's earthquake films—Ushihara Kiyohiko's *The Earth Rages* (*Daichi wa okoru*, 1923), Ikeda Yoshinobu's *Cursed Day* (*Onoware no hi*, 1923), and Ōkubo Tadamoto's *Facing Death* (*Shi ni menshite*, 1923)—were filmed after the company had evacuated the capital, on Makino Studio sets in Kyoto as well as outdoor locations around Kansai.[13] Even smaller companies made *shinsai eiga*, such as Osaka Films, which began shooting *Love of the Earth* (*Daichi no ai*, 1923) on November 1.[14] It seems only Nikkatsu's *shinsai eiga* were filmed in Tokyo, in actual ruins.

In contrast to the sensationalized earthquake documentary films discussed in the previous chapter, Nikkatsu earthquake melodramas were advertised with solemnity. A full year after the *shinsai eiga* were first released, they were brought before the public once more and promoted as "commemorating" the catastrophe. As fictional, character-driven narratives, earthquake dramas featured a very different address than documentary films. Documentaries were advertised as factual record with terms like *jissha* (literally, "true pictures," or actualities, referring to their use of documentary photography and film), whereas earthquake melodramas adopted familiar *shinpa* melodrama conventions, including the genre's typically tragic endings and stark moral contrasts. These emotional, moralizing narratives enabled Nikkatsu to market its melodramas as having an important role in memorializing the quake. Publicity and reviews of the earthquake melodramas emphasized their narrative templates for moral and emotional reflection. At the same time, the earthquake melodramas pointedly distinguished themselves from melodramas of the past. In marked contrast to conventional *shinpa*, which typically unfolded in bourgeois domestic interiors and relied heavily on dialogue delivered by the narrator (*benshi*), *shinsai eiga* melodramas were marketed as ushering in a new standard of realism by virtue of their topical material and documentary mise-en-scène. *The Earth Shakes* (*Daichi wa yuragu*, dir. Suzuki Kensaku) and *In the Ruins* (*Haikyo no naka*, dir. Mizoguchi Kenji) were filmed on location in Tokyo in September, less than three weeks after the disaster. Publicity images published in *Nikkatsu gahō* show exterior scenes that were filmed in Asakusa and other unspecified outdoor locations (fig. 2.1).

The distinct character of documentary and melodrama film advertisements delineates separate functions for these genres. Whereas advertisements for Shōchiku's and Nikkatsu's earthquake documentaries emphasized lurid realism, scale, spectacle, detailed visual description, and the inclusion of famous landmarks, the publicity and discussion of earthquake melodrama films emphasized imagining and remembering. As opposed to the actualities' "see and know" rhetoric, melodrama ads invited the audience to *re*experience. When used with respect to the melodrama films, the Nikkatsu executives' terms *shajitsuteki* (realistic) and *shinkoku na riarizumu* (serious realism) do not denote documentary realism as much as they highlight the blurring of fiction and reality in character-driven films. I will return to this overlap and the importance of dramatic protagonists later in the chapter.

Though neither film survives, detailed descriptions of *The Earth Shakes* and *In the Ruins* show how they incorporated conventional melodramatic elements into plots with wide audience appeal. The populism of earthquake melodrama films contrasts strongly with *bundan* (literary establishment) writing on the disaster, which was criticized at the time

FIGURE 2.1 A two-page spread in *Nikkatsu gahō* (November 1923) shows on-location shooting for *The Earth Shakes* and *In the Ruins*.

for its lack of social engagement.[15] Suzuki Kensaku's film *The Earth Shakes* concerns a rich family—consisting of a patriarch, his wife, and their three daughters—and their relationship to their servants and the wider community. The film merges a culturally conservative notion of the earthquake as heavenly punishment with a politically progressive message of class equality. The aristocratic family's class snobbery and frivolous preoccupations are shown to be their downfall. The Mizoguchi Kenji–directed *In the Ruins* is a more uplifting drama about lovers reunited by the catastrophe, which provides an opportunity for them to begin a new life together. I examine these films in greater detail below.

In *The Earth Shakes*, a wealthy family is unwilling to let go of its pride despite the humbling disaster. They balk at the idea of a new, postearthquake society founded on commonly shared experiences of physical hardship and deprivation. According to the plot summary in *Nikkatsu gahō*, a wealthy, "class-conscious" (*kaikyū ishiki no surudoi*) husband, wife, and three daughters are accustomed to a frivolous existence and provide their servants with few comforts. One especially industrious servant, Yūzō, slaves away morning and night, in stark contrast to the family's indolence. Yūzō's body is strong, but he has no special aspirations or formal education. He is a simple person, described as thankful for every sunrise and sunset and deeply grateful for his lot in life. His humility before the simple grandeur of nature is contrasted with the materialism of his employers. The wealthy family suffers "divine punishment" (*tenken*) when they are forced to watch the earthquake and fires reduce their great mansion and gardens to ash. Their home destroyed and riches lost, the family experiences the frailty of a bare existence they never knew before. Faced with physical extremes, they find themselves helpless in the face of cold, hunger, and fear. With the exception of the daughter Ranko, the family clings stubbornly to its illusions of superiority until the very end. The family's inability to acknowledge the earthquake's great equalizing force leads to the ultimate demise of the clan.[16]

As this plot description makes clear, in *The Earth Shakes*, the collective experience of bodily duress is portrayed as containing its own moral truth. The film synopsis underscores this message with passages that describe the disaster's heavenly wrath: "Within just a few hours, all of great Tokyo is reduced to burnt ash. Class, status, and all of man's devising are destroyed without a trace. Above the charred plains of great Tokyo, nothing but earth and human beings remain. Even the masters of wealthy households are now merely human."[17] This transformation of the city's multitudes to a single, suffering humanity was a common theme in earthquake reportage and fiction. Newspaper articles frequently characterized Tokyo as an "inferno" (*shōnetsu jigoku*) where men, women, and children suffered and died regardless of age, gender, or social standing. Agonized bodies were portrayed as nearly stripped of humanity as terror, pain, thirst, and hunger took over. Such rhetoric was narrativized in films like Shōchiku's *In the Face of Death*, which *Kinema junpō* described as a tragic compilation of earthquake shorts (*shinsai aiwa shohinshū*). In the several episodes that make up this film, which was shot in Kansai, a father and daughter from the countryside, sisters who work for a business, and a fearless ex-con face different circumstances (sadness, madness, or noble death).[18] The message of the film seems to be that everyone in the city suffered, no matter how virtuous or powerful.

Shinsai eiga countered accusations of sensationalism with a concept of "moving history" that emphasized tribute and posterity. Viewers of the Osaka Kinema earthquake melodrama film *Day of the Tempest* (*Arashi no hi*), which was filmed in Kansai and released in Tokyo in October, were urged to "Cry! See the meaning of life in the depths of your tears!" (fig. 2.2).[19] When *The Earth Shakes* played at the Sanyūkan in Asakusa in May 1924, the ad read: "Against scorched earth as far as the eye can see, the beauty of humanity is revealed in this major commemorative film [*kinen daieiga*]."[20] Similarly, *In the Ruins* was described as a major film "commemorating" the unprecedented, explosive quake when it played at the Sanyūkan in June.[21] This aegis of commemoration for Nikkatsu screenings in 1924 suggests the studio's ongoing commitment to the program it promoted in late 1923, when Kozono Suenori said that *shinsai eiga* would commemorate what earthquake survivors had lived through, offering realistic representations that reflected those extremes.

Filmmakers exploited the earthquake's real-life tragedy for its emotional intensity, which melodramatic conventions directed toward moral argument. There is no mistaking the *shinpa* conventions on which *shinsai* melodramas relied. *The Earth Shakes* features the typical *shinpa* predicament of ossified class differences betraying the promise of modernity by blocking opportunities for upward mobility. In the film, aristocratic snobbery is held up as anathema to a compassionate, enlightened society

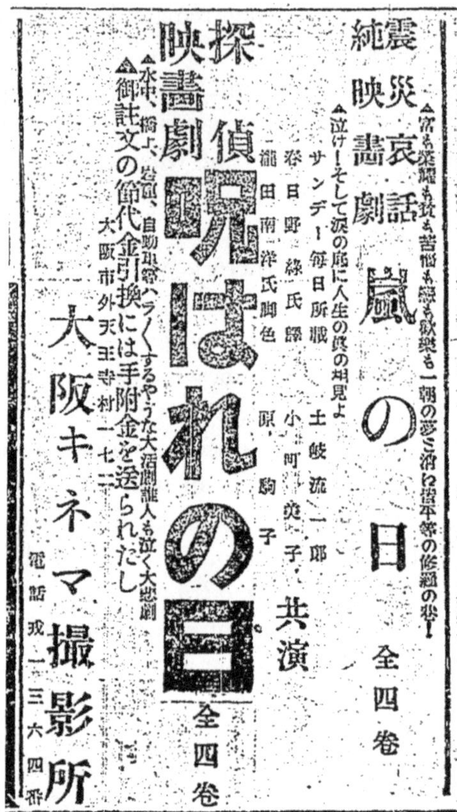

FIGURE 2.2 Ad for *Day of the Tempest*: "Cry! See the meaning of life in the depths of your tears!" *Tokyo asahi shinbun*, October 24, 1923, morning edition.

capable of rebuilding itself. Despite conventional narratives, the *shinsai* melodramas featured a new emphasis on the body. In *The Earth Shakes*, the daughter Ranko's story drives home the film's theme of moral purification through bodily duress. Observing how selflessly Yūzō and the servants struggle to help her family survive, the young lady feels ashamed of her own sloth. As the plot summary notes, after experiencing hardship firsthand, Ranko is finally able to understand the meaning of the word *work*. Even though her sudden willingness to take up physical labor scandalizes her family, she joins the efforts of Yūzō and the others. Struggling alongside them, she feels invigorated, noble, and refreshed. In *The*

FIGURE 2.3 Publicity still of *The Earth Shakes*. Courtesy of the National Film Archive of Japan.

Earth Shakes, as in other affective earthquake representations, helpless, low physical reactions (such as tears, shame, and suffering) evince common humanity, and moral truths are revealed through weeping and hard labor—in other words, as immanent in the physical substrate of existence (fig. 2.3).

The Mizoguchi Kenji film *In the Ruins* also draws heavily on familiar *shinpa* structures: class differences tear lovers apart, and only a disaster that rattles the status quo can restore priority to human feeling. In the chaos of the earthquake, Natsuko is separated from her husband, Morita. While looking for Morita in Asakusa, Natsuko runs into her long-lost lover, Akira. The unexpected reunion reduces them to tears, prompting the recollection of their long history with one another. When they were young, Akira lived with Natsuko's family. They hoped to marry until Natsuko's father suddenly gave her to Morita to repay a debt. Devastated, Akira dropped out of college and joined a group of laborers. Finding each other once again, the reunited lovers make their way to a refugee site (*hinanjo*) and recall their history in what was presumably presented as a flashback in the film. Back in the present, Natsuko is unable to locate Morita, but now reconciled with Akira, she can enjoy her life at long last.

As this description indicates, recall plays a crucial narrative function in *In the Ruins.* Though strictly speaking, it is the earthquake that instantly reconfigures the main characters' relationship, the reconstruction of their histories effects a series of reversals of fate that lends the film a suspenseful, affective structure. In other words, the film shifts the moment of crisis from the present to the past, and occulted truths, hidden motivations, secret histories, and moral crossroads give the film's melodramatic narrative a reflective, contrastive, and extended temporal shape.[22] Akira and Natsuko's recollections bring psychological depth and dramatic tension to the narrative of *In the Ruins*, even though the central conflict—Natsuko's marriage to Morita as an obstacle to romance with Akira—is already resolved in the "present" of the film. As the film shuttles between past and present, the viewer is invited to reflect on their own relationship to the past—engaging in the very process of "commemoration" encouraged by Nikkatsu's advertisements for its fictional earthquake films. In this sense, films like *In the Ruins* perform the affective mapping theorized by Jonathan Flatley, whereby texts seek "to produce a particular kind of affective experience in their readers, and at the same time to narrate this very experience."[23] Flatley uses affective mapping to analyze melancholic literary texts that, he argues, allow readers to view their emotional lives analytically and as formed by specific historical contexts. Once this is accomplished, readers are able to remediate the sense of loss that stems from trauma by imagining other possible histories and/or futures. Flatley calls these "non-depressive" melancholic texts, for rather than dwelling on loss, he argues, they foster the conviction that the world could be other than it is.

The *shinpa* melodrama plot structures of fictional earthquake films are addressed to loss and social transformation, making them available for analysis in Flatley's terms. However, they do not necessarily perform the political function he describes. Flatley emphasizes the world-making potential of nondepressive melancholic narratives, implying that it is possible to distinguish between "compensatory" and "apolitical" (= bad) and "non-depressive" and "political" (= good) melancholic texts. However, the commercially exploitative melodramatic earthquake films are not easily read in such black-and-white terms. Flatley explores (textual) melancholy as a means for regaining interest in, and thus gaining political purchase on, the world, but he does not pursue what it might mean to prefer intense experiences over constructive or sense-making (and ideally politically transformative) representations. Rather than judging the political efficacy of the earthquake films, I would like to suggest that the most compelling implications of Flatley's argument lie in his theory of reading. Although the lack of extant *shinsai* melodrama films makes close visual and narrative analysis of the films impossible, this limitation prompts us toward intertextual interpretations and inferential readings that imagine how historical readers/spectators *might* have engaged with these films. Without films, we are required to resort to the prosopopoetic kinds of "reading in" Flatley discusses and become far more sensitive to the affective structures and textual strategies that work across texts.[24] As Flatley argues,

> There must be just enough noncomprehension to necessitate reading into the text, since it is the breakdown of clear understanding that motivates one to guess at meanings. Such speculation involves an imaginative imitation of the writer, "getting behind" (as [Henry] James liked to put it) the writer so as to see the world as the writer does. As part of this mimesis, the reader must also create or project that person behind the text with whom s/he will identify.[25]

Flatley suggests that such moments are capable of soliciting especially powerful emotions from the reader because they require acts of "imagination and imposition."[26] This act of drawing on one's experiences to interpret someone else's narrative and, in the process, projecting oneself into the text "is analogous to the reenactments of past emotions Freud observed in the scene of analysis that he called transference."[27] Flatley's theory of prosopopoetic reading helps suggest how publicity, criticism, and behind-the-scenes reports might be read to imagine the address of non-extant earthquake melodrama films. This reading strategy directs our attention to the connections between paratextual materials and film texts, prompting us to make use of information that historical viewers would have used when developing their own understanding of, and identification with, actors/characters in the films. At the same time, as Flatley suggests, it is also crucial to recognize the limitations of this kind of reading. For instance, Flatley analyzes *The Turn of the Screw* as a cautionary tale about the power—and danger—of taking prosopopoetic reading too far: "The final moments of the story [in which Miles dies in the governess's arms] can be read as a severe cautionary against taking reading in too seriously, for when reading in gets caught up in institutional modes of the will to knowledge, the flirtatious, mimetic moments can be steamrolled by the imperative to uncover secrets and produce knowledge."[28] According to Flatley, the frame narrative of *The Turn of the Screw* models the relationship of "affective transference" between reader and narrator, while the governess's tragedy cautions against taking the "will to knowledge" too far.[29]

We can now return to the question of how Nikkatsu actors' bodies helped cement connections between fiction and reality, past and present, films and intertexts. As I have already discussed, *Nikkatsu gahō* articles strongly emphasized the actual experiences that were channeled into the actors' performances, which lifted the performances into the realm of the "real" and elevated the films above mere fiction. At the same time, the actions of characters in these fictions (for example, the characters performing "remembering" in *In the Ruins*) create a structure for the audience's engagement, opening an "empty space for the perception of similarity," a kind of scene or template that makes it possible for the audience to insert themselves into the world of the film by drawing on their experiences, too.[30]

The Actor's Body

Shinsai eiga infused *shinpa* melodrama with life-like realism through the use of earthquake survivors and location shoots. Photography of Tokyo's ruins lent documentary authenticity to these tragic tales of the Great Kanto Earthquake. These films offered something distinct from earthquake documentaries and their compiled views of different Tokyo neighborhoods and famous landmarks. What distinguished *shinsai eiga* from earthquake documentaries was their use of actors in fictional, character-driven narratives.

Plot summaries of Nikkatsu's *shinsai eiga* were printed in the November 15, 1923, special earthquake issue of *Nikkatsu gahō* next to *jitsuwa* of the disaster written by Tokyo-based Mukōjima studio actors.[31] Behind-the-scenes commentary on the films encouraged readers to make connections between the *shinsai eiga* and *jitsuwa*, often pointing to how actors' actual experiences contributed to their performances, enhancing the authenticity of the films. Actors in *shinsai eiga* helped anchor the reactions of the spectator, allowing the *benshi* to guide the audience through a strictly controlled and focalized response to the film. However, there were also times when real life punctured the fiction rather than sustaining it, such as when actors broke down on set, unable to control the emotions unleashed by reenactment. Behind-the-scenes articles in *Nikkatsu gahō* underscored how the actors' uncontrollable emotions breached the line between fiction and reality, certifying to the truthfulness of the stories at the same time they threatened to undermine the diegetic integrity of the films.

Publicity articles encouraged audiences to read into the performances even further than the fiction required, by looking for evidence of actors' real-life experiences. For instance, a cartoon in *Nikkatsu gahō* depicts the actress Sawamura Haruko looking bedraggled against Tokyo's ruins (fig. 2.4). The caption reads, "Since she's an actual victim of the disaster, who knows if she's an actress made up as a refugee or a refugee made up as an actress?"[32] Publicity for *In the Face of Death* in the November 1923 issue of *Shōchiku gahō* (Shōchiku illustrated) showed photographs of main actress Takao Mitsuko as herself and as her character in the film. Takao's *jitsuwa* (in the same issue) was linked to the film by a review by Itami Saburō, who attributed the power of Takao's performance to the fact that she had "tasted this kind of fear" herself.[33]

Jitsuwa were among the most popular forms of earthquake narrative. According to Alex Bates, "These personal accounts allowed an imaginative connection with the event that more dispassionate reports could not offer."[34] *Jitsuwa* were emotional, and often incredible, tales of heroism and sacrifice (*bidan*) or the strange (*ibun*). As Bates observes, these stories were usually narrated in the first person and, as the term suggests, presented as "true tales." Yet the existence of third-person *jitsuwa* narratives with "an impossibly omniscient narrator and many extraneous flourishes" shows that many of these stories conspicuously blurred the lines between truth and fiction.[35]

In films that drew on *jitsuwa*, actors' performances helped prompt audience identification and emotional response. At the same time, any

FIGURE 2.4 Cartoon of Nikkatsu Mukōjima actress Sawamura Haruko, who starred in *The Earth Shakes*: "Since she's an actual victim of the disaster, who knows if she's an actress made up as a refugee or a refugee made up as an actress?" *Nikkatsu gahō*, November 1923.

breach of believability could be attributed to a "break through" of all-too-authentic emotion, for studio publicity repeatedly emphasized how actors broke down during filming and could not sustain their roles. Several anecdotes in the November 1923 issue of *Nikkatsu gahō* describe incidents where performances disintegrated into reality as memories of the actual earthquake came flooding back. In these incidents, the hysterical actor's response helplessly bridged fiction and abreaction, memory and enactment through traumatic "acting out."

For instance, in "From the Post-Earthquake Studio," cinematographer Yokota Tatsuyuki describes how a low-tech re-creation of the earthquake for *The Earth Shakes* caused havoc on set. Yokota's account plays up the grotesque dimensions of the situation by emphasizing the gap between what the actors had actually lived through and the paucity of the simulation, which nevertheless triggered real fear among the quake survivors. As shooting started, the crew violently shook backdrops and dropped white powder on the actors from above. Part of the film set was knocked over for effect, while the actors staggered back and forth in an attempt to create a believable illusion of the heaving earth. As this was happening, and while the cameras continued to roll, actress Suzuki Utako suffered a genuine nervous collapse. Actresses Mizuki Kyōko and Sawamura Haruko got dust in their eyes and began running around, raising a big fuss. In his account of the chaos, Yokota is simultaneously pitying and derisive toward the actors, highlighting the pathetic contrast between Suzuki's real paralysis and Mizuki's and Sawamura's dramatics: Suzuki's hysterics illustrate the powerful reality effects of film and performance, while Mizuki and Sawamura are ridiculed for making much ado about nothing.

Yokota's ambivalence toward this scene can be connected to the beginnings of star discourse in Japan. His sly derision can usefully be compared with similar rhetoric found in American film magazines during the rise of the star system. As Gaylyn Studlar has argued, this kind of knowing address to magazine readers was instrumental in constructing star personae and shaping the public's relationship with screen performers. By providing insider knowledge with a few winks and rolled eyes, columnists "offered their readers a superior, distanced awareness of the star-making process while simultaneously perpetuating an illusion of intimacy with the stars."[36] It is worth pointing out that Yokota's account offers magazine readers a position of moral superiority by cynically showing how the desire for realism backfires on set, resulting in Suzuki's real nervous breakdown and Mizuki's and Sawamura's slapstick hysterics.

In another anecdote, a reporter from *Nikkatsu gahō* who visited the shoot of *In the Ruins* describes Suzuki Kako and other actresses thrusting out their hands for treats he had brought to the set, crying "Me too! Me too!" According to the actresses, these desperate pleas were used as a strategy to maintain the "mood of the earthquake" (*shinsai kibun*) while shooting.[37] Such behind-the-scenes anecdotes encouraged magazine readers to anticipate highly realistic films in which the backdrop of the devastated city and actors' real experiences provided indexical links to the Great Kanto Earthquake. At the same time, Yokota's emphasis on the pathetic gap between the re-creation and the "real thing" (reinforced by mockery of what happens when this distance breaks down) implies a demand for skillfully *manufactured* performances.[38] Accordingly, the *Nikkatsu gahō* reports can be linked to two aspects of an emerging star discourse: on the one hand, fascination with and access to actors' private lives, and on the other, appreciation for the screen actor's craft and the magic of movie-making.

Tokyo location shooting contributed a layer of life-like contingency because location shoots meant that aftershocks could be captured by the camera, unexpectedly, at any time. The *Nikkatsu gahō* reports encouraged movie viewers to scrutinize actors' bodies as closely as the landscape, for their bodies were characterized as sites where spontaneous or unconscious physical reactions to trauma might also erupt at any time. Nikkatsu used the audience's supposed hunger for realism to promote its newest films, simultaneously feeding a growing interest in (and commodification of) actors' private lives. Instructing magazine readers on how to decode the actors' performances in semi-fictional representations of the quake, *Nikkatsu gahō* articles encouraged the public to appreciate the work that went into making films while guiding this interest toward actors' personalities and real-life experiences. Although the circumstances of the postearthquake Japanese film industry are quite different from the those of the Hollywood examples Studlar analyzes, *Nikkatsu gahō* clearly also "encouraged a type of so-called fetishistic, 'I-know-but-nevertheless' balancing of knowledge and belief" that allowed its magazine readers to, on the one hand, enjoy a fantasy of the realism of earthquake fiction films that was enhanced by the presence of earthquake survivors while, on the other hand, be confirmed in their knowledge of the gap between representation and reality.

Here we find the true significance of actors' bodies for the realism of the earthquake melodrama films. Nikkatsu actors' performances provided psychological anchors in narrative films that were intended to perform a public, commemorative function. At the same time, reports of their erratic behavior on and off the set were used as evidence of severe trauma that could not be put into images or words. These incidents authenticated the realism of *shinsai eiga* precisely by threatening to disrupt the diegesis, reminding audiences of what could not be shown. *Nikkatsu gahō* reports assured magazine readers of the true-to-life realism of the fiction films while encouraging them to scrutinize the image for accidents and mistakes that would provide a glimpse of the reality behind the fiction. Actors who overidentified with their roles suffered from a collapse of mental functioning that signified the collapse of representation itself: their helpless bodily reactions demonstrated the failure of composure in the face of horror. Press reports rationalized these breakdowns by suggesting that some experiences were utterly impossible to visualize or intolerable to reason and conscious recall. This idea was repeatedly emphasized in film workers' *jitsuwa* or first-person testimony.

This *shinsai eiga* publicity could be compared to what Jennifer Bean has discussed as a marshaling of "perilous realism" to shore up "stardom's institutional framework [and] its absorption of print and image technologies" in 1910s American cinema.[39] Analyzing the hype around American serial queens' real-life daring, Bean shows how reports of actresses' difficulties during filming contradicted images of ease with testimony of duress. She argues that by introducing somatic instability into what was visually assumed to be mastery, this star discourse conjoined "multiple epistemological models that confirm the credibility of a player's performance by quickening, rather than refusing, the contingencies of vision. In order to portend meaning unavailable to or, in fact, *occluded* by sight, reports from the players—'in her own words'—became something of a genre itself."[40] Bean compellingly argues that in this manner, early cinema's "imagination of disaster"—its proclivity for accidents, surging crowds, pitfalls, and crashes—was redirected and reshaped by star discourse. Behind-the-scenes reports helped produce a multidimensional realism alongside (and in spite of) an increasingly standardized and regulated film text. Rather than detract from diegetic absorption, Bean contends that sensational female action star biographies reinforced the referential bonds between film diegesis and reality. The star's body provided a linchpin for these overlapping realities, anchoring the contradictions between them and thus providing stability for a cinema whose representational norms were rapidly changing. Thus she argues that the body functioned as "the most privileged site for exploring the effects of an unevenly regulated apparatus."[41] Disaster was a privileged subject precisely because it introduced the potential for mastering shocking reversals, discontinuity, and accidents. The Nikkatsu earthquake melodramas help us trace similar structures in transitional period Japanese cinema, although, I would argue, on much different terms.

First, fictional films made about the Great Kanto Earthquake immediately after the disaster are obviously not a case of manufacturing peril simply to amplify star status, even though first-person earthquake narratives certainly drew attention to and increased the depth of actors' public profiles. Although Nikkatsu used earthquake melodramas to sustain its Tokyo production during a time of crisis and did, I think, exploit the tragedy to push a new program of realism, there is more to be said about the function of these films. What I am most interested in here is how the "intractability of the body," as Bean puts it, crossed different mediums, textual systems, genres, and even the line between consciousness and unconsciousness, allowing for a rich representation of an inconceivable experience that could not be adequately expressed in words or images alone.

In order to understand how contemporary viewers may have experienced Nikkatsu's earthquake melodramas, we cannot rely on the films (which no longer exist) or even descriptions of the films. It is also necessary to examine the filmmakers' and actors' first-person accounts of the Great Kanto Earthquake, which were published alongside publicity for the films.

Nikkatsu Actors' Jitsuwa

As I have already discussed, the November 15, 1923, issue of *Nikkatsu gahō* included commentary on *The Earth Shakes* and *In the Ruins* that focused on actors' personal identification with their roles. In addition to detailed plot summaries, the magazine published photographs of the Tokyo-based actors filming in the rubble. However, the highlight of the issue, the first to be published after the Great Kanto Earthquake, was a featured section of Nikkatsu actors' *jitsuwa*, or "true stories" of their experiences. Besides this first-person testimony describing the events of September 1, the issue also included first- and third-person anecdotes about filming and everyday life after the disaster. The editors commented on the earthquake's persistent psychological and emotional effects, and Nikkatsu employees confessed unshakeable feelings of dread and nervousness. Behind-the-scenes articles highlighted how actors in *shinsai eiga* roles found themselves helplessly reliving their experiences or else striving to retain this "earthquake mood" to produce believable performances.

Yokota Tatsuyuki's irreverent description of the chaos during the shoot for *The Earth Shakes* shows that the overlap between fiction and reality was sometimes described in a comic mode. More examples of such patently absurd overlapping between reality and comedy appeared throughout the *Nikkatsu gahō* issue. Kitō Shigeru's *jitsuwa* "In My Memory of That Day" describes confusion at Mukōjima on the day of the earthquake in an account that swings between surrealism and pathos.

> In front of the company gate there was a crack in the earth about a foot wide where muddy water was flowing out. . . . The splashing sound of the river *jabu jabu jabu* was getting louder. Now everyone had taken refuge at the field used for location sets [*rokashon setto*] not in use. There were cracks running up and down here, and the neighborhood residents were laying out boards and storm shutters and trembling *gata gata gata*. It was a strange and sorry sight to see Segawa Tsuruko crying while still in costume. The *bento* shop was warped just like an expressionist set. Both Inagaki-san's and Kitamura-san's houses had collapsed, and it seemed strange to me that the second floors remained intact, like half a house. When I saw that the concrete smokestack of the textiles factory had snapped in half, the Asakusa Jūnikai immediately crossed my mind.[42]

After the worst was over, Kitō walked through the neighborhood with a group of others to try to get an idea of the damage. Out on the street he observed Kōsaka Toshimitsu filming the city for what later became the Nikkatsu earthquake documentary. Rows of collapsed houses lined the Shitamachi streets, and Kitō recounts hearing the blood-curdling cries of strangled voices issuing from deep inside the wreckage, as if from blocked throats. Kitō grabbed at trees as he walked to steady himself against successive aftershocks as if he were "catching the horizontal swinging bars at school." Everyone else was wandering about in half-crouching positions holding onto the trees, and he says, "When we saw each other's postures, it became funny and gave rise to grim smiles."[43] In "One Day Later and I Would Have Perished," Nikkatsu actor Koizumi Kasuke describes walking along the train tracks back to his home in Hongō. He tried to leap onto a train full of passengers, but as soon as he jumped onboard the train slowed to a stop—"I couldn't help but laugh at my confusion at having jumped onto a train so crowded with fleeing people that it couldn't move." He also notes that Tokyo's buildings were "all warped and contorted like expressionist stage sets."[44]

Comparisons of Tokyo's landscape to expressionist sets and buildings to broken bodies brought home the fragility of the human being in a disintegrating landscape. Bodies and buildings shook in sympathy, and both were subject to sudden collapse. When *The Earth Shakes* was shooting in Tsukiji, the crew observed a Western-style brick building topple and become a pile of ruins, a reminder that buildings could collapse at any time, long after September 1. Real aftershocks made it into the footage of fictional films, creating continuity between fiction and "real life" (*seimei-gake*). Some aftershocks were so fearsome that the crew was compelled to run for shelter. According to *Nikkatsu gahō*, the inclusion of this footage in the finished film contributed to the film's realism: "there's no shortage of this kind of actuality [*jikkan*] [in the film], and it contributes to the mood of fear."[45]

Similarly, another *Nikkatsu gahō* anecdote suggests that Mukōjima actresses didn't just put on "victims' faces" for the camera, since they were, in actuality, miserable. The blurb describes a film magazine reporter, presumably the author of the anecdote, visiting the studio with a photographer. Their visit happened to coincide with the arrival of a certain unnamed playwright. The photographer attempted to shoot the actresses assembled around the playwright, but the dramatist "had a terribly malicious tongue and the actresses had probably never in their lives encountered someone so disagreeable." He mocked their unseasonably light clothing, and when they couldn't take it anymore, he joked that their sullen faces would spoil the photographs. Afterward, once their "victims' faces" had been "exposed to the camera," the actresses confided that they truly had only the lightest of kimono to wear against the cold. According to the magazine, these words conveyed the "post-earthquake mood, you could say, or a taste of misery."[46]

In *jitsuwa* in the magazine, actors' descriptions of homelessness and wandering dwelt on their feelings of loneliness and exposure. In her *jitsuwa* "Five Hours in the Middle of the Water," Senō Matsuko related her sense of being totally isolated and vulnerable in the burning landscape. She described only narrowly escaping the fires in Asakusa, after which everything seemed like a dream. She remembers shaking off a little girl who had latched onto her *obi* and would not let go. She fled from a man who attempted to help her. In her hysteria, she thought he was trying to strangle her, but it occurred to her that such a death might be preferable to being horribly burned alive in the fires. At midnight on September 1, she was still moving across the city, crawling underneath smoke and flames. To avoid the fires, she jumped into the river. It was low tide, so she was able to find a foothold about the size of half a tatami mat along a stone wall where others were taking shelter from the flames. There were four men squeezed onto the outcropping and a woman with a dead baby who had gone insane. Boats in the river were burning, and a nearby bridge went up in flames, but even as the fires crossed from one side of the river to the other, she and the strangers around her were safe. They walked along the river in the water and eventually climbed out at the police box near Yanagibashi.

> I didn't know whether it was night or not, but everything all around me was bright, and fields of fire surrounded me like nothing I had ever seen in dreams or reality. I sat on the gravel where frequent temblors reminded me that it was still yet possible I would die, and I waited for time to pass. My kimono was mostly in shreds and my hair was in disarray, but there was nothing I could do about that. Instead, I used some newspaper as clothing and leaned limp and exhausted against a chest of drawers. At that time, all I could think was that everyone in Tokyo was dead, and I was the only person who had been saved. There was truly no one else there.[47]

Eventually strangers passing by Senō gave her a wadded kimono and *haori*, as well as a child's flannel garment that she tore to make bandages for the burns on her face and blisters on her feet. She slowly made her way to Kamata in a crowd of people. On the way, she was aided by many more strangers, some whom she spoke with, some whose names she never learned.

The darkest story in the special earthquake issue of *Nikkatsu gahō* is that of Uesugi Rokurō, who saved his daughter and sixteen-year-old niece only to lose them in the panic at Yoshiwara, where he later found their bodies. Uesugi was visiting a neighborhood bath near his house in Senzoku-chō in Asakusa when the earthquake struck. He ran home without even a loincloth and pulled his niece and daughter from the shaking building where they had been left alone while his wife ran errands. Several hours later, they were in a crowd of refugees that had gathered in Yoshiwara Park when flames encroached on the crowds, driving them closer together. Uesugi thought it would be safest on the east side of the park, but a grove of plum trees drew the flames. He broke off branches from the trees and threw water on the wood in a desperate attempt to protect against the approaching fire. There was barely any standing room as the crowd thronged closer and closer together, and people began to cry for help as the panic created an avalanche of living bodies. Uesugi didn't realize they were being pushed closer toward the pond, since the heat was becoming utterly unbearable. Suddenly, a voice cried out repeatedly, "Get into the pond! Get into the pond!" and everyone made a mad dash for the water, causing a stampede.

> I gripped the children close as I was pushed by the avalanche-like mob, pushed out as far as the middle of the pond. From that moment on, I didn't have a single thought of trying to survive. Realizing that if we were pushed underwater, we could die, I held the children tightly, praying "If it comes to that and we must breathe our last, at least let the children feel no pain." Then just like that, I think we were pushed down into the water. I can only remember that part as if it were a dream. Suddenly I was vaguely aware of looking around me. There were piles of dead bodies all around, and I realized, my heart leaping in my chest, that I was alone. I alone had come up from the waters. When had the children been taken from my grasping hands? Why had I alone been saved? As if in a dream, I trampled dead bodies underfoot as I made my way back to the burned-out ruins of the hospital. There I came to as I watched the hot water pouring off the rain pipes. . . . At that instant, no sooner had I thought "Ah! I have a wife and child!" then once again I rushed back toward the pond, but the dead bodies were like mountains. At that point, somehow I no longer had any thought of dying, but I wasn't clearly conscious of whether I had been rescued by someone or if I'd gotten out myself. I slept there just like that. As it was getting dark and night fell, I was helped by an old woman passing by, but at that time I wasn't even wearing underclothes. I was stark naked. I was completely nude. It's like tracing a dream, trying to think back to that time, but I remember feeling that I was being held down by many clinging hands.[48]

After wandering in confusion, Uesugi made his way back to the Nikkatsu film studio. He remembers getting as far as the gate before meeting stage technician Kamehara Yoshiaki, who constructed the sets for Mizoguchi

Kenji's expressionist film *Blood and Soul* (*Chi to rei*, 1923). Uesugi collapsed in tears. "At that point I was in a total stupor. It's no wonder Kamehara-san said that at the time I was like a man gone insane." Uesugi joined other refugees taking shelter within Mukōjima's gates. On September 3 he was able to recover his niece's and daughter's bodies, which were found floating in Yoshiwara pond, but it took him more than a week to locate his wife's corpse.

Newspapers reporting on the Great Kanto Earthquake likened the chaotic city to a body in pain. Battered by the quake and incessant aftershocks, scorched by firestorms, and shrouded in smoke, the city itself seemed to heave and cry out in distress. Articles frequently repeated the four-character phrase *abikyōkan* or "shrieking in agony" to describe the capital, whose streets groaned with ongoing temblors and the restless movement of desperate crowds. Like other commonly used phrases—"unprecedented" (*mizou*), "reduced to ashes" (*shōdokashita*), "inferno" (*shōnetsu jigoku*, literally "burning hell")—the expression "shrieking in agony" underscored the utter vulnerability of the city and the people in it. Many of the most affective representations of the disaster were associated with the terrors and hardships of the masses. Even when tales of individual heroism and suffering were presented in collections of *jitsuwa*, their compilation in digest form conveyed the collective experience of the quake as the sum of many irreducible, individual horrors.[49] In one of the first reports to come out of Tokyo, an *Osaka asahi shinbun* correspondent from nearby Takazaki gave a breathless description of the metropolis turned inside out. In these tumbling sentences, a litany of horrors strains against the limits of grammatical phrasing and punctuation:

> an endless number of refugees head in the direction of Yamanote toward Aoyama, among them in the disarray the wounded are borne on stretchers as they gasp for breath, and they number possibly several thousand. In the crowd, parents are separated from their lost children, and people raise their voices in screams. Surrounded by flames, refugees abandoned places of refuge and escaped danger by leaping into the river, where the bodies of those who were wounded by fires that swept overhead come floating by. Then, there is the sight of those being engulfed by raging flames, who struggle desperately against the most appalling end. And yet there is still more, several hundred thousand people running this way and that looking for a single cup of water—which requires several hours—shoving each other and parched. The army and police patrol together and wives and daughters from

> good families shove each other aside to get to their bread first. And numbers of refugees bearing scant household effects and furniture increasingly occupy the city's wide-open spaces and streets. In places like Ueno Park, Aoyama, Sugamo, they lay out straw mats and shutters to sleep on. Not only that, as if the entire city is expecting another earthquake to hit, they sleep outside in the open, nor does anyone go into buildings anymore. Shattering early autumn's dreams, this scene of hellfire and the suffering of the imperial city's people is beyond words to describe.[50]

Descriptions of the earthquake groped at what language could not adequately express by using parataxis and ellipsis, as well as references to avant-garde films and dreams. Screams, faints, prereflective acts, and loss of consciousness all figure strongly in earthquake representations, underscoring trauma as an experience that seemingly had no object and that moved the body in uncontrollable ways. Traumatic experiences that eluded representation or consciousness were nevertheless testified to by bodies out of control.

In the aftermath of the Great Kanto Earthquake, representations of the body and the language of bodily pain provided an idiom for substantiating and communicating otherwise intransitive, uncontrollable, instinctual, irrational, and absurd responses to the tragedy. In newspaper reports, bodily sensation and movement were mapped onto the shifting, erupting, disintegrating city space of Tokyo. In the same manner, in *Nikkatsu gahō*, the body of the actor became a vehicle for discussing the unimaginable and the unrepresentable. The body's inarticulate and uncontrollable behavior bore witness to extreme experiences that could not otherwise be expressed.

Nikkatsu actors' "acting out" of their own real-life, traumatic experiences in fictional *shinsai eiga* linked films and paratexts via the body. As I have argued, intertextual readings of the films through publicity and *jitsuwa* allow us to retrieve the importance of the body as a physical sign where a dual inscription of traumatic memory (as both conscious recall and compulsive repetition), past and present, and fiction and reality could be read.[51] Recognizing this, we can see that what was apparently a contradiction in how the films were presented—as perfect re-creations and as fictions punctured by documentary events—points to overlapping expectations placed on actors' bodies and constructed across a diverse field of representations and texts. Bodies were the bearers of audience identification in narrative fiction films that plotted out structures of rememoration, but they also offered physical evidence of real trauma and its aftermath. The body was where these overlapping significations accumulated and where representation itself threatened to collapse.

CHAPTER 3

"Realism" and Modernity

Earthquake documentaries and melodrama films allow us to explore the important role that cinema played in representing the disaster and harnessing emotion toward different ends. Analysis of these films and their intertexts demonstrates how filmmakers appealed to postearthquake audiences with the promise of realism, even though the full extent of the disaster and the worst of its horrors could not easily be represented directly. This is not to say that filmmakers, spectators, and authorities were agreed in their understandings of "realism" and aligned in their interests, nor that the Great Kanto Earthquake was even the most important force in producing interest in cinema's power and reach. However, public unrest and the challenges of reconstruction heightened the stakes for thinking about cinema's persuasive sensory realism, and after the earthquake, widespread demand for information and entertainment helped film and publishing companies recover and expand, inaugurating an age of mass media. The increasing ubiquity of commercial culture and popularity of the movies amplified concern with cinema's ability to channel spectator emotions and produce powerful reality effects.

By the time of the earthquake, the industrialization of American cinema and Hollywood's rise to global prominence had vividly demonstrated cinema's broad appeal and extensive relationships with commodity culture. Transformations in American cinema during the period 1908 to 1917 led to the standardization of production techniques and narrational practices, the rise of the feature-length film, and the star system, all of which radically altered the nature of cinema's address to the spectator.[1] The ease and transparency of films made according to this "classical" system developing in the 1910s, together with Hollywood's takeover of international film markets, fueled widespread discussion of cinema as a "universal language" and the "most democratic art." These developments changed the terms in which the film spectator was conceived. As Miriam Hansen has argued, the transition in the American industry redefined the film spectator from "a participant in a concrete and variable situation of reception to a term that informs the structure of the film as product" and entailed a shift "from a collective, plural notion of the film viewer to a singular, unified but potentially universal category, the commodity form of reception."[2] In other words, the film spectator addressed by American classical narrative cinema was no longer an individuated member of a heterogeneous audience whose reception of the film varied depending on ethnicity, language, cultural background, class, and gender, as well as the specific exhibition situation in which viewing took place. Instead, the structures of classical cinema posited a spectator for whom visual pleasures transcended (and even suppressed) individuality. The abstract and ideal spectator was "a consumer."[3]

The imbrication of American cinema and consumer culture made it possible for cinema to become a mass-cultural form. The standardization of film industrial and textual practices was motivated by the need to appeal to the greatest number (and therefore widest variety) of ticket buyers, so, appeals to class and ethnic differences were increasingly supplanted by a more general "consumerist script" that encouraged fantasies of class mobility and material abundance.[4] The immigrant and working-class audiences who patronized cheap, store-front theaters were succeeded by the middle-class and upwardly mobile clientele of the movie theater.[5] The turn to feature-length films necessitated longer, more complex narratives that required a spectator's sustained attention; as a result, absorption, identification, and emotional involvement were increasingly encouraged over distracted viewing. Although cinema's showcasing of fashion and luxury items could be distracting to some viewers, such consumerist spectacles generally contributed to the consolidation of an inviting and inclusive cinematic address that pulled the spectator "into" a coherent fictional diegesis.[6]

Discussions of film "realism" around the time of the Great Kanto Earthquake must be understood within a transnational film historical context. What was at issue was not simply cinema's ability to register the world in front of the camera but its associations with Western modernity, which included the technological, economic, and social underpinnings of cinematic realism and its capitalist-consumerist address. For intellectuals and authorities, this produced two primary concerns: first, a concern with cinema's relationship to Westernization and, second, a concern with the potential of the masses to transform culture and society through their influence on popular culture. Discussion of these issues predates the Great Kanto Earthquake but becomes even more urgent after the disaster. In *tenbatsu* (divine punishment) discourse, it was argued that the earthquake was heavenly retribution for the evil, decadent commercial urban culture that had taken root in Tokyo.[7] After the earthquake, the "people" (*minshū*) and the "masses" (*taishū*) became keywords as rapid urbanization and media expansion transformed Japanese society.[8] Mass media such as cinema helped generate new concepts of individual and collective identities that were tied to emergent technology and new social formations. Commentators disagreed as to whether these new identities were authentic and whether the public's sentiments were legitimate—particularly when they posed a challenge to established values and could be dismissed as a mimicking of Western culture. For these reasons, it is important to consider film realism not just in terms of medium-specific properties and textual practices, but also (and in some contexts primarily) as a set of questions relating to cultural authenticity, cultural authority, and cultural appropriateness. Realism has a cultural politics.[9]

This cultural politics is perhaps foregrounded most clearly in the aesthetic and pragmatic arguments for and against "realism" at Nikkatsu's Mukōjima film studio. In contrast to studios like Shōchiku and Taikatsu, which were established in 1920 as "reform studios," Nikkatsu (est. 1912) had to navigate a difficult transition from earlier practices to the "pure film" (*jun'eigageki*) practices that brought Japanese cinema more in line with international norms. This is why Mukōjima studio publications, Mukōjima film workers' memoirs, and Mukōjima studio-affiliated fan magazines offer a rich source of arguments for and against reform, attesting to a variety of positions on "realism." Nikkatsu took a cautious position, resisting the pure film movement's call for the outright elimination of the female impersonator (*onnagata*) and other theatrical conventions. The studio bulletin *Kakushinseru Mukōjima satsueijo* (Reforming Mukōjima studio, 1923) includes many arguments for retaining the *onnagata*, including cultural and economic justifications. Nikkatsu film director Wakayama Osamu observed that despite strong realistic motivations for using actresses in female roles, socially and culturally it was not feasible to use women because "common decency in contemporary Japan forbids this."[10] Wakayama argued that visual, bodily realism was at odds with cultural authenticity.[11] In the essay "Regarding the *Onnagata*" in the same bulletin, director Suzuki Kensaku argued against using strictly formal criteria or designations such as "new" and "old" to assign critical value to different film practices, saying that unstable representational codes and changing formal distinctions could not be used as reliable ontological categories (*naimen hontai* or "inner essences").[12] Suzuki's remarks touch on a common concern that the "modernity" cinema was so often associated with was none other than the very conditions of precarity and flux.[13] Yet there are also examples of pure film reformers adopting the rhetoric of cultural authenticity to argue for the adoption of Hollywood norms. For instance, in *Kinema rekōdo* (Kinema record), a film journal aligned with the pure film movement, several articles in late 1913 and early 1914 criticized foreign-made "Japanese dramas" (*Nihon-geki*) and used their misrepresentations of Japan to argue for film reform. However, the rhetoric of cultural authenticity was generally conservative.

Before the earthquake, many Nikkatsu-affiliated film critics described their ideal cinema as one that would deal with inner experience and essences rather than resemblances. In the Nikkatsu-affiliated magazine *Mukōjima*, articles celebrated the sensitive artist's unique inner vision and denigrated the slavish imitation of outward appearances made possible by mechanical reproduction. *Mukōjima* and *Nikkatsu gahō* magazine critics warned that without the guidance of a strong artistic vision, the camera's ability to capture what was in front of it resulted merely in surface tracings of reality. In stark contrast to *Nikkatsu gahō* articles written after the earthquake that embraced documentary realism, pre-earthquake *Mukōjima* and *Nikkatsu gahō* articles castigated filmmakers for clinging to optical realism. For example, in the June 1, 1923, issue of *Mukōjima* magazine, Ōi Tadasu asserted that "the power of film only begins when we use it to depict the internal, abstract circumstances of things that only people with very high sensitivity can sense."[14] According to Ōi, too many filmmakers were simply concerned with film's ability to automatically reproduce the external, superficial aspects of reality. He compared such filmmakers to children scribbling with pencil and paper, as if the simple fact of inscription—the automatic registration of light passing through the camera lens to register on film—was greatly pleasing to their childish curiosity.

There was also a general tendency among critics affiliated with Nikkatsu to argue that the influence of Western culture would undercut the artistic integrity of Japanese films, undermining their ontological claims to reality, because Westernized films bore little resemblance to real life in Japan. Critics attacked the copycat reproduction of Western culture and the rampant spread of its images through the global circulation of cinema. They warned against the superficiality and materialism of mass-mediated image culture. In the June 1923 issue of *Mukōjima* magazine, Yamamura Fuyuo argued that the realities constructed by cinema were inauthentic as long as these "realities" were nothing more than a rote copy of what was put in front of the camera.[15] He condemned the slavish imitation of foreign culture in Japanese films, stressing the importance of cultural fidelity, organic community, and original artistic vision. Arguing for authenticity instead of realism, Yamamura asserted that only the pure subjectivity of the sensitive artist could authenticate the artwork, and at no cost should inner vision be subordinated to the mechanical reproduction of external reality. In rejecting the mere mechanical reproduction of reality and the uncritical adoption of Western norms, Yamamura offered a cultural nationalist notion of "purity" that challenged the "purity" of the pure film movement, which wanted Japanese filmmakers to adopt standard Western film practices. Ōi Tadasu's and Yamamura Fuyuo's articles show how discussions of realism were not limited to the camera's direct inscription of the phenomenal world, but were also engaged with aesthetic questions and cultural anxieties about what was "natural" and real. For critics like Yamamura, this was an important concern because the flashy, kaleidoscopic visuality of modern urban culture was glaringly out of harmony with national values.

Interestingly, after the Great Kanto Earthquake, Nikkatsu magazine articles were no longer so quick to elevate rarefied artistic subjectivity if it contradicted general tastes. This change in attitudes at one of Japan's most conservative film studios is a strong indicator of a general shift in attitudes toward film realism and mass culture after the Great Kanto Earthquake. To take one example, actor Mikoshiba Morio's numerous essays in *Nikkatsu gahō* point to new assessments of cinema as mass culture while revealing how the connections between cinema and consumerism prompted concerns about cinema's potentially harmful effects. Mikoshiba's essays are worth examining more closely, for this ambivalence toward cinema's power and scope is an important theme in 1920s popular discourse on cinematic desire and identification.

Mikoshiba's article "Film's Value as the People's Art" ("Minshū geijutsu to shite no eiga no kachi"), which ran on March 1, 1925, shows the emergence of a positive discourse on cinema's mass appeal in which film is duly recognized as a powerful cultural medium, similar to the press in terms of the reach of its influence and its reflection of popular tastes.[16] In articles like this, cinema's appeal to the lowest common denominator and its tendency to change with the vagaries of the times are newly assessed as proof of cinema's inherently flexible, democratic qualities.[17] It had not been long since Mori Iwao noted in an April 1, 1922, *Kinema junpō* column that cinema's mass audience and appeal to low tastes stood in the way of its recognition as art. Mori described critics as undecided as to whether popular entertainment could truly produce quality aesthetic works. In contrast, he noted, for the censors it was not cinema's artistic potential as much as its powerful address to a large (and potentially unruly) public that was the dominant concern. The question "Is It Art or Not?," Mori sardonically observed, stumped the sharpest critics but gave "feeble-minded" censors little pause. Even if critics and intellectuals were still divided, censors had already realized that film was far too powerful and influential to be given a special exemption as "art."[18] This hesitation regarding cinema's mass appeal and cinema's claims to be art contrasts strongly with Mikoshiba's 1925 article, in which he enthusiastically embraces cinema as the "people's art" (*minshū geijutsu*) and argues that cinema is privileged above all other arts, because it alone is first and foremost a popular entertainment (*minshū goraku*). Interestingly, Mikoshiba also turns to the censors to make his point, opening his article with an image of the sheer volume of film footage that censors must screen to keep up with the rapidly expanding film industry. In Mikoshiba's assessment, there is no contradiction between cinema's mass appeal and its aesthetic potential. Film, he argues, is an integral part of ordinary people's everyday lives and should be admired for its ability to keep pace with changes in lifestyle. Just as the gramophone and the 1,000-yen piano are no longer luxuries but common middle-class commodities, he writes, cinema isn't just entertainment but a "necessity of life" (*seikatsu hitsujuhin*).[19] Thus, for Mikoshiba, cinema is "popular" (*minshūteki*) in the truest sense of the term—because it represents ordinary people and their everyday concerns. He uses the American housewife as an indicator of film's inclusiveness and everydayness: even she goes to the movies twice a week.[20] But he can only claim cinema as universal and everyday by drawing a strong distinction between mass-mediated representations of modernity, on the one hand, and the virulently disintegratory and antisocial tendencies of modernity as represented by modernism, on the other. According to Mikoshiba, whereas popular cinema "contemplates and recognizes aspects of the age from a stature which is at the same height as the masses," avant-garde cinema is the solipsistic invention of abnormal and overreactive imaginations. For all his enthusiasm for popular commercial culture, Mikoshiba firmly rejects faddish modernism, insisting that visions seen by a mob do not beget a popular consciousness: "Even if [films] are widely seen by the crowds (*gunshū ni ōku mirareta*) that is not enough to make them popular—they must take the people (*minshū*) or social conditions (*setai*) as their subject matter."[21]

Here we see Mikoshiba's ambivalence. Even his celebration of popular cinema contains suspicion of urban decadence and unease regarding film's radical appeal to the senses. Suspicion and unease emerge when he compares the ceaseless and unpredictable growth of cinema to the expansion of Tokyo itself, which "year by year has become prosperous and vast, though there is nothing in the way of systematic organization, nor the virtue of being steadfast, nor foundation to be found."[22] His statements on the city and the avant-garde suggest serious doubts about the chaotic epiphenomenon of modernization—from its fleeting, atomistic sensations and their representation, to the urban environment itself.

This concern with excess and its effects extends to Mikoshiba's October 1, 1926, article "Philosophy for the Actor" ("Yakusha shosei tetsugaku"), in which he humorously dissects the film actor according to the various "economies" the actor must obey, providing a systems-based analysis of different emotive gestures and their impact on the audience.[23]

He describes the modern actor as a machine and the director as a foreman. He argues that acting should be a mechanically regulated economy of savings and expenditures, and he criticizes profligate actors and directors who push performance toward excess. For instance, Mikoshiba argues that tears are meant to moderate distress by flushing away emotions in a kind of hygienic physiological reaction (*eiseiteki seiri sayō*). Therefore, if the actor wants his audience to cry, he must refrain from showing tears and reserve that capacity for the viewer. Mikoshiba describes the actor's provocation of emotional responses in intensely intimate terms, as when he compares the actor's ability to produce intoxication with the sweetness and mystery of a kiss. He cautions the actor to avoid any unnecessary expressions, while simultaneously warning that being too stingy with one's talent threatens the whole economy. Once again, it seems that Mikoshiba's primary concern is the issue of self-control. He cautions his fellow actors that self-centeredness and vanity tend to increase with mastery of the craft, so it is imperative not to be too self-indulgent. Once again, he holds up avant-garde "subjectivist art" (*shukan shugiteki geijutsu*) as the epitome of "onanism" (*jii*) and "self-conceit" (*unubore*). Avant-garde works are dismissed as "masturbation films [*masutābeishon eiga*] that no one else can understand."[24]

As Mikoshiba's essays suggest, despite transforming attitudes toward mass culture brought on by a sea change in the number of magazine titles, newspaper circulations, film theaters, and films produced in Japan, cultural modernization was hardly a journey toward free-signification and limitless self-expression. The phantasmagoria of modern culture and the fluidity of the modern subject remained important topics of debate. The Great Kanto Earthquake amplified an existing sense of cultural crisis in which the threat of fragmentation and irrepressible energies was very real. Responses to the earthquake included attempts to describe the causes and consequences of social and psychic fragmentation, as well as proposals as to how to best channel its release of anarchic forces and reorganize the ruins of the city into a meaningful whole. Notions of the earthquake as heavenly punishment (*tenbatsu* or *tenken*) called for moral straightening with reconstruction. Surprising though it may be, *tenbatsu* discourse was also prevalent in postearthquake film magazines, despite the blame that such theories cast on cinema. *Tenbatsu* discourse is another area where we can analyze the cultural politics of mass culture in modernizing Japan.

One example is Shōchiku screenwriter Ishikawa Hakuchō's personal narrative of the disaster in the October 1923 issue of *Kamata*, the first issue of Shōchiku's Kamata studio magazine to appear after the earthquake. Ishikawa was on a shoot in the nearby city of Kamakura when the disaster struck. He gradually made his way from Kamakura back to the Kamata studio just outside Tokyo, in a journey that lasted from September 1 until the evening of September 2. In spite of the horrible suffering and heroic acts he witnessed, Ishikawa was convinced that the earthquake was well-deserved punishment for modern moral decline.

> From Katase to Kamata, how miserable was the punishment that nature wrought [*shizen no chōbatsu*]. What I myself witnessed was so sorrowful that you can't possibly imagine the sights of which I could tell. The European battlefields, the Russian Revolution, the labor movement—these things have made me abhor civilization [*bunmei*], and I resent the sad lifestyle that we, who have no choice but to live with these things, must lead. This earthquake has made me lose my faith in civilization.[25]

Ishikawa described the darkness and terror of the Great Kanto Earthquake as chastening its victims—"people went about in the streets so brimming with fear and anxiety that even the light of the sun appeared dim, and they all but forgot themselves, seemingly drifting about in a fearful dream, as if in utter shock."[26] Yet he also found that ordinary people were capable of extraordinary kindness and courage in times of extreme duress. Near Yokohama he came across a group of five or six men in front of a house that had been completely obliterated by the quake. The men exhausted themselves trying to lift a large column, while another man stood by, dumbstruck, staring fixedly at the scene with a child in his arms. The man's wife had rushed into the violently shaking home to save their youngest child despite her husband's attempts to hold her back. The column fell on the wife and baby, and both died. Ishikawa also reported emotional exchanges between strangers who were heading different ways. Some were making their way toward Tokyo, while others were fleeing the city for Yokohama. En route to separate destinations, these travelers stopped, tearfully shared stories, and wished each other well. They expressed such intimacy in parting, Ishikawa said, that it seemed their spirits warmed one another in a mutual embrace. Disturbingly, his account contains a single passing reference to the "Korean disturbance" (partially censored in the text), but he seems to discount this ethnic violence and emphasizes the good deeds he witnessed during his journey. Ishikawa speculated that these reminders of the "beautiful coexistence of bygone times" were only possible because of the earthquake's wrath. He wrote with dismay that once everything was rebuilt, "they'll be at it again in sickening competition. Struggling once again without blood or tears or even feelings. The winner, the loser, even though they will all meet the same end, they'll curse each other and hate each other like the unfeeling human beings that they are."[27] Invoking the notion of the Great Kanto Earthquake as punishment several times throughout the article, Ishikawa declared, "Having given serious consideration to [cold-hearted competition and strife], I have thought, how many times would I welcome nature's excoriation, whether this earthquake or some other punishment, to return again and again, if it would only make such incredibly self-centered human beings stay faithful to their human emotions!"[28] Commentators such as Ichikawa believed that the transformations accompanying modernization—swelling urban populations, the rise of commercial culture, turbulent mass politics, the mechanization of society, technological warfare, class conflict—were essentially dehumanizing. Ichikawa suggested that modern competition and conflict inhibited cooperation, empathy, and understanding—and ultimately the ability of anyone to feel anything authentically at all.

Despite *tenbatsu* discourse, the Great Kanto Earthquake did not wipe Tokyo's new urban cultures off the map—it hardly even slowed the growth of mass culture. The earthquake destroyed twenty of Tokyo's twenty-two theaters, forty-three of its fifty-six cinemas, and sixty of its ninety-one dancehalls. One year later, Japan's entertainment and media industries were even stronger than before.[29] In mid-October 1923, it was reported that thirty new movie theaters were being planned for the entertainment district of Asakusa alone, including ten to be completed before the end of that year. By November, there were already seventy-seven movie theaters up and running in Tokyo, up from the twelve that had survived the earthquake.[30] By fall 1925, 185 film theaters were operating in the city of Tokyo, compared with 112 in the entire greater Tokyo metropolitan area in 1922.[31] Yearly film attendance in Tokyo increased from 9,252,521 in 1917 to 15,193,324 in 1926, when an estimated 157,385,449 tickets were sold throughout Japan.[32] This expansion helped bring about a large-scale transformation in attitudes toward mass entertainment.

In the immediate aftermath of the disaster, Tokyo film and publishing companies were sustained by demand for information about the disaster and entertainment relief. The rebuilding of studios, presses, labs, shipping depots, and theaters provided an opportunity to implement new technologies and scientific management techniques, contributing to a modern revival of Japan's media industries. Edward Mack argues that the earthquake allowed Tokyo publishers to update their printing technology and created opportunities to expand capacity, negotiate more flexible shipping arrangements, and distribute books through sales networks that had previously been limited to magazines. The publishing industry grew so fast that total book and magazine sales nearly doubled between 1921 and 1925. During this time, publishing expanded at an average of 15.36 percent a year, the fastest rate since 1897–1902. In the two years immediately following the earthquake, the publishing industry grew at a rate of approximately 19 percent. Despite fears that Tokyo-based publishing would never recover from the disaster, Kansai-based firms gained only a momentary advantage over Kanto competitors. Mack and others link the resiliency of Tokyo's print industry to the high demand for news, images, testimony, and other forms of information about the quake.[33]

If we look at the impact of the Great Kanto Earthquake on the Japanese film industry, we see similarly that film production initially dropped but quickly rebounded, and ticket sales continued to rise steadily. Whereas in 1919, there had been approximately 7.3 million film admissions in Japan, by 1924 admissions rose to 54 million and nearly tripled that by 1926.[34] A total of 537 Japanese films were released between December 1923 and December 1924, with 575 American films and 635 European films shown in Japan in 1924.[35] In early 1927, *Kinema junpō* estimated that the Japanese industry would produce about 700 films in the upcoming year.[36] Examining the startling postearthquake figures for different media industries, scholars such as William O. Gardner, Mark Driscoll, Miriam Silverberg, and Edward Mack have argued that the efflorescence of mass culture should not simply be measured as an increase in production volume, since the rise of mass culture also entailed the emergence of new and diverse forms of production and consumption. Japan's rapidly shifting media ecologies contributed to new methods of ascribing cultural value, new expressions of subjectivity, and new techniques for exciting jaded consumers.[37] By magnifying ongoing, often alarming shifts and leveling in Japan's modern culture, the earthquake also played an important role in guiding film critics, authorities, and other observers to make connections between cinema and large-scale demographic change.

It was also in this decade that Japanese educational film production began in earnest.[38] Makino Shōzō, "the D. W. Griffith of Japan" and "father of Japanese cinema," established the first educational film production unit in 1920. According to Makino's son, legendary yakuza film director Makino Masahirō, his father quit making fictional films for Nikkatsu after hearing reports of children imitating the potentially dangerous acrobatic hijinks of star actor Onoe Matsunosuke.[39] The films of "Medama no Matchan" (Matchan the Eyeball), as Onoe Matsunosuke was affectionately known, were disparaged by film reformers for their reliance on theatrical spectacle. Makino's ninja films with Onoe incorporated kabuki-inspired makeup (*kumadori*) and stylized fight choreography (*tachimawari*). Makino used in-camera editing to create kabuki-esque quick changes known as *hayagawari* plus surprise entrances and exits, which in theater were facilitated by black-clothed stagehands, trapdoors, and a revolving stage. Reform film critics who wanted to "modernize" Japanese cinema ignored Makino's use of trick editing, instead advocating the use of editing to create "realistic" space and visual narration rather than special effects.[40] Onoe Matsunosuke's biggest fans were disparagingly referred to as "nursing mothers" (*komori onna*) and "snot-nosed brats" (*hanatare kozō*).[41] Makino's decision to give up magical ninja films and turn to educational filmmaking suggested that Japanese cinema was finally "growing up." Along with other developments in the early 1920s, the emergence of educational filmmaking indicates new appreciation for and redirection of the persuasive power of the medium.

Within the government, this new attitude was apparent in the Ministry of Education's entry into film production, as well as the centralization and standardization of film censorship laws. The government showed very little interest in cinema during the earlier part of the century, despite an early 1910s theater-building boom that was stimulated in part by widespread enthusiasm for films of the Russo-Japanese War (1904–5). In contrast, the government quickly took an active interest in the emerging medium of radio in the early 1920s. As Gregory Kasza notes, the state imposed far more rigid controls on radio than it had on either cinema or the press.[42] He suggests that the government possibly wished to avoid the mistake it had made with film, for cinema's potential as a purveyor of information was not fully recognized for many decades.[43] A new appreciation of cinema and mass media in the early 1920s led to revised media policies, the ascription of a new public role for cinema, and new public recognition for filmmakers. The government's involvement in film production followed a slow and uneven process, but it later had important consequences for Japan's wartime media policy and film control. Public prestige for motion pictures was unimaginable until the early 1920s, at which point the state's new cognizance of film as an important medium can in part be traced to the earthquake, the rapid growth of the mass audience for cinema, and the sociopolitical context in which this expansion occurred.

With the growth of mass media and the swell of popular political movements, the 1920s is often viewed as a period of democratization and cultural liberalization. At the same time, this was also a time of increased government involvement in media and tighter restrictions on public assembly and free speech. Beginning in the Meiji period and continuing into the Taishō and early Shōwa eras, Japan's media policies demonstrated authorities' sustained interest in creating and controlling national polity by careful administration of mass communications and popular political discourse. Despite the possibility that these media could be used to express opposition and promote pluralism, the government used newspapers, radio, and film to control the new publics they created. As Kato Shūichi has argued, in the Taishō period, developments in modern mass media and communications, along with the emergence of an educated urban class, created the necessary conditions for popular political participation and prepared the way for "the manipulated mass society of the future."[44] Takemura Tamio similarly describes the Taishō era's bourgeoning popular culture as creating the necessary conditions for total mobilization.[45] In 1925—a year particularly emblematic of these contradictory currents—the Diet approved the right to vote for all men over the age of twenty-five who were not receiving public assistance. This was indeed an important achievement for Taishō-era progressive movements, which had agitated for greater popular representation in Japanese government. However, in the same session, Japan's elected leaders passed the repressive Peace Preservation Law, which severely restricted political speech and free assembly. It became the template for even more restrictive censorship codes, such as the 1939 Film Law.[46]

Miriam Silverberg, Takashi Fujitani, Yoshimi Shun'ya, Noriko Aso, and others have shown how in the late nineteenth century, Meiji modernizers used modern visual forms to showcase industry, celebrate the expansion of empire, inculcate national values, and encourage consumption. These representations created a "modern subject" by modeling the proper relationship between the spectator and the state. The same interest and caution in using spectacle to harness popular energy can also be found in Japanese officials' approach to media representations of the Great Kanto Earthquake.

In 1923, authorities who cautioned media producers not to stir up the public with sensational depictions of the earthquake were mindful of Japan's recent history of agitation and dissent. Writing on early twentieth-century transformations, Japan historian Andrew Gordon describes "fear of political disorder, fear of gender disorder, and cultural concern to answer the question, Who are 'we Japanese'?"[47] The first two decades of the twentieth century saw the turbulent rise of popular politics, spurred by the mobilization of the public behind two very expensive wars: the Sino-Japanese War of 1894–95 and the Russo-Japanese War of 1904–5. To build taxpayer support for these campaigns, the government encouraged an outpouring of national fervor and commended its citizens' sacrifices, which fueled public expectation that ordinary people had an important role to play in national politics. In World War I, Japan provided arms and other supplies to the Allied forces in the Pacific. This and the hefty indemnities China paid Japan after the Sino-Japanese War helped fuel the development of heavy industry and began a transition away from light manufactures and an agrarian economy. The indemnity payment of 360 million yen was equivalent to approximately four and a half times Japan's annual budget the year before the war.[48] A great deal of that sum was funneled directly into the military budget and into subsidies for the steel and iron industries. The Russo-Japanese War further contributed to the development of industry and the emergence of a mass society. War demonstrations helped legitimize large public gatherings and the press encouraged outspoken, patriotic editorializing. A growing class of urban wage laborers and the new middle class began to organize for better working conditions and political representation in recognition of their contributions to empire. Frequent riots took place in Tokyo between 1905 and 1918, spurred in part by demands for a stronger constitutional government and increased popular representation in national government.

The Treaty of Portsmouth ending the Russo-Japanese War in 1905 sparked the first of many riots. The war had been eight times as expensive as the Sino-Japanese War and produced four times the number of casualties: 60,000 were killed in battle and 20,000 succumbed to disease. The treaty awarded Japan no reparations and no significant territorial gains.[49] It only allowed Japan to take over Russian railway lines in southern Manchuria, the Russian lease over Port Arthur, and half of Sakhalin Island. This was hardly a significant concession, even though it set the stage for Japan's future campaigns on the continent. The Japanese public was outraged by the Treaty of Portsmouth. A September 5 rally in Hibiya Park in protest of the treaty launched a three-day riot that killed seventeen people. Mobs destroyed 70 percent of the city's police boxes.

The majority of riots in Tokyo between 1905 and 1918 originated in Hibiya Park. Protests against streetcar fare increases on March 15, 1906, erupted into a three-day riot during which dozens of streetcars were smashed and company offices attacked. From September 5 to 8 later that year, rioters again destroyed streetcars and police boxes while protesting the increase in fares. A February 11, 1908, protest against tax increases exploded in violence. In 1913, a February 10 rally for constitutional government that took place outside the Diet created a mob that smashed police boxes and attacked government newspapers. This time, there were 253 arrests and 168 injured, including 110 law enforcement officers. Later that year, on September 7, a rally for a strong China policy in Hibiya Park grew out of control, resulting in attacks against the police and Foreign Ministry. The push for an aggressive China policy remained a theme in the February 10–12 riots, when demonstrators protested against naval corruption and for stronger constitutional government. On this occasion, rioters attacked members of the Diet, stormed newspapers, and destroyed streetcars and police boxes, leading to 435 arrests. A February 11, 1918, rally for universal suffrage led to police clashes with demonstrators. The 1918 rice riots lasted from August 13 to 16 and led to 578 arrests. As Gordon points out, a strong undercurrent in most of these demonstrations and riots was criticism of clique government and impassioned demand for greater representation of the people's voice in national politics.[50]

In 1923, images of earthquake survivors occupying Tokyo's city parks and open spaces, including a wide area in front of the Imperial Palace, surely brought to mind the throngs of demonstrators that had gathered in Hibiya Park. Film footage, photography, paintings, and sketches of crowds running from the early September firestorms echo depictions of the Tokyo riots. Even the three-volume 1926 *Tokyo shinsairoku* (Record of the Tokyo earthquake), published by the Tokyo municipal government, placed the disaster, relief response, and reconstruction within a longer history of the city's physical and social transformations, from the decline of the Tokugawa shogunate to the present day, and in the immediate context of Tokyo's modern excesses. According to the prefatory remarks to this substantial collection of earthquake reports, Japan's participation in World War I had thrust the nation (*kokka*) into the center of international activity, and the public (*kokumin*) had suddenly found itself confronted with an onslaught of international intellectual currents. An earlier paradigm of cultural exchange, characterized by careful synthesis of Eastern and Western thinking, was transformed by a headlong rush into the new. Japan's successes and its exposure to Western modernity encouraged arrogance, hedonism, and a taste for indolence acquired from a world wearied by war and looking for respite. Meanwhile, resentment toward the war's nouveau riche fueled restless egalitarian sentiments. Society became rash, frivolous, and exorbitant while "the high tones of imperialism changed into the shriek of the populace" (*teikoku shugi no kōchō o minshū no zekkyō ni henji*) under the influence of the Soviet revolution and Germany's defeat in World War I. According to *Tokyo shinsairoku*, this "shriek" voiced "arguments for racial equality, the rise of the proletariat, demand for women's rights, and insistence on the *suihei mondai* [the issue of ongoing discrimination against former 'untouchable' castes]." The preface draws a strong connection between these political developments and the rise of a decadent urban culture:

> the populace was swept by a craze for the pursuit of pleasure. . . . [In Tokyo] there are nouveau riche who throw away millions on books, postcards, and curios; young nobles who spare no expense on lavish banquets; intellectuals who scream for the pressing need for sex education; gentlemen who live apart from their wives, who stick by them through thick and thin, so they can enjoy cohabitation with their lovers.[51]

As Charles Schencking points out and *Tokyo shinsairoku* attests, on the eve of the earthquake, "To many observers, Tokyo had become a center of hedonistic consumer culture, entertainment, decadence, political unrest, and labor agitation and a breeding ground for dangerous thoughts and questionable behavior."[52] This *tenbatsu* discourse fueled reconstruction fervor. Many of the commentators who described the Great Kanto Earthquake as *tenken* or *tenbatsu* were quick to promote the earthquake as a "golden opportunity" (*kōki*) to reconstruct the city and redress moral and ideological regress.[53]

As I have argued, the Great Kanto Earthquake was instrumental in prompting officials to pay closer attention to the ways that mass media could be used to shape public sentiment. The earthquake is a key historical moment in early debates on film's reality effects and its potential use for education and propaganda. By drawing attention to the power of cinema, the catastrophe shaped vernacular understandings of film realism, accelerated government involvement in the Japanese film industry, and inaugurated government-sponsored filmmaking in Japan. Earthquake documentaries and melodramas used new strategies to harness spectator identification and mobilize film's publicity apparatus to produce a multidimensional realism. Publicity for the earthquake documentaries demonstrates a drive to commercialize the Great Kanto Earthquake by packaging its atrocities into consumable experiences. Advertisements, commentary, and *jitsuwa*, or personal testimony, of actors and staff at Nikkatsu Mukōjima were also instrumental in publicizing the earthquake melodrama films and pushing a new program of realism.

In the chapters that follow, I move on from the earthquake to shift attention toward questions of gender and emotion. In popular discourse on cinema's persuasive sensory realism, the most impressionable spectators were imagined to be women. Mass culture was frequently described as feminine or feminizing due to its associations with overpowering, destabilizing, superficial, materialistic, or unreasonable forms of identification and desire. Women's bodies and subjectivities provided a popular idiom for thinking about the allure of consumerist fantasies, and a gendered lens allows us to see how discourse on cinematic realism was also often focused around similar issues of identification and desire. Many scholars have examined how gender issues informed the politics of mass culture in interwar Japan, and I will demonstrate how attention to gender can also enrich our understanding of the politics of film realism, celebrity, and identification, and enhance our appreciation of how interwar commentators regarded cinema as a sensory-affective medium.

PART II

The Power of Cinema: Identification and Emotion

CHAPTER 4

Desire and Identification

The Aspiring Actress Problem

In the mid-1920s, a score of sensational articles about "aspiring actresses" (*joyū shigansha*) appeared in Japanese newspapers and film magazines. These stories chronicled the plight of young girls who risked peril by running off to movie studios, hoping to become stars. Many came from rural areas of Japan and left their employment or family homes without permission to pursue dreams of acting. They were imagined as especially vulnerable to exploitation because they were unworldly and narcissistic. Articles with condemnatory titles, such as "Miserable Aspiring Actresses Lured by the Hell of Vanity!" ("Kyoei jigoku ni akogareru, kanashiki joyu shigansha!"), savaged aspiring actresses for their selfish delusions and unreasonable attachments.[1] According to these articles, aspirants believed that if they simply showed up at a film studio they would be hired on the spot, not realizing that film companies were inundated with applicants and most hopefuls were rejected. Newspapers chronicled how, in the course of their misadventures, aspiring actresses were robbed, raped, kidnapped, captured by authorities, and returned home. Unscrupulous studios took advantage of aspirants by levying unreasonable fees. Other "studios" and "agencies" were exposed as fronts for prostitution rings.

Although the aspiring actress articles take many forms (news item, editorial, fiction, satire), I group these representations together because of their many similarities. First, many articles cite multiple examples of women's victimization to imply an epidemic of movie-struck girls and related crimes. Second, the reports typically characterize the women as a "mob" or a "throng," using the language of mass hysteria to describe their delusional behavior. Finally, the reports blame the victims and their pathological obsession with the movies for what happens to them. That is, rather than describing the women as happenstance victims of a film-related crime wave, the cases are treated as a single phenomenon, with roots in specifically female character flaws. Aspiring actresses are repeatedly characterized as vain, narcissistic, self-centered, and overinvested in images. They are depicted as modeling their behavior on careful study of the movies (*katsudō kenbutsu*), which results in an attenuated grasp on reality.

These tales were not just moral lessons; they were also entertainment. They were written to chastise young women and warn parents, but they titillated with their lurid descriptions of wayward women and overstimulated female bodies. The prevalence of these reports makes the aspiring actress panic a prime example of the increasing attention to cinematic realism and its somatic effects in 1920s Japan, an era in which discussion of cinema's reality effects took on new dimensions because of the proliferation of permanent film theaters and the emergence of regular distribution networks, as well as the new salience of star publicity for studio branding. It is clear that several industrial and sociocultural factors played an especially important role in giving rise to aspiring actress discourse.

One important factor is transition in the Japanese film industry. In the early silent period in Japan, female impersonators were used instead of actresses in women's roles. It was only in 1920 that Japanese reform studios such as Shōchiku and Taikatsu (1920–22, dissolved when its production wing was absorbed by Shōchiku) were created with the policy of using women in female parts. Some existing studios, such as Nikkatsu, continued to use impersonators as late as 1923. Even after women became standard in female roles, acting, with its long-standing associations with prostitution, remained a disreputable profession in Japan.[2] Filmmaking was generally considered a low vocation and frequently linked to organized crime and social ills. Thus, the aspiring actress panic can partly be linked to a period of dramatic change in Japanese film practices, during which women became more visible in Japanese films and the modernizing industry attempted to improve its image. Aspiring actress articles reflect numerous traits of this industry in flux: new demand for actresses, the rise of star culture, the emergence of predatory businesses and scams that targeted film workers, new awareness (and apprehension) of cinema's ability to span the urban-rural divide, and more energetic efforts on the part of the Japanese film industry to foster professionalism and channel fan attachments in productive ways. This last fact is especially evident from the way these articles were deployed by the Japanese film industry itself (though it may seem counterintuitive) in an attempt to correct the public's mistaken impressions regarding film production practices.[3] This explains why several film magazines associated with major film studios published news items and editorials excoriating misbehaving aspirants. In many ways, these cautionary tales were part of the new marketing of the "Hollywood of Japan" as the Japanese film industry—newly concentrated and united in the wake of the Great Kanto Earthquake—attempted to hitch itself to positive images of tourism, cultural living, recreation, and other new forms of middle-class leisure culture.[4]

A second major factor driving aspiring actress discourse is the fact that, in Japan as well as in the United States and in Europe, women were becoming increasingly visible outside the home. Giuliana Bruno, Shelley Stamp, Anne Friedberg, Miriam Hansen, and other feminist film historians have examined how public spaces like movie theaters offered women new opportunities to look and be looked at, while at the same time film theaters were regarded as notoriously difficult spaces to survey and control.[5] As these scholars point out, and the aspiring actress panic confirms, there was something transgressive about the perspectives that films opened up to women. Films extended imaginary visual mastery over expansive topographies, affording exciting and sometimes erotic experiences of looking, as well as access to spaces that were previously off-limits. This allowed female spectators to enjoy powerful and empowering experiences of mobility they could not enjoy in real life. As Stamp has argued, the movies thus participated in the reconfiguration of social and sexual geographies: "The way that cinema enabled a fictive remapping of a viewer's relation to social space—although potentially liberating for women—was for the same reason threatening to many commentators."[6] An aspiring actress's obsession with the movies was, of course, not simply an obsession with her own image and the idea of becoming a star. It also reflected rural women's fascination with the big city and the worlds of possibility that films explored. The aspiring actress panic revolved around cinema's ability to transform both identity and space.

"To the Depths of Hell"

Commentators writing about aspiring actresses attributed women's desire to enter the film industry to impulsive, materialistic desires instilled by films and magazines. The desire to become an actress was interpreted as a sign of vanity and blamed on women's innate predisposition to imitation and daydreams. According to many writers, the aspiring actress exhibited a deeply problematic, narcissistic identification with film stars, as well as an inability to tell the difference between fantasy and reality. The darkest stories reasserted the connection between acting and prostitution.

In Japan, actresses were banned during the Edo period in an attempt to curtail unlicensed prostitution. They gradually reappeared in the Meiji period during the push to update Japanese stage practices. Actresses became perceived as necessary for performances of European realist plays, such as Henrik Ibsen's *A Doll's House* (written in 1879 and first performed in Japan in 1911), and for the creation of a modern Japanese theater.[7] This "new actress" (*shinjoyū*) was strongly implicated with the arrival of European cultural influences and the development of new and progressive forms of femininity. For instance, when the Tokyo Imperial Theater launched an actress school in 1908, a flurry of newspaper articles publicized the trainees as "new women" (*atarashii onna*).[8] The school was highlighted in the fifty-part *Tokyo asahi shinbun* series "Women of Tokyo," which profiled women writers, screenwriters, nurses, and "new actresses" and reported on women and social ills, such as prostitution, sex crime, double suicide, and sexually transmitted diseases. One installment was devoted to the Tokyo Imperial Theater acting school's ten female students, whose ages ranged from seventeen to twenty-three.[9] When the powerful Kansai-based Shōchiku theater company decided to recruit actresses in 1912, the *Tokyo asahi shinbun* launched a special twelve-part series called "The New Actress" ("Shinjoyū," November 11–27), which enthusiastically embraced actresses over the female impersonator's artifice while acknowledging ongoing cultural resistance to women on stage. According to the first part of the series, the Yūrakuza theater, Masagoza theater, Bungei Kyōkai (Arts and Letters Association), Doyō Gekijō (Saturday Theater), Jiyū Gekijō (Free Theater), and Kindaigeki Kyōkai (Modern Drama Association) were suddenly inundated by "new actresses, new new actresses, and new new new actresses."[10] Part seven dubbed the phenomenon an outbreak of "actress fever" (*joyūnetsu*).[11]

Aspiring actress stories from the 1920s are far more alarmist in their depictions of women's desire (and failure) to become movie stars. The *Tokyo asahi shinbun* article "From Vainglorious Dreams, Descent into Women's Hell, Women Who Fail to Become Celebrated Stars Lead Precarious Existence" ("Kyoei no yume kara, ochiyuku onna jigoku, appare sutā ni narisokone ukikusa no yō na onna no mure," October 3, 1925) attributed women's false hopes of stardom to highly publicized stories of café waitresses or geisha breaking into the movies. According to the reporter, Shōchiku's Kamata studio was overwhelmed with aspiring actresses showing up at their door. Every day, three or four girls arrived at the studio without warning, only to be turned away. As if rejection wasn't enough, the article intoned, "As a result of their disillusionment, their comeuppance is to sink to the depths where fallen women go."[12] The article identifies another problem: some girls manage to get in front of a camera only to discover that they have no stomach or skill for moviemaking. According to the article, this is more proof that "their looks [*gaimen*] are splendid and their personalities [*naimen*] are unbearably awful."[13] After disobeying parents and running away, such willful women cannot or will not return home. Because of this, the article notes, the cheap inns near Kamata are crawling with disappointed hopefuls. It warns that many female students are fooled by fake actor recruitments and fall prey to criminal schemes.

Some film companies charged applicants exorbitant admission prices to join their studios. The article "Two Girls with Actress Fever to Police: 'Please Take Us In'" ("Joyūnetsu no futari shōjo, tomete kudasai to kōban e," August 1, 1927) reveals how Japan Film Ltd. (Nihon Eiga Kabushiki Kaisha) in the Tokyo neighborhood of Takinogawa drew aspiring actresses to the city with recruitment ads. Once the women arrived at the studio, they were shocked to discover that they were required to pay a thirty-yen guarantee fee.[14]

In some cases, crime syndicates took advantage of aspiring actresses. Officials investigating mail fraud found that a corrupt clerk at the Kyoto Gojō post office was kidnapping aspiring starlets. The clerk stole complimentary tickets that large theaters such as the Kyoto Minamiza, Kabukiza, Meijiza, and Kyotoza sent out to Shōchiku affiliates. Police were investigating the stolen tickets when a detective discovered that the clerk had also intercepted correspondence from actresses responding to Shōchiku Shimogamo studio recruitment ads. The clerk pocketed their photographs and résumés and destroyed the envelopes, using these documents to entrap the women. He posed as a studio employee and invited two women to an offsite screen test, luring them to a building where all the entrances had been nailed shut, where he planned to hold them against their will and rape them. According to the report, seven or eight other people were implicated in the plot.[15]

In a similar case from 1926, two men from the Tokyo-based joint stock company First International Film were arrested for cheating actress applicants. Their recruitment drive attracted 560 women. Among these, twenty-eight girls were extorted for "confidence money" and sexually assaulted at a local inn. It took several days for the local Kyōbashi police station to investigate the victims' allegations. The newspaper observed that the women involved all wore Western clothes and appeared to be students.[16] Another incident in Tokyo was reported in the May 31, 1929, article, "Villains Lure Women with Film Actress Recruitments, Two Women Terribly Deceived, Lose Way Fleeing Evil-doers" ("Eiga joyū boshū de onnatachi o tsuru akkan, sanzan na me ni atta onna futari, ma no te o nogarete sa mayō").[17]

Finally, there is the case of the Diamond Cinema company and the disappearance of amateur actors who accompanied production staff to China. Diamond Cinema started out as a Japanese cinema research group founded by Nozaki Etsurō in May 1925. It assembled actors by recruiting twenty-four amateur men and women between the ages of eighteen and twenty-three. According to the *Tokyo asahi shinbun* investigation, more than half of the company were college students at the height of *eiganetsu* (film fever). Women were allowed to join for free, but men were charged five yen a month. Nozaki's associate, Kanda Hiderō, worked with recruits on their expressions and gestures and served as the company's film director. Their first films included a biopic of politician Tanaka Shōzō, who famously protested the pollution caused by the Ashio copper mine. According to the *Tokyo asahi shinbun*, these productions were poorly planned and shoddily made. After a couple of months, Kanda broke with Nozaki, who left the company to pursue projects overseas. In mid-July 1925, Kanda took a group of actors to Dairen (Dalian), a port city in China that had been partially controlled by Japan since the Russo-Japanese War. Kanda was known by a number of aliases, including the name Sawada Sadao. On the continent, he was known as the Strong Arm (*ratsu'ude*) and involved in disreputable business dealings. One of the missing actors was eighteen-year-old actress Nemoto Midori (stage name Sano Mikiko), who had appeared in the Tanaka Shōzō film. Kanda told Nemoto he was planning to shoot an exotic drama in Dairen. Because the purpose of the voyage was location scouting, he would not guarantee any paid shooting on the trip. He collected travel fees of thirty yen from each company member who elected to go. Soon after the company departed to China, the actors' families received suspicious telegrams requesting money. Six or seven days before Nemoto's expected return to Japan, a college student who had also been on the trip suddenly returned to Tokyo to inform her parents that the trip had been a deception. Nemoto's family contacted the Dairen authorities, but they were unable to locate her. The planned date of her return came and went with no news. Finally, Nemoto's parents received a telegram from Dairen, allegedly from their daughter, which read: "Cinema. No filming planned. Returning. Send kimono." Her whereabouts were still unknown.[18]

Another *Tokyo asahi shinbun* article, "Telegram of Death Arrives, Sender Unknown. On Kiyoshi's Family, Who Was Lured by an Ad for a Compensated Trip to Manchuria and Mongolia, and Died in Dairen" ("Sashidashinin fumei de, kita shibō denpō, Manmō shisatsu no ue sharei no kōkoku ni tsurareta, Dairen de taoreta Kiyoshi no jikka") discusses the tragic story of a youth from a well-to-do family in Nagano prefecture who had been tricked into joining Diamond Cinema. Uchida Kiyoshi traveled with Diamond Cinema from Dairen to Hōten seemingly without incident. However, communiqués from the tour became increasingly suspicious, the name of the group leader changed frequently, and Uchida's family began to suspect that their son was being held against his will. In order to figure out what was going on, relatives went to Tokyo to find out anything that they could, but they were unable to trace their son. Finally, a telegram from an unknown sender arrived with the news that Uchida was critically ill and his family should send money and clothing immediately. The family responded with money and a telegram demanding their son be returned. The response they received read simply: "He has died. Send 150 yen."[19] Yet another article probed the company's history: "The True Character of Ringleader Kanda Hiderō, Known as the

Strong Arm in Manchuria and Korea. Wife Is Shōchiku Actress Takakura Kaneko" ("Manchō chihō de shirareta ratsu'ude, danchō Kanda Hiderō no sosei, tsuma wa Shōchiku joyū Takakura Kaneko"). The paper asked, "Exactly who is this Diamond Cinema and its ringleader Kanda Hiderō, who is responsible for making young men and women cry under the cold Dairen sky?"[20]

Many aspiring actress articles warned that criminals targeted naive youth with promises of stardom. See the article "Young Women Ruined Trying to Become Film Stars, Disobeying Parents Leave for Tokyo without Permission, Swindled by Studio Chiefs Who Sell Them Off, Wake from Illusions with Ocean of Tears" ("Eiga no sutā o kokorozashite, mi o horobashita wakai musume, oya ni somuite mudan de jōkyō, umauma satsueijochō ni uritobasaru, me ga samete umi no namida," December 25, 1925). This article makes a common assertion that victims are rural girls who are unfamiliar with urban dangers. For instance, eighteen-year-old Kanemitsu Kikuyo believed she had the good looks to achieve an actress's lifestyle (*joyū seikatsu*). She appealed to her parents for support, using the pretext that she was interested in the arts, but they remained firmly opposed. Four months later, Kanemitsu left home without permission and became a café waitress in Shinjuku. In her spare time, she hung around the studios studying actresses, which made her an easy target for the chief of the Tōyō film studio. He claimed he was starting his own venture and, if Kanemitsu invested some money, he would make her a star.[21] In a side article, a law enforcement official commented that these swindles were extremely common because women wanted to believe in silver screen destinies and were easily lured by false advertisements. Police regularly investigated suspicious announcements from "such and such actress training school." According to officials, "The duped individuals are generally not from Tokyo. They are usually girls from the countryside who don't know anything about the big city. The advertisers are also doing this with the objective of luring country girls."[22]

In 1926, Matsumoto Yoshirō, a reporter for the *Asahi* newspaper, compiled cases of "miserable aspiring actresses" for two articles in *Nikkatsu gahō*: "Miserable Aspiring Actresses Lured by the Hell of Vanity!" ("Kyoei jigoku ni akogareru, kanashiki joyū shigansha!," February 1926) and "To the Depths of Hell: Details of Crimes That Accompany Descending Throng of Actresses" ("Naraku no dontei e, mizukara shizumu joyū shigansha no mure, sore ni shitagau hanzai no iroiro," October 1926) (fig. 4.1).[23] Matsumoto blamed young women for becoming so obsessed with movies that they became obvious targets for sex traders or con men. According to Matsumoto, the women were at fault for "destroying their very bodies and souls, sinking to the lowest of the low."[24]

"Miserable Aspiring Actresses Lured by the Hell of Vanity!" admonished irresponsible would-be actresses, emphasizing the punishment, shame, and remorse that awaited them. In the introduction of the article, Matsumoto cautioned that women who ran away to film studios would find themselves with no money to get home, nothing to eat, and no place to stay, and would likely end up among the "painted ladies" at one of Kyoto's "dubious snack bars."[25] One of his anecdotes describes a twenty-year-old from Hiroshima prefecture whose fascination with the movies began as a young girl. In her youth, she frequented the shows of a touring film company that visited her town once or twice a year. Later a permanent movie theater was built and showed programs that changed every week, intensifying her unhealthy obsession. She became fixated on a particular film star, which led to daydreams about what it must be like to be an actress with adoring fans, and so she ran away to Kyoto. The city was famous for its concentration of film studios, and Matsumoto refers to it as the "capital of temptation."[26] After making the rounds of all the film theaters in the entertainment district Shinkyōgoku, the girl quickly ran out of funds. According to Matsumoto, she ended up in a Kyoto police station, weeping "tears of remorse into her sleeve" in the "cold murky darkness" of her cell.[27]

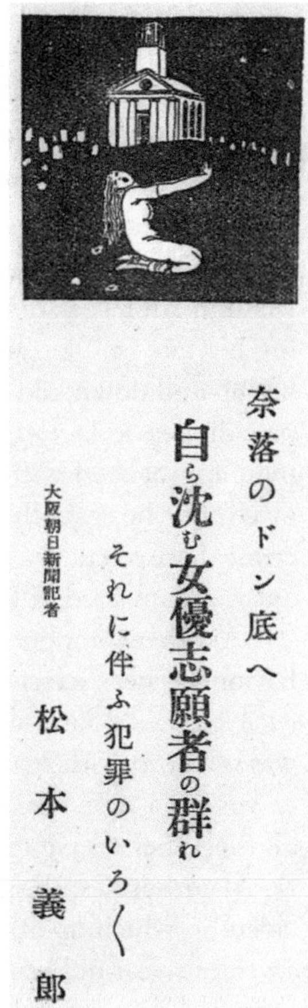
奈落のドン底へ
自ら沈む女優志願者の群れ
それに伴ふ犯罪のいろ〱
松本義郎
大阪朝日新聞記者

FIGURE 4.1 *Nikkatsu gahō* headline (October 1926): "To the Depths of Hell: Details of Crimes That Accompany Descending Throng of Actresses."

In "To the Depths of Hell: Details of Crimes That Accompany Descending Throng of Actresses," Matsumoto describes the case of a nineteen-year-old from a village in Shiga prefecture, a graduate of the village supplementary school, who pored over film magazines and "peeped" in movie theaters while "dreaming of becoming a glamorous film actress" with a monthly salary and fancy clothes.[28] She gathered all her money and made the pilgrimage to Kyoto, only to be rejected by the Nikkatsu, Makino, and Tōa studios in turn. Dispirited and broke, she was pondering her fate in Okazaki Park when a lecherous ice cream vendor looked her up and down and inferred her desperate state: "Her sunken eyes and pale distressed face! The unsteady gait of one worn down by life!"[29] The man approached with friendly overtures, and the girl thought she was saved, but he sexually assaulted her and sold her into prostitution. The crime discovered, the girl was sent back to her hometown, and her assailant was convicted of kidnapping.

Another component believed to contribute to the aspiring actress's behavior was her excessive desire for expensive commodities. In his *Nikkatsu gahō* exposés, Matsumoto describes an eighteen-year-old housemaid who was obsessed with makeup and frittered her time away idly dreaming of becoming a star. She coaxed her master's daughter to run away with her, and together they escaped to Kyoto. Despite the efforts of local and national authorities, the girls were never found. Matsumoto describes an incident in which up-and-coming starlet Sunada Komako was robbed by a seventeen-year-old aspiring actress who worked as a servant in Sunada's home. This young girl from Aomori prefecture had "dreams of becoming a glamorous film actress." Matsumoto writes that for a girl from the country (*inaka*), it must have been a shock for the maid to suddenly find herself in "Kyoto, Hollywood of Japan":

> Not to mention that, after joining the household of a hot new item [*saikin uridashi*] like film star Sunada Komako, she must have thanked heaven for making her more fortunate than any other woman in the world. At the same time, how she must have stolen envious glances at Miss Komako's standard of living [*nichijō seikatsu*], and by and by come to imagine herself in the same light, spending day after day brimming over with the powerful emotions that evoked.[30]

In fact, Matsumoto is sympathetic to the hardships that struggling low-ranked actresses face. He observes that each studio in Kyoto boasts several hundred actresses (presumably counting extras and casual workers). Countless women carry *meishi* (business cards) declaring their studio affiliation. Yet extras go days without work, he says, making life extremely precarious for these women. Those who work on the lowest rungs don't even make enough to buy face powder, and it may take several years or even decades for an actress to succeed. Matsumoto assumes that even successful actresses sometimes weep "tears of disillusionment and homesickness."[31]

Finally, the vanity of actress hopefuls was repeatedly emphasized in these articles (fig. 4.2). This vanity was posited as the link between film viewing and mimetic behavior. It was purportedly the aspiring actress's obsession with her own image that led her to confuse the screen with a mirror in which she saw herself. As Hideaki Fujiki has observed, images of stars "destabilized the socially coded gender divisions that had existed in the creation and circulation of visual images in Japan," and this disruptive quality led authorities to regard improper forms of looking and investment in star images as a social problem rather than a personal matter.[32] By the late 1920s, Marxist-influenced film critics joined conservative intellectuals in warning the public "not to imitate the appearance and conduct of stars or to desire images of them."[33] Because of heightened consciousness of the links between film stardom, Westernization, and consumer culture in the 1920s, not to mention the disordering effect of star images on gendered space and visibility, Fujiki argues that "the dyad of the star and the female audience [was] one of the socially most conspicuous, 'modern' phenomena in Japan at the time."[34] Similarly, Anselmo observes that female film fans' tendencies toward imitation were heavily emphasized in the American film press, peaking around 1916–17, underscoring the strong link "between young femininity and mechanically reproduced mass culture."[35] In the Japanese aspiring actress discourse, this brand of femininity often leads to criminal and pathological behavior. For instance, the *Tokyo asahi shinbun* article "Beautiful Domestic at Imperial University Dorm Goes Arson Crazy Watching Movies, Possessed by French Actress" describes "an extremely beautiful young girl" who set fire to her employer's home several

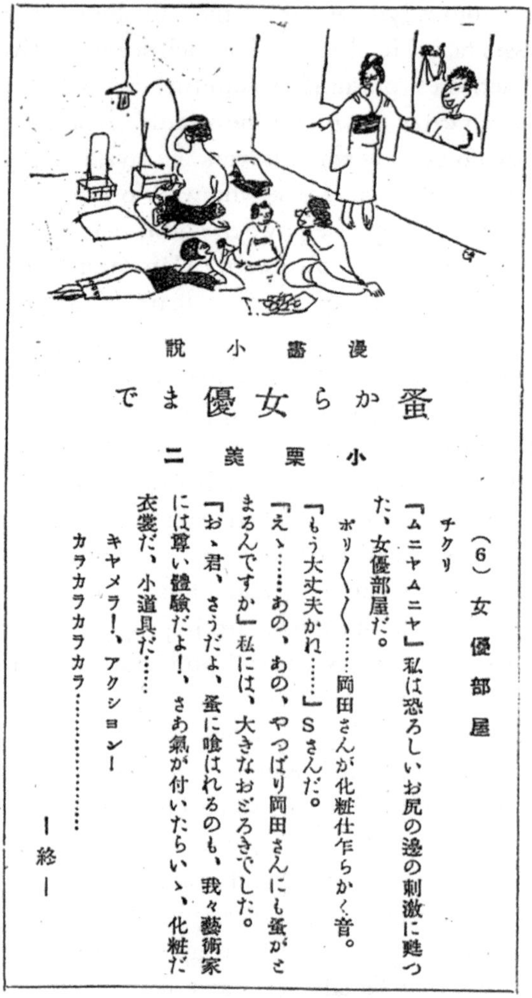

FIGURE 4.2 A panel from the manga "From Fan to Actress" by Oguri Yoshiji from *Nikkatsu gahō* (October 1926): a voyeuristic look into the private lives of actress initiates who have been "bitten" by the movie "bug."

times in one week after watching "a Western movie in which a beautiful young girl her own age sets fire to her master's home, is driven out, and at the end of her wandering becomes a famous French actress."[36] It seemed the girl was so enthralled by the film that she simply acted out its plot, identifying completely with the French actress and believing that the character's glamorous fate would also be hers. All of the key components of the aspiring actress panic are present in this story: infatuation with the movies; identification with an actress, which is reinforced by awareness of one's own good looks and confirmed by others' solicitous behavior; narcissism, which encourages delusional behavior; and imitation, for the aspiring actress seemed to imagine her dreary life as only a rehearsal, a performance, or something else somewhere between the real and the unreal.

The tone of the aspiring actress articles varies, but as Matsumoto's articles show, these tales could be both moralizing and sensationalistic. The narration is more knowing than the victim, often salacious and punitive, savoring the aspiring actress's violent comeuppance. In film magazines in particular, many aspiring actress articles have a conspiratorial tone, as if the writer is inviting the reader to join him in admonishing the aspiring actress. The writer shows off an intimate knowledge of female desire that is touted as superior to the subject's knowledge of her self, since the woman is figured as delusional and unable to control her compulsive behavior. Matsumoto in particular seems to enjoy publicly shaming the women in direct proportion to the heights of glory they imagined they would achieve.

Another example of this conspiratorial tone can be found in the article "Notes by a Young Aspiring Actress on Kamata Sightseeing from the Letter She Sent to Her Lover" ("Joyū shigansha no wakaki onna ga Kamata kenbutsu no shuki, sono jōnin ni okutta tegami yori"), which was published in the July 1924 issue of *Katsudō sekai* (Movie world).[37] In this article, a woman's letter to a male friend is presented with editorial commentary. The letter writer describes a visit to Shōchiku's Kamata studio, and her effusive description of Shōchiku is picked apart in parenthetical asides. These asides presume intimacy with the magazine reader, mercilessly mocking and antagonizing the letter writer while appealing to the reader for consensus. In the letter, the woman tries to justify why she went on a tour of the studio with another man. "You know, I've watched Kamata films forever," she writes, "They're like a bright paper lantern I've always carried with me, you see? Yet, I am a woman! I'm so timid that when I see someone yawn in the dark it's enough to make me shriek." Says the magazine: "(Oh yeah, right . . .)"[38] The letter writer apologizes for visiting Kamata without the addressee, who happened to be working that day, but she asks if he would take her out next Sunday when he is free. The magazine: "(It's surprising how many young ladies are playgirls these days. The most popular new wooing technique: 'Mr. A, do you like me? No? Well, S always tells me that he likes me. But I'm going to see B, so you'll be sorry!' Scheming chatter.)"[39] When the woman refers to the addressee with the too-familiar pronoun *anata* (akin to "darling" here) one too many times, the editor is absolutely overcome, interjecting, "Ye gods, please keep her from saying that word 'darling' one more time!" When she says it again, it's "Aah, god!" in parentheses.

As with Matsumoto's cautionary tales of aspiring actresses—which, though rhetorically addressed to female readers, licked lips at female shame—it is difficult to identify the *Katsudō sekai* article's intended reader, its actual readership, and how this article was received. The tone of the editorial asides suggests a covert exchange between men that reflects prevailing cultural attitudes, but it is important to note that this "male" editorial commentary for men is layered over a woman's address to a male intimate. This layering of voices and gendered addresses makes the article potentially accessible and thrilling to readers of any gender, despite the pronounced misogyny of the commentary. For instance, the snide editorial asides (exaggerated for humorous effect) have the potential of heightening readers' transgressive pleasure in the venturesome female letter writer, even though her pluck is being picked apart. In other words, whether or not readers agreed with the commentary, they could be entertained by how the letter writer's presumptuousness sends the editor into comic fits of aggravation. Readers sympathetic to the letter writer may have been thrilled that a female fan's words and actions could be interpreted as unseemly and threatening to the status quo. Anselmo has argued that in the United States, women's letters to film magazines show that female fans embraced the stereotype of "movie-struck girl" as an identity label, attesting to "popular culture's prevalent understanding of 'ardent' fandom as a juvenilized and feminized behavior."[40] These girl fans even "wholeheartedly endorsed pathological associations between their investment in movie stars and acute infectious diseases."[41] According to Anselmo, the reasons for this may lie in the fact that even articles that were critical of fans' "intemperate behavior . . . suggested that film fandom was as much linked with female rebellion as with girls' independence and individuality."[42] Similarly, the commentary in "Notes by a Young Aspiring Actress on Kamata Sightseeing from the Letter She Sent to Her Lover" allows readers to occupy a position of moral superiority (albeit by sidling up to male power) while also identifying with the letter writer's excess. The reader can enjoy the female writer's romantic and cinematic indulgences, even while these fantasies are deflated by the sardonic editor's remarks.[43]

In addition to Anselmo's research, silent film historiography provides corroboration for this interpretation with examples from other national contexts. In the article "Wages and Sin: *Traffic in Souls* and the White Slavery Scare," Shelley Stamp observes that in 1910s America, large crowds of women flocked to see films that depicted the perils of sex trafficking.[44] Stamp asks, what would cause such large numbers of women to gather at movie theaters to see these films, in precisely the very urban neighborhoods that white slavery films warned about? She suggests that films such as *Traffic in Souls* (dir. George Loane Tucker, 1913), *The Inside of the White Slave Traffic* (dir. Frank Beal, 1913), and *The Exposure of the White Slave Traffic* (A&A Inc., 1914) offered female spectators "a form of mastery over city life available only at the cinema."[45] Although female characters in *Traffic in Souls* are presented as vulnerable once they venture out alone into the treacherous city, female spectators watching the film gained access to a thrilling yet secure virtual experience of urban spaces they would not otherwise have been able to enter. Similarly, writing about silent cinema and modernity in Naples, Italy, Giuliana Bruno argues that cinema extended the erotics of *flânerie* and its anonymous visual pleasures to women.[46] Because of women's limited mobility, Bruno argues, their visual pleasures were primarily limited to looking and buying. The commercial cinema screen provided an extension of the shop window and a new means of exploring the world. This was especially meaningful for female spectators, because it made available previously forbidden "spaces of the gaze as sites to traverse and trespass."[47] Although the movie theater was a public space, it was also a dark, phantasmatic space that dissolved the rigid divisions between public and private. Bruno describes the film theater as a space of spatiotemporal juxtaposition, of fleeting encounters both on and off the screen. In this sense, the theater mirrored the rapidly transforming urban metropolis, which was a space of relentless change and violent sensations. Cinema reflected and extended the urban environment, allowing women new forms of pleasure and desire by allowing them new and exciting experiences of space.[48]

Ambivalent images of female film fans reflected the ideological contradictions created by women's increasingly active social, sexual, and economic roles. Why, then, was this negative discourse frequently found in fan magazines and even adopted by self-professed young female film fans? Anselmo suggests that whereas movie-struck girls were often depicted as vacuous, narcissistic, materialistic, pleasure-seeking, and passive (since they hoped to be "discovered" and "made" by Hollywood), in fact "many girl fans soberly envisioned acting as a guaranteed means to secure a profitable and edifying lifestyle" and were on a "search for self-improvement and social mobility."[49] Young actresses who succeeded often correlated their success with careful self-study and self-critique, closing the circuit between film fan and film star. That young women demonstrated such "willing and public adherence to such a pejorative stereotype" as the movie-struck girl reflects a powerful identification with a strong, desiring subject position that far outweighed the negative terms in which such desires were perceived.[50] In adopting the stereotype, female film fans proved their devotion to cinema. What others saw as excessive consumption or obsession could be flaunted as a sign of subcultural expertise. Moreover, Gaylyn Studlar suggests that the contradiction between women's economic potential and their social and cultural status was so great during the transitional period leading to the emergence of classical cinema that women's participation in the entertainment industry could only be expressed within a cautionary discourse that seemingly robbed them of their agency. In the United States, this transition took place during the 1910s. The same factors played a role in aspiring actress discourse during the transitional period in the 1920s in Japan.

Indeed, the Japanese press seemed to imitate the American portrayal of movie-struck girls by design. This was likely a strategy to legitimize the modernizing Japanese film industry by strengthening its connections to Hollywood. Just as Kyoto's appellation "Hollywood of Japan" invited the public to compare the migration of Japanese film companies from Tokyo to Kyoto to the movement of American studios from New York and Chicago to Los Angeles, it contributed to romantic notions of the "Hollywood" lifestyles of Japanese filmmakers and actors, bestowing the comparatively impoverished Japanese film industry with an aura of glamour. After the Great Kanto Earthquake, film magazines began to promote studio tours and visits to stars' homes. This kind of publicity strengthened associations between film and middle-class leisure culture, connecting cinema to pursuits such as tourism, home design, and cultural living, as well as to consumer products such as fashion and makeup.

Two Models for Understanding Cinema, Delinquency, and Space

The terms by which the aspiring actress was constructed as a social problem reveal growing concern with cinema's expanding address, its powerful sensory-experiential dimensions, and its potential influence over spectators, and show how "excessive" responses to cinema were given gendered overtones. In particular, the aspiring actress panic reflects the rapidly transforming cultural geography of modernizing Japan, for this media phenomenon gave expression to apprehensions regarding the increasing mobility of women, the rapid rise of cinema, and the spread of urban consumer culture.

What is at issue in the aspiring actress panic is not simply the power of cinematic fantasies that blur the line between fiction and reality, encouraging vain female spectators' reckless identification with their favorite stars. The panic foregrounds the distance-spanning power of media and problematizes obsession with the movies made possible by the widening circulation of films and film magazines. Journalists described cinema as enthralling naive country girls, motivating them to close an impossible distance between themselves and a world whose dangers they were woefully ignorant of. Studios were blamed for taking advantage of these unworldly hopefuls and exploiting the very gaps and vulnerabilities the "marketplace of mass culture" claimed to transcend.[51] The panic shows that, far from resolving the urban-rural divide, the widening ambit of mass culture exacerbated deep concerns about the uneven geography of modernization.

Concern with the immoral influence of cinema was not new, but the rise of the mass audience transformed the terms by which the connection between cinema and social ills was conceived. A link between juvenile delinquency and cinema had existed since at least the 1910s, but the aspiring actress panic represents a marked shift away from narrow concern with the environment of the urban movie theater and entertainment district. In contrast to earlier focus on the immediate spaces of film reception, the 1920s panic directed its concern toward cinema's ability to act at a distance. Even though the aspiring actress panic still drew explicit connections between cinema and adverse social transformations via specific cinematic sites, articles on cinema and juvenile delinquency in the 1910s and 1920s differ in how they understand the cultural geography of cinema. In particular, there is a shift from concern with the unique social, psychological, emotional, and even physiological effects of movie theaters—spaces of film reception—to the role that "film factories" or movie studios, as spaces of film production, play in creating troubling new behaviors across long distances. As the very spaces associated with cinema transformed, so did sensational discourse on cinema as an agent of bad cultural modernization.

Concerns with bad cultural modernization can be traced to the 1868 Meiji Restoration, which brought an end to the feudal order and initiated a series of reforms aimed at creating a modern nation-state. With this far-reaching political and societal restructuring, the problem of juvenile delinquency took on new salience. Meiji reformers' aggressive modernization policies promoted rapid industrialization, while government bureaucrats designed comprehensive programs for molding the populace into patriotic citizens and obedient imperial subjects. In this context, David Ambaras argues, juvenile delinquents "symbolized the dangers of uncontrolled social change and the defects of existing social arrangements."[52] Delinquency was regarded as an unavoidable consequence of social upheaval as well as a sign of incomplete reform. Meiji authorities policed delinquent youth in an effort to fix the structures of the new society and ensure the successful establishment of a new status quo.

By the twentieth century, state-run reformatories and special elementary schools were created to discipline wayward young subjects and shape them into obedient and productive members of society. Ambaras discusses how reformers often used students as a point of contact with families and their wider communities, which allowed officials to encourage the spread of newly inculcated behaviors beyond institutions of learning and correction.[53] The 1900 Reformatory Law (revised 1908) shifted authority over delinquency away from the judiciary branch so that youths could be detained even when they had not been convicted of crimes. This gave the government more leeway in intervening in young men's lives. No precise definition of delinquency existed, nor was one necessary for the institutionalization of troubled youth.[54] Reformers addressing delinquency drew heavily on colonial discourse, presenting themselves as "colonizing agents who could assimilate both 'dark' urban slums and the 'savage' minds of adolescent schoolboys to the norms of Japanese modernity."[55]

Japan began building a colonial empire after the Meiji Restoration, first establishing the Imperial Japanese Army in 1871. The army invaded Taiwan in 1874 and used military force to establish trade relations with Korea in 1876. Consecutive military successes in the Sino-Japanese War of 1894–95 and Russo-Japanese War of 1904–5 emboldened the Japanese and led to the annexation of Taiwan in 1895, the establishment of Korea as a Japanese protectorate in 1905, and the formal annexation of Korea in 1910. During this period, delinquents were often compared to recalcitrant colonial subjects. Ambaras argues that the attitude of reformers and government officials toward lower-class urban populations, reformatory inmates, and special elementary school students was not unlike that of colonizer to colonized. He provides examples of reformers comparing their wards to Koreans who were unresponsive to administration and creating analogies between poor families displaced by urban reorganization and the indigenous Ainu people driven off their land by the Japanese settlers of Hokkaido. Delinquent reform programs resembled programs for assimilating Koreans and Taiwanese into the Japanese empire.[56] Ambaras refers to this phenomenon as "internal colonization" and links it to various other institutions of acculturation, such as the juvenile reformatory and the special elementary school, that were used to produce acquiescent subjects.[57]

Like the reformatory and the colony, the movie theater and the film studio were places where new forms of sociality were imagined to take hold. In the 1910s, Asakusa's movie district was often described as a breeding ground for criminals and delinquents, a heterotopic space where one might be contaminated through contact with social and cultural Others. Serious concern with moral corruption at the movies in Asakusa first appears around the beginning of the 1910s. At this time, social problem articles in the *Tokyo asahi shinbun* begin to make frequent allusions to the specific social, psychological, and physiological impact of movie theaters and their environs. The sudden appearance of these concerns can be linked to a 1907–10 theater building boom. Until 1907, Tokyo's Asakusa Denkikan theater (built in 1902, converted to a movie theater in 1903) was the only permanent film theater in Japan.[58] Between 1907 and the end of 1909, the number of permanent film theaters in Tokyo increased from one to forty, and theaters began to pop up in Osaka as well. Beginning in 1908, new film theaters appeared in rapid succession in Nagoya, Kyoto, and Yokohama.[59] Growing demand for cinema sustained the new theaters, and the theater building boom contributed to the emergence of a popular film culture and drew attention to its existence. Around this time, Aaron Gerow argues, commentators began to perceive cinema as a distinct moral and regulatory problem. According to Gerow, it was not until the infectious popularity of the French crime serial *Zigomar* (dir. Victorin-Hippolyte Jasset, 1911–12) that cinema was experienced as a "mass cultural phenomenon" in Japan.[60] Japanese newspapers ran special articles on the *Zigomar* craze, turning the phenomenon into a media sensation. Education officials expressed alarm over the powerful influence of film on children, and the *Tokyo asahi shinbun* criticized the Tokyo Metropolitan Police for allowing the films to be released.[61] In response, the police declared that they would ban all future *Zigomar* films and knockoff productions. Gerow argues that this phenomenon, "arguably the first example of a truly mass modern entertainment fad in Japanese history, was made possible by the theater-building boom."[62] It allowed commentators to perceive cinema as a distinct medium for the first time, with specific cultural, institutional, and economic practices. This concern with the medium was grounded in specific concerns with the space of reception. Gerow writes,

> Not only the films themselves but also cinema as a modern spatial experience assaulting the senses seemed to contribute to the motion pictures' influence. As [the *Tokyo asahi shinbun*] had previously stressed, the movie hall represented a dangerous, crass, and almost obscene form of physicality, harming not only the spirits of spectators but also their very bodies (as such, cinema eventually became the object of legal and educational, as well as medical, forms of correction).[63]

What is perhaps most striking about the *Tokyo asahi shinbun*'s description of film culture is its emphasis on the atmosphere of the urban movie theater and the temperament of Asakusa crowds. In these and other 1910s articles on delinquency, attention to the space-based culture of motion pictures (and its leakage beyond specific exhibition situations) takes precedence over attention to what exactly is being shown onscreen. In the first article of the *Tokyo asahi shinbun Zigomar* series (October 5, 1912), the reporter describes the films' influence as spreading from the theater into the streets. He hears the strange word Zigomar everywhere he goes—spoken by children, adults, and soldiers—in the streets, on the train, and all around Tokyo. Whatever "Zigomar" is, the writer contends, it must surely be contagious. Children everywhere play at being Zigomar, and people see Zigomar's likeness everywhere in the crowd. "Zigomar" circulates from "mouth to mouth" ("kuchi kara kuchi e tonaerareru," "kuchi kara kuchi e tsutaerareru ni itatta") while sequels and knockoffs like *Nihon Jigoma* (Japanese Zigomar) and *Shin Jigoma* (New Zigomar) prolong the life of the original film.[64] This commentary highlights the power of cinema to spawn imitations. The article focuses more on the phenomenon of imitation than the content being imitated.

Even before the *Zigomar* craze, Asakusa crime was a veritable newspaper genre. Articles on this topic posited connections between criminality and modern space. A 1911 *Asahi* report linked crime to large gatherings of people and made a pointed connection between cinemas and crowds, arguing that the "kind of crowd is more important that the abilities of the criminal." The reporter noted that among many important influences on urban crime, surely "the motion pictures have the most corrupting influence on men and women's manners. *Where* motion pictures are, there is indecency."[65] Large crowds near theaters provided criminals with potential victims and concealment for their crimes. Associations between cinema and criminal activity grew stronger throughout the 1910s, as the dark space of the theater and the chaos of the entertainment district became increasingly linked to anonymous encounters, indecent behavior, and illicit acts in newspaper reports on crime. Quasi-ethnographic fascination with bizarre crimes and random encounters in Asakusa reached its apotheosis in the 1920s and 1930s theme of *ryōki* (curiosity hunting) in nonfiction and fiction, most notably in Edogawa Rampo's erotic and grotesque *tantei shōsetsu* (detective stories).[66]

However, while tales about Asakusa crime and social deviancy offer many interesting examples of women flaunting social norms, these are weak prototypes for the aspiring actress. Ambaras finds that in general, in comparison with male delinquency, female delinquency in the Meiji and Taishō eras is far more difficult to trace. There is little information on reformatories for girls, and female juvenile delinquency is not even mentioned in the Diet's formulation of the Reformatory Law. Unlicensed female sex workers, even those who fell within the age range targeted by the Reformatory Law, were not classified as delinquents.[67] Licensed prostitution and other forms of sexual and affective labor performed by geisha, café waitresses, and dancehall employees may have been frowned upon, but these occupations were also seen as important outlets for normal male heterosexual urges. The most likely forerunner of the aspiring actress is the delinquent schoolgirl.[68] Like the delinquent schoolgirl, the new actresses of stage and screen provided a site for imagining the malleability of modern identity and the potential confusion of right and wrong in the process of acquiring new social norms and a modern education.[69] This malleability was the source of erotic fascination and moral apprehension.

Prior to the aspiring actress panic it is the *space* of Asakusa, as a liminal space, that is connected to depraved girls' licentiousness and abandoned responsibilities in articles such as "Women Attempt Double Suicide, One Seriously Wounded, One Unharmed, Hidden Crimes of Depravity among Us" ("Onna dōshi jōshi o hakaru, ichinin wa jūshō ichinin wa buji, koko ni mo hisomu darakusei no zaiaku"), a story that ran in the *Tokyo asahi shinbun* on May 6, 1909.[70] Here, Asakusa is presented as a liminal space of play where two female employees of the Kanagawa Electric Joint Stock Company went to escape their dreary lives. They dreamed of running away in search of better prospects, but after getting mixed up with corrupt college boys, their horizon of opportunities rapidly narrowed. The women had concocted a ruse to spend a night away from the factory dorm, hoping to meet a friend who would help them find new jobs. The meeting fell through, and they found themselves stranded in Tokyo. A college student offered them a place to stay in exchange for sexual favors. The next day the women returned to their jobs, no closer to deciding what to do; if anything, the reporter suggests, their debauched night whet their appetite for rebellion. The women continued to feel exploited by their boss, who worked them mercilessly while incentivizing them with false promises. He cajoled them with talk of free time in Asakusa, movie tickets, and spending money, but none of these perks ever materialized. Desperate, the girls ran away and met up with the student and his friend for movies in Asakusa, where they spent the night once again. After this episode, they no longer had the courage to go back to work. They tried to appeal to nearby relatives for help but ended up wandering the streets, resolved to die. Early morning on May 5, the girls joined hands and jumped in front of an oncoming freight train, but they overshot the track. One girl fell safely, but the other's legs were severed at her thighs. Although Asakusa is only mentioned a few times in this article, these references help dramatize the girls' dilemma. In the popular imagination of the time, Asakusa was an in-between space and a gateway to corruption. In the story of the girls, Asakusa is a place that is neither work nor home. It is both a lure (in the boss's promises) and a trap, a corrupt college boys' playground from which the girls cannot return until morning. As the place where the girls lose their innocence, it also suggests a space between childhood and adulthood.

In the 1910s, Asakusa became increasingly notorious as the place where misfits went to escape from reality, where fugitives hid, where criminals found victims, and where deviants satisfied weird desires.[71] In the fifty-six-part *Tokyo asahi shinbun* series "Juvenile Delinquents Rampant through the Entire City" ("Manto akushōnen no ōkō," February 23–April 24, 1910), examples of bad behaviors in areas of Tokyo such as Nihonbashi, Kyōbashi, Azabu, and Yotsuya filled several installments at a stretch. Film theaters were foregrounded in the four installments dedicated to "Real Cases from Asakusa," in which the local police chief contended, "In the testimony of every elementary school pupil, the torment endured at motion picture venues [at the hands of delinquents] is the absolute worst."[72] According to the chief, authorities were assiduously combating delinquency at Asakusa theaters. However, he noted, it was far easier to censor film prints than it was to police space. Police examined *benshi* scripts (*setsumei kōjōkaki*) and plot summaries (*sujikaki*) to cut out offending material; even so, preventing public indecency in the audience was much more difficult, as shown by the large number of theater expulsions for "obscene behavior." Occasionally, the chief reported, small daggers or pistols were deployed in crimes inside the theater. Weapons could generally be detected by plainclothes cops, in which case offenders were immediately removed, but it was virtually impossible to prevent men and women from mixing in the dark, where their immoral behavior was not easily surveilled. The chief complained about the disproportionate amount of attention Asakusa received for movie-related crimes. He griped that the area didn't have a "monopoly" on film in Tokyo and suggested that the newspaper look into other wards and examine the bad influence of movies there.[73] He embraced Asakusa's movie town as something to be proud of: "Typically, when you hear 'motion pictures,' you can't help but think of Asakusa Park. Compared to motion pictures in every other neighborhood in the city, the motion pictures in Asakusa are the most representative and, moreover, the most sophisticated."[74] The overriding concern with the space-based behavior of delinquent types is similarly evident in installment 54 of the "Juvenile Delinquents" series. This installment gives detailed descriptions of three main types of corrupt individuals: (1) effeminate men who use ribbon to tie their *haori* (lightweight, thigh-length kimono jackets) and hang out at *karuta* card games and with theater groups; (2) brawling men who wear *geta* (wooden sandals) no matter what the weather is like, who get into fights and prowl parks, where they intimidate victims with knives and guns; and (3) corrupt female students whose shame is going into "places the public knows very well—these days it's the motion pictures and such—where they fervently grasp young middle school students' hands." The article includes a section called "Daraku no basho" (Corrupt places) that lists the most corrupting city places as card games, baseball fields, and movie theaters. These are the places most liable to "lead to the depravity of bad students and bad schoolgirls."[75] The "Juvenile Delinquency" series demonstrates the degree to which film was closely associated with Asakusa. These articles also highlight the extent to which 1910s concerns about cinema and delinquency were typically directed toward film-related behaviors and places, rather than the film industry itself.

Long before the advent of cinema, Asakusa was an important entertainment district. During the Edo period, Sensōji (Asakusa Kannon Temple) was an important pilgrimage site. After losing the official backing of the shogunate in 1625, Sensōji survived by drawing income from commercial entertainments that appealed to Edo commoners. Nam-lin Hur has described how Asakusa games, gambling, festivals, theater, *yose* (vaudeville), *misemono* (attractions), and prostitution fostered a lively, unregulated space for "prayer and play."[76] In the Meiji and Taishō periods, Asakusa was sustained by the enormous influx of laborers and lower-middle-class workers to Tokyo. The majority of these transplants settled in the Shitamachi neighborhoods of Honjo, Fukagawa, Shitaya, and Asakusa on the eastern side of Tokyo. Tokyo's *sakariba* (entertainment centers) transformed together with Meiji modernization policy and the state's attempts to populate new, modern spaces with new, modern behaviors.[77] It was due to the influence of domestic expositions and other Meiji city planning projects, Yoshimi Shun'ya argues, that the atmosphere of vice found in Edo pleasure districts, such as Asakusa, increasingly gave way to bustling recreation sites devoted to the display of commercial goods (fig. 4.3).[78] Nevertheless, as Seiji M. Lippit has suggested, even as late as the 1930s Asakusa was strongly associated with alternate realities (for example, in Kawabata Yasunari's novel *Asakusa kurenaidan* [The scarlet gang of Asakusa]). Asakusa retained a cultural memory of older times and liminal spaces that resisted modernity and the tendency of the Meiji state to reduce difference to the same. In Lippit's analysis, the cultural borrowings, recyclings, and juxtapositions found in Asakusa's carnivalesque atmosphere threatened the uniformity of national culture and gummed up "the model of the marketplace" in which different elements could be reduced to exchange value to be bought and sold.[79] We could extend this argument to say that Asakusa was a heterotopia in Foucault's original sense, in that it epitomized the "hidden presence of the sacred" with its spaces of play, spirit worlds, and erotic worlds, which paralleled and contested officially sanctioned sites of cultural production, proposing alternative (even deviant) forms of sociality.[80]

The 1910s commentary on Asakusa connects cinema and juvenile delinquency via spaces that seem resistant to modernizers' reforms and that even seem to encourage wayward social reproduction. In contrast, the 1920s aspiring actress panic focuses on the eagerness of young girls to become film stars. In particular, commentators in the 1920s seem hyperaware of the transvaluation of women's bodies during a period of rapid modernization and mass cultural development. This panic hinges on the extent to which the woman's body—as a source of labor, reproduction, and caregiving—has quickly transformed into a mass cultural commodity invested with imaginary desires. This panic becomes full blown after the Hollywood scandals of the early 1920s and coincides with the startling expansion of the Japanese film industry after the Great Kanto Earthquake. It exhibits new and distinct concerns compared with the earlier "new actress" theater craze of the 1910s.

FIGURE 4.3 Postcard of Asakusa Park circa 1922, a bustling space of commercial display.

Reading and Mapping Desire

The aspiring actress panic mobilizes the language of mass hysteria in describing film studios and police stations utterly overwhelmed by large numbers of hopefuls, suggesting a mass rebellion of women who reject their social and economic subordination. Yet these narratives inevitably depict women being thwarted by the unresolvable contradiction between film fantasies and harsh social realities. The aspiring actress panic stages the tension between realistic social expectations and the increased independence, visibility, and mobility of women in modernizing Japan. In this sense, these narratives enact melodramatic scripts: they demonstrate the incompatibility between normative social dictates and women's desires during a period of social change.

As Laura Mulvey points out, melodrama is a mode for highlighting social problems that have no easy solution. She writes, "the strength of the melodramatic form lies in the amount of dust the story raises along the road, a cloud of over-determined irreconcilables which put up a resistance to being neatly settled in the last five minutes."[81] Moreover, Steve Neale observes,

> Melodramas tend to deal in terms of subject matter with desire and its vicissitudes. As a genre marked by emotional hyperbole, by what Peter Brooks has called 'grandiose emotional states', melodrama involves extremes of polarised emotion: love and hate, joy and despair, and so on. These extremes mark and are marked by the vicissitudes of desire: its coming into existence, its realization (brief or lasting) or its failure, and in particular the blockages to its fulfilment. The constantly changing and apparently arbitrary course of events articulates and intensifies these vicissitudes, and, in turn, is motivated by them. Blockages, barriers, and bars to the fulfilment of desire are constantly introduced as events change course.[82]

Dramatic irony is key to the functioning of melodrama, since spectators know "the facts of the situation, the characters' true feelings, how and why they act, think and feel as they do," due to the "hierarchical point of view structure" that organizes melodramatic narratives.[83] This uneven distribution of information encompasses misunderstandings and misrecognitions among characters and privileges the film spectator with knowledge that not all characters in the film share. Yet despite the fact that the audience is empowered by knowledge and therefore in a "superior" position vis-à-vis the characters, we as viewers cannot control how the narrative unfolds: in this respect we are powerless. This is why so many film scholars, Neale included, have argued that melodrama's powerful emotional effects are amplified by knowledge discrepancies that cause us to wish "if only."[84] Importantly, he argues,

> if melodrama is, as a genre, especially concerned with love and desire and is therefore especially marked by certain characteristics of fantasy, pleasure will come from the pleasure of fantasy itself, a pleasure which resides in the process of articulation of a wish rather than in any representation of the attainment of its object: 'The pleasure of fantasy lies in the setting out, not in the having of the object.' In any story, pleasure comes primarily from the process of its telling, rather than from the nature of its ending.[85]

It does not matter whether the ending is happy or sad, because "Point of view and hierarchical structures of relative knowledge . . . allow a degree of separation-in-identification with the characters and scenario which binds the spectator into the fantasy and generates empathy with the protagonists, while permitting a retention of the fantasy whether or not it is fulfilled by *these* characters in *this* film. It is always too late, yet it might have been possible."[86] As melodrama often deals with periods of social transition or social upheaval,[87] this also contributes to its dramatization of misaligned perspectives and moral conflicts and its production of "dialectical images" that simultaneously show how the world is and how it was, how things are and how they could be.[88]

If aspiring actress stories did not invite the reader's wish—"if only"—the appearance of these articles in fan magazines would be difficult to explain. Why would film studios and fan magazines, which depended on the public's embrace of cinema, risk alienating a key demographic (female spectators and consumers) while strengthening associations between film and vice? The only reasonable explanation is that to a certain extent, the aspiring actress problem was a manufactured discourse that both the studios and the fans could embrace. A number of factors support this interpretation.

First, the aspiring actress panic laid blame on amateurs and illegitimate companies, lending established female actors and film studios an air of professionalism and legitimacy at a time when actresses and filmmakers were generally considered a suspicious lot. In the 1920s, the film profession was rapidly transforming. For instance, just prior to the Great Kanto Earthquake, Nikkatsu's Mukōjima studio in Tokyo created a director apprentice system, professionalizing filmmaker training by creating "assistant director" positions. This was a step toward recognizing filmmaking as an occupation that required skills and qualifications. Notably, Mukōjima filled these assistant director positions with university students and graduates, whereas previously the majority of film studio employees had no more than high school educations.[89] Taking such developments into account, one can reasonably hypothesize that established studios sought to enhance their own legitimacy and hasten the professionalization of the industry by casting aspersions on upstart companies and amateur hopefuls.

Second, despite the generally cruel and moralizing depiction of female film fans in these sensational articles, the aspiring actress panic bestowed public recognition on intense film passions. As a "what not to do" discourse, the aspiring actress panic supplemented more affirmative descriptions of fan behavior, allowing studios and journalists to shape discourse on film fandom by reprimanding "bad" behavior and celebrating "good" film fans. By publicizing cases of dangerously obsessed fans or ardor that resulted in bad judgments, studios and journalists could focus general disapproval of film fandom on a limited number of incidents wherein the fans involved were clearly "doing it wrong." Female readers could still obtain pleasure from these articles by recognizing their own passions in the stories (albeit depicted at pathological extremes). At the same time, this strategy allowed studios and magazines to increase profits by encouraging fans to channel their enthusiasm toward acceptable outlets, such as film magazine consumption. Film companies could distance themselves from bad film viewers by sensationalizing the horrible things that happened to incorrigible aspiring actresses, offering these stories as object lessons and outrageous tabloid entertainment.

In conclusion, the aspiring actress panic indexed many crucial transformations in the Japanese film industry, including the shift toward actresses in female roles as standard practice; the spread of permanent film theaters across Japan; the expansion of film journalism and of mass media in general; and the ongoing industrialization of Japanese cinema, which necessitated the training and professionalization of film workers, more concerted attempts to control the film industry's public image, and more carefully managed publicity, both positive and negative. In 1920s Japan, distance-spanning mass media made new subjectivities available for nationwide consumption, and new ways of understanding cinema's influence and its ability to move bodies took account of cinema's growing impact beyond the urban milieu. In contrast to 1910s discourse on Asakusa delinquency, which was concerned with the immediate environment of urban film spectatorship, the 1920s aspiring actress discourse represented the increased reach of cinema in terms of its powerful pull on young women from all over the country who, inspired by cinema to abandon their proper places, descended on film studios. In aspiring actress stories, women were on the move. Their rebellious bodies struggled against the more traditional gendered trajectories mapped for them. That these women were perceived as dangerously disruptive to normative values is clear from the disparaging characterizations one finds even in mainstream, mass-circulated venues such as the *Tokyo asahi shinbun*. Like tales of Asakusa delinquency, stories about aspiring actresses drew explicit connections between cinema and social transformation via specific cinematic sites, but the 1920s panic reflects new ways of thinking about media and space. Like melodrama, the aspiring actress panic offered a temporary resolution of tensions created by ongoing social transformation, giving expression to the forbidden wish and its negation. Despite a momentary confusion of image and reality in the stories, plus a brief liberation from gender scripts and social norms, the aspiring actress was quickly reabsorbed into the social order. She was sent back to her family or her mundane factory job. Her excessive sexuality was recoded, recuperated to more familiar forms—she was shown to be "just" a bad girl, a sex worker, a flirt, or a victim of sexual assault. The panic shows the failure of modernity to transcend the gaps between city and country and erase social and economic disparity overnight. Instead, film studios exploited feelings of longing—and journalists exploited cultural anxieties—produced by the rise of cinema and other forms of distance-spanning mass culture.

CHAPTER 5

Intimacy and Alienation

Murayama Tomoyoshi, Modern Media Celebrity, and Film

In Japan, no artist was more sensitive to the emergence of new forms of media celebrity and consumer desire than Murayama Tomoyoshi (1901–77). Murayama was an original cofounder and leader of the collective Mavo (1923–25), an anarchic, modernist coterie that agitated for the integration of art and everyday life.[1] Mavoist works tapped into popular fascination with the rapidly transforming urban environment and its media culture. Its theatrical antics contributed to the artists' notoriety and enhanced their celebrity. Members included Ōura Shūzō, Yanase Masamu, and Ogata Kamenosuke, and the group published an eponymous journal coedited by Murayama, Okada Tatsuo, and Hagiwara Kyōjirō. Murayama's earliest works were based on the idea of "conscious constructivism," which incorporated influences from anarchism, expressionism, Italian futurism, Soviet constructivism, and dada. He also experimented with cinema. He was one of the first Japanese artists to use modern media celebrity and commercial culture as aesthetic materials. Murayama paid close attention to how film and popular media redrew the boundaries between public and private, and reality and fantasy—and he explored these boundary transgressions by incorporating autobiographical material in his works. In addition to experimenting with many different forms of media, Murayama was also a master of self-publicity, making him the quintessential artist of Japan's media age.

Murayama was a leader in exploring mass media and mass culture as new arenas of expression and using the marketplace to promote his art.

From the very beginning of his career, he worked in a wide variety of media and at the intersection of different genres. In the 1920s alone, his works included paintings, sculptures, collages, set designs, commercial illustrations, scripts and screenplays, performances and actions, criticism and translations, and mixed-media constructions. His belief that the rise of cinema as a mass medium was a major cultural development put him in the company of a small number of artists and intellectuals—including Kikuchi Kan, Gonda Yasunosuke, Tanizaki Jun'ichirō, and Kawabata Yasunari—who were similarly invested in the social and aesthetic possibilities of mass culture and film.[2]

In the years immediately before and after the Great Kanto Earthquake, Japanese writers and intellectuals in elite social circles worried that the commercialization of literature and rise of mass media would erode their autonomy and special social privilege, leading to a decline of intellectual culture and the fine arts. By late 1924, with the emergence of the so-called neoperceptionist school (*shinkankakuha*) and the establishment of the breakaway literary journal *Bungei jidai* (Literary age) under the leadership of Kikuchi Kan, writers in the *bundan* journal *Shinchō* (New currents) began to talk of a "new age" (*shinjidai*), "new authors" (*shinshin sakka*), and even a "new *bundan*" (*shinbundan*). The main developments driving the new age were variously identified as a growing split between proletarian literature and bourgeois literature, the emergence of the neoperceptionist school, the establishment of *Bungei jidai*, the creation of literary columns in mass-circulated newspapers, the rise of "crass" or "popular" literary forms (*tsūzoku bungaku*—represented by the serialized newspaper novel), and the growth of the commercial market for literature. In roundtable discussions published in *Shinchō* in early 1925, writers discussed whether these transformations would lead to the demise of the *bundan* and whether high literature would be vulgarized to reflect common tastes. Socialism and commercialism were compared on the basis of their shared emphasis on utility and lowest-common-denominator appeal. Some writers suggested that socialism and commercialism were both fundamentally anti-intellectual, whereas others simply made a pragmatic distinction between "literary literature" or "high literature" (*geijutsu bungaku*) and "popular literature" or "low literature" (*tsuzoku bungaku*).[3] Murayama's position seems especially revolutionary considering that around the time of his debut solo exhibition in 1923 and subsequent rise to fame, many in the creative elite believed that stronger connections between art and everyday life, ushered in by socialism or commercial culture, would be accompanied by anti-intellectualism and resentment against the special status of professional artists, writers, and critics.

A skillful publicity artist, Murayama used media to his advantage, carefully planning his public appearances, magazine interviews, magazine essays and fiction, commercial designs, and commissions for film and theater to propel himself to a new level of celebrity. In addition to pursuing carefully selected, well-publicized projects, he created a unique personal brand using fashion. He made a memorable impression with his trademark *kappa* haircut—a helmet-shaped bob that he wore down to his jawline that vaguely resembled the tresses of the mythical water creature called the *kappa*. This hairstyle complemented his wife and collaborator, writer Murayama Kazuko's own "Dutch cut." Observers pointed to their interchangeable hairstyles as an example of modern gender fluidity.[4] Murayama sometimes donned a knit cap with a narrow brim and a *rubashka* shirt, a garment that originated as Russian farmers' clothing, as a sartorial allusion to his political sympathies. According to Takizawa Kyōji, Murayama made every attempt to be seen in this outfit whenever he had to meet the media; as a result, the look became a kind of Mavoist trademark.[5]

This chapter examines Murayama Tomoyoshi's public image and his engagement with cinema after the Great Kanto Earthquake. It focuses on his fascination with the new forms of affect and celebrity emerging from commercial mass culture, which Murayama linked specifically to film. He was especially interested in the revolutionary forms of intimacy and estrangement engendered by modernity, which resulted from new technologies and media forms that reconfigured the boundaries between private and public. In particular, he linked these specifically modern forms of intimacy and estrangement to the rise of commercial mass culture and its new strategies to sell sex and market celebrity personas, new attempts to shock and stimulate consumers, and new ways of extending, prolonging, and gratifying desire. Technology and media forms created fresh varieties and new intensities of sensation. These sensations emerged within a rapidly expanding consumer market that subjected all aspects of everyday life—including desires, emotions, and the body itself—to commodification. In their scope and power, the impact of these transformations on the pleasures, social relationships, and fantasy lives of urban middle-class consumers could perhaps only be compared to the vast impact the internet and social media have had on notions of identity and connectivity more recently.

By the 1920s, over the course of a mere half a century, Japan had transformed from a rigidly hierarchal, caste-based feudal society with strict sumptuary laws and codes of behavior to a rapidly industrializing and increasingly pluralistic society with a very developed urban consumer culture. Although it was still generally a relatively impoverished, agrarian-based society dominated by a small and powerful elite, it was also evident to contemporary observers that Japan was fast becoming a mass media society in which, at least in fantasy and through media, urban consumers could imagine going to strange faraway places and altering their identities. As Jeffrey Angles and others have observed, this tendency was particularly marked in the playful commercial culture known as "ero guro nansensu":

> People often describe the popular culture of the Taishō and the first decade of the Shōwa [roughly, the 1910s to mid-1930s] as exhibiting a fascination with *ero, guro, nansensu* エロ・グロ・ナンセンス (eroticism, grotesquerie, and nonsense). . . . [In the works of some of the best known interwar writers, such as Tanizaki Jun'ichirō, Akutagawa Ryūnosuke, Kawabata Yasunari, and Satō Haruo,] protagonists adopt new identities, participate in dramatic crimes and murders, toy with various forms of nonheteronormative sexuality, and transgress expected gender roles, all to experience the world in new ways. . . . Some postwar scholars have tended to think of the fad for *ero, guro, nansensu* as inspired in large part by publishers, newspaper editors, reporters, and other cultural figures eager to market their products to an ever-growing reading public. More recently, other cultural critics have interpreted the prewar fad for the erotic and the grotesque as reflecting people's desire to escape the difficult economic circumstances and increasingly repressive political developments of the 1920s and 1930s for an alternative space of imaginative play. By turning to a world of eroticism and the bizarre, these critics argue, people were able to fantasize about lifestyles and moral codes that resisted incorporation in the productive goals of the nation-state.[6]

Angles points out that such desires were not new and can also be found in mid-nineteenth-century Tokugawa-period popular culture. However, in the 1920s and 1930s fascination with "curiosities" (*ryōki*) took on new dimensions because of Japan's gradual acquisition of colonial territories and growing confidence in its imperial ambitions, along with accelerated industrialization and urbanization and the explosive rise of mass publishing.

Murayama's interest in different degrees and modalities of experience is apparent from his prolific output across many different forms of expression: sculpture, painting, literature, screenwriting, playwriting, dance, theater, set design, children's illustration, commercial design, criticism, and more. When it came to film, Murayama produced set designs, movie theater decor, theoretical writings, scripts, and movie theater pamphlet illustrations. By working at the intersections between film, theater, visual arts, and popular media, Murayama's work is typical of the so-called new art movements (*shinkō geijutsu undō*) of the 1920s, which were characterized by their dynamism.[7] This dynamism can be understood not only in terms of reaction and forward movement but above all in terms of artists' tendencies to move between different media forms. *Shinkō geijutsu* artists explored lateral connections between different media, collapsed the boundaries between different genres and practices, promoted multimedia experimentation, and paved the way for new theories of "synthetic art" or *sōgō geijutsu*. Like other *shinkō geijutsu* artists who were influenced by post-impressionist movements from abroad—expressionism, futurism, cubism, constructivism, symbolism—Murayama did not always necessarily recognize or respect differences between different schools of modernism. Instead, his works and writings juxtapose different aesthetic styles, sometimes in unexpected combinations.

At the age of twenty, just before beginning his career as an artist, Murayama traveled to Berlin and spent most of 1922 in Europe. During this sojourn he became attuned to modern media celebrity and the commodification of desire. Hagiwara Ken suggests that Murayama was deeply shocked by the erotic spectacles he witnessed in Europe and was even repulsed by their staging for an affluent, hedonistic audience.[8] Yet surely Murayama was not simply offended by these presentations, for he reveled in repeated retellings and representations of his own transactions with prostitutes and his erotic obsessions with performers. His work carefully examines the ambivalent relationships between art and commerce, between sexual liberation and commercialization, and between self-expressive and objectifying presentations of the body. Murayama's experiences abroad also made him sensitive to Japan's semicolonial relationship to the West, where he became highly aware of the feminization and racialization of Japanese bodies and Japanese "national character" in Western discourse. His later political artworks embraced experiences of abjection and humiliation as grounds for mutual recognition and understanding among women, colonized people, and the international proletariat. In the late 1920s, Murayama became a leader in the Japanese proletarian arts movement, going on to publish several books on proletarian arts and film. His earlier artworks already contain the proposition that the experience of abjection offers a position from which to critique global capitalist imperialism and the Japanese empire.

In addition to discussing Murayama's formative experiences abroad, the works I discuss in this chapter—the libretto for a multimedia operetta titled *A Linked Heart Comedy, Life of an Artist (Or, An Operetta, Life and Heart of an Artist)* (*Rensa shinzō kigeki, geijutsuka no seikatsu (aruiwa, operetta, geijutsuka no seikatsu to shinzō)*, 1923) and an experimental film scenario called *Actress* (*Joyū*, 1926)—demonstrate Murayama's early interest in how commodification shapes everyday life and the social, providing new opportunities to express, share, and consume. These works incorporate autobiographical materials and examine the commodification of women's bodies and sexuality, as shop attendants, singers, dancers, prostitutes, and film actresses, within a modern consumer economy. These representations allow Murayama to explore how feelings of intimacy and alienation become increasingly linked and intensified with the commodification of emotion, sex, and desire. *Life of an Artist* and *Actress* incorporate confessional materials, exposing Murayama's private life for public consumption and demonstrating his strong identification with female performers who turn their bodies into commerce and art. In their use of film technology and references to cinema, these works reveal the centrality of cinema for thinking about how fantasy, desire, and identification are mobilized in commercial mass culture.

Spectacle, Intimacy, and Alienation: Sojourn in Berlin

Murayama Tomoyoshi was born in the Suehirochō neighborhood in Tokyo's Kanda district. His father was a medic in the navy who died shortly after moving the family to Numazu to open a tuberculosis sanatorium in 1910. After his death, Murayama's mother converted to Protestantism and began working for the magazine *Kodomo no tomo* (Children's companion), where she also began publishing her short fiction. Through this connection, Murayama sold his first work as an artist in 1920, a drawing for the magazine.[9] Murayama studied philosophy at Tokyo Imperial University for a year before interrupting his degree to pursue the study of early Christianity at Humboldt University in Berlin. However, upon arriving in Berlin in 1922, Murayama realized that he would have to pass a Latin test and decided to abandon his original plans.[10] From February to December 1922, Murayama made it his new goal to see as much European theater, dance, and art as he could. Berlin was a major center for modernist art movements. Murayama was exposed to expressionism, futurism, constructivism, cubism, dadaism, Bauhaus, and Neue Tanz. The hub of dada activity had shifted from Zurich to Berlin in 1917, and Murayama arrived just after its peak. Japanese artists Nagano Yoshimitsu and Wadachi Tomo-o introduced Murayama to important artists and tastemakers, including Herwarth Walden of the Galerie Sturm, Ukrainian sculptor Aleksandr Archipenko, and Italian futurist Filippo Tommaso Marinetti. In March 1922, Murayama and Nagano contributed work to the "Great Futurist Exhibition" at the Neumann Gallery in Düsseldorf. In late May, they participated in Düsseldorf's First International Congress of Progressive Artists. Murayama writes vividly of the First International Congress reception, which included a provocative performance by Dutch dancer and dadaist Theo van Doesburg and seventeen-year-old Niddy Impekoven.[11] The congress represented an important turning point, contributing to a general shift in European modernism from expressionism to constructivism and leading to the emergence of constructivism as an organized international movement centered in Germany at the time. El Lissitzky, Hans Richter, and Hannah Höch participated in the exhibition, and artists debated the meaning of the exhibition itself. Was "constructivism" a new aesthetic and political program, or was it simply a convenient label for a provisional group of artists looking for opportunities to show work?[12] It is unclear whether Murayama participated in the congress meetings, but upon returning to Japan he immediately began to exhibit "conscious constructivist" works.

While in Germany, Murayama saw plays in Berlin, Munich, Dresden, and Leipzig. He attended performances at large venues such as the Volksbühne (opened 1914; 2,000 seats) and the Berlin Grosses Schauspielhaus (opened 1919; 3,500 seats), as well as more intimate performances at galleries, cafés, and salons in private homes. At the Volksbühne and Berlin Grosses Schauspielhaus, Murayama was awed by the size of the auditoriums and theater audiences and the grand scale of stage sets and theatrical casts. In Japan, the only comparable venue at that time was the Teikoku Gekijō (Teigeki or Imperial Theater, opened in 1911; 1,700 seats), a Western-style horseshoe-shaped theater with an orchestra pit, housed in a four-story building in the French Renaissance style. The Teigeki stage was fitted for both kabuki and European-style theater performances, with ticket booths, a cloakroom, bathrooms, lounges, a shop, and a restaurant in the same building. In his autobiography, Murayama writes that the Volksbühne "opened my eyes to the new architecture," stimulating an interest that later expressed itself in his stage designs.[13] Although he considered himself a visual artist when he first returned to Japan, over the ensuing decade Murayama increasingly dedicated himself to set design, stage directing, playwriting, and film.

It is possible to identify three themes in Murayama's writing on theater and performance in Germany. First, he wrote extensively on the grand scale of large theaters and their impressive architecture. Second, he paid close attention to audience reactions, breaches of the fourth wall, and the thrilling use of crowds—aspects that increased the sense of audience participation in mass spectacles. Finally, in marked distinction to his writing on grand theatrical spaces and mass spectacle, he frequently wrote of the intense, sometimes uncomfortable, situations he encountered within performance settings. These writings reveal his fascination with voyeurism and exhibitionism, as well as his emerging identity as a Japanese avant-garde artist.

Hagiwara Ken has already discussed Murayama's impressions of mass spectacle, crowd participation, and theater architecture in productions by

Karlheinz Martin and Max Reinhardt.[14] Murayama was attentive to how the performances he attended were intensified by their settings within spacious theater architectures, the use of dynamic set designs, the intermingling of audience and performers, and enthused audience response—not to mention the context of turbulent post–World War I Germany. He was electrified by the German proletarian plays known as *Massenspiele*, which used expressionist techniques, thrilling action sequences, pictorialist staging, and large numbers of extras to create moving spectacles of triumphant masses. Yet Murayama was not simply interested in large-scale spectacles and dramas of the crowd. He wrote frequently about charged performance situations that took place in far more intimate settings and produced very different sensory-affective intensities. These experiences were just as overwhelming and influential for his work. They included provocative performances that involved nudity, sexuality, or intimate interactions between performers, and which were often staged in close quarters. Analyzing Murayama's reactions to these performances, it is evident that these intimate dramas made him more self-conscious of his position as a foreigner in Europe, contributing to his discomfort as an outsider. These feelings of conspicuousness also heightened the eroticism of being party to such brash displays. Although these spectacles excited Murayama's sexual curiosity, he was embarrassed by their performance in public settings where viewers could be viewed. He felt particularly conspicuous because of his racial difference, which made it difficult for him to blend in with the crowd. Accordingly, he found himself empathizing powerfully with performers (especially women) who were exposed to the open scrutiny to which he, as a Japanese in Europe, was often subjected. These performances had a strong impact on how Murayama viewed his identity and performed his relationship to the public.

In his autobiography, Murayama writes of these intimate performances as if his own sexuality was on display. He suggests that he felt a stronger sense of shame and shock than did other audience members because modern art and performance in Japan were not yet so permissive. In addition to these performances, Murayama writes repeatedly about other scenes of sexual shame. While in Europe, he repeatedly visited prostitutes, and he was marginally involved in a trial in which a German girl accused a Japanese acquaintance of rape. Murayama returns repeatedly to these experiences in his artworks and writings. His representations of these events emphasize how, for him, both the shame and *jouissance* of desire were intensified because of his racial otherness and other differentials (gender, class, culture) that set him apart from German society at large, as well as from his sexual partners.

The Misremembered Play: La Ronde

I am particularly interested in two incidents that Murayama recounts in his memoirs, which have also been discussed in Hagiwara Ken's essay "Berlin, 1922": Murayama's viewing of a risqué performance of the poem *Venus* by Arno Holz and his viewing of the play *La Ronde* by Arthur Schnitzler. Both performances took place in Germany.

According to Murayama's account, he was taken to a private recitation of *Venus* that took place at a midnight salon in the home of a countess. Murayama and Wadachi Tomo-o had been invited there by poet Fred Antoine Angermayer and his wife. Other attendees included Wassily Kandinsky, Emil Jannings, Mary Wigman, Lil Dagover, and over 100 other guests. The poem was recited from memory by a large man, a baritone from the Staatsoper. Partway through the reading, a masked woman emerged from behind a black curtain. Murayama describes the baritone embracing the woman's thighs and violently groping her breasts, exposing them to the audience. The recitation went on in this manner for over an hour. Murayama writes, "Of course, we didn't have strip shows or underground theater then. I was utterly astounded to see the likes of a woman's exposed breasts caressed in front of a crowd of people, all in the name of art. This scene has been seared into my brain to this very day."[15]

That same year, along with Wadachi, Murayama attended a performance of *La Ronde*, a play written by Arthur Schnitzler in 1896–97 that, due to censorship regulations, was not performed on stage until 1920.[16] *La Ronde* is set in contemporary Vienna. It consists of ten scenes that take place before or after sexual encounters between men and women. The play has a discontinuous, episodic structure, with each scene revolving around a different pairing. Except for the last scene, the only actors who appear in each scene are the two involved in the coupling. There is an iterative quality to the play's unfolding, for in each new coupling, one partner reappears from the previous scene. The characters are the Whore, the Soldier, the Parlor Maid, the Young Gentleman, the Young Wife, the Husband, the Little Miss, the Poet, the Actress, and the Count. Through these liaisons, *La Ronde* reveals how different levels of Viennese society are linked by sexual exchange; at the same time, the play shows how the nature of the "exchange" varies dramatically depending on the social relation between the parties involved. Characters are not always who they say they are, as we know from previous scenes or learn in scenes that follow. Yet this does not mean that duplicitous characters' sexuality is in their own control. The play's interactions reveal the expectations, anxieties, pressures, and limitations that apply to different members of society, including the elite, and influence how individuals conduct themselves in public and private. Much of Schnitzler's dialogue revolves around sociosexual anxieties and protocols. Conversations touch on past lovers, the proper relation between husband and wife, adultery, the rules of seduction, (degrees of) sexual desire, experience and inexperience, vanity and sexual prowess, and sexual expectations for different genders and different social classes. The title *La Ronde* alludes to the fact that the play travels full circle, from coupling to coupling, concluding with a different pairing involving the same prostitute with which it began.

Twenty years after its first publication, the first uncut public performance of *La Ronde* was held at the Kleines Schauspielhaus in Berlin in December 1920. The premiere was hugely successful, and the play was still popular when Murayama visited Europe.[17] Murayama marveled at the cyclical construction of the play and the audacity of showing men and women together in bed on stage, which was still very shocking at the time. In his autobiography, he wrote, "The play had an utterly unique concept of using a chain-like succession of links to create the connections between scenes: the play is a series of bed scenes, each revolving around one male-female couple, one member of whom is paired with a different partner in the next scene."[18] He noted that having only two actors on stage in such intimate scenes drew attention to the quality of the acting, while the dialogue was dense with information about each character's class, occupation, and situation in life.[19]

La Ronde's depiction of intimacy seems to have struck a powerful chord in Murayama, for its themes appear frequently in his early work. Repeatedly in the play, men and women accede to unsatisfactory, unexpected, or unwanted sexual arrangements. The Young Wife is ashamed of her affair with the mediocre Young Gentleman, but her sexual curiosity is rebuffed by her Husband, who drugs and rapes the Little Miss in the next scene. The Count is too drunk to remember sleeping with the Whore and too meek to fend off the Actress; he seems to cherish his male friend Lulu far more than the women he reluctantly and regretfully has sex with. Gendered expectations and class disparity contribute to misunderstandings. Because of frequent misunderstandings and misgivings, the play's serial structure, and the refrain of infidelity, the drama of *La Ronde* is steeped in jealousy and remorse. No character seems completely in control of his or her partners' sexual activity or their own. Partners cheat and lie, and class boundaries are far more permeable than most of the characters can admit or feel comfortable with. The play is a study in guilt, suspicion, and poor impulse control.

Hagiwara points to one aspect of Murayama's description of the play that is particularly fascinating: his recollection of *La Ronde* is not completely accurate. Murayama misremembers there being a Japanese character played by an actor in yellow face, even though there is no such character in the play. His description of this misremembered scene focuses on his own feelings of discomfort and self-consciousness. He describes his awareness of the audience's "stolen glances" in his and Wadachi's direction, as well as tittering, smirks, and sympathetic looks as the scene with the Japanese lover played out. Murayama was deeply impressed by Schnitzler's critical strategy of positioning the audience as voyeur to a series of sexual encounters and thus implicating them in the play's social satire. However, at that moment, he was keenly distressed by the uncomfortable experience of becoming part of the spectacle. Whether he misremembered or invented this incident, this and other European anecdotes demonstrate Murayama's strong consciousness of his racial difference and his awareness of how that difference framed others' perceptions of his gender and sexuality. His account of viewing *La Ronde* foregrounds the same emotions that are highlighted in early works such as *Life of an Artist*: shame, embarrassment, and implication in someone else's embarrassment, all within a theatrical or performative context. These experiences became an integral part of Murayama's artistic biography and aesthetic imagination.

Constellations: Race, Gender, and Sexuality in Der Meister

Hagiwara suggests that Murayama conflated *La Ronde* with another play he saw in Germany, *Der Meister: A Comedy in Three Acts* by Hermann Bahr. This is plausible because *Der Meister* features a Japanese character named Dr. Kokoro.[20] Hagiwara does not elaborate further on his reasoning, so I would like to explore the possible basis for such confusion here.

Although there is no interracial love scene in *Der Meister*, the play ends with a striking gesture of intimacy between "the master," Duhr, and his colleague, Dr. Kokoro. Duhr is an arrogant physician who has been refused the title of "Doctor" by the local university, but he nevertheless practices medicine. Throughout the play, he shows himself to be an overly confident and selfish man who refuses to take advice while constantly meddling in the affairs of others. In contrast, just as his name Dr. "Heart" suggests, Dr. Kokoro is a sounding board for other characters' repressed emotions and resentments. His primary role in the play is to advise characters and provide a distanced commentary on the action, while Duhr actively pressures others to make decisions against their true feelings and better judgment. When he can take it no more, Dr. Kokoro begs Duhr to express his vulnerability, intervening at a point when Duhr's stoicism and bluster have led to his humiliation, paining Kokoro as a helpless onlooker. Duhr protests against Dr. Kokoro's counsel, arguing that his "Oriental point of view" is unenlightened, but Dr. Kokoro disagrees.[21]

> KOKORO: No, no. You make a mistake, master. The people of the West and the people of the East . . . just the same . . . under their skins. Every kind of people have emotions . . . must have emotions. You try to substitute reason. . . . What you call it? . . . Utility! But it does not go. . . . It is false, false.[22]

Duhr asserts that Western civilization is more advanced, for unlike Orientals, Westerners are no longer slaves to their emotions and impulses. Kokoro responds critically and prophetically, "Who can say? You think you live wisely. . . . I think you are only practical instead of wise. Take yourself, for instance . . . your marriage."[23] Kokoro sees into the heart of matters, even predicting Duhr's marital troubles, which will blindside Duhr later in the play.

After Duhr's inevitable fall, and in the very last moments of the final scene of the last act, Kokoro confronts Duhr, asking how he can remain so pragmatic and composed after everyone has abandoned him, including his wife. Kokoro believes that his arguments for the heart have been proven correct, but Duhr refuses to admit defeat, and once again, Kokoro finds himself debating the master as the play draws to a close. He enjoins Duhr: "He is the true master who runs bravest with his passions," running quickly "over the road of life . . . in what direction the reins are pulled. And passion pulls the reins."[24] The play ends with an intimate but queerly ambivalent reconciliation between the two men. This scene may be key to Murayama's conflation between *Der Meister* and *La Ronde*, so I quote it at length here:

> DUHR: [*reflecting*] Then, if I understand you rightly, man is not master of his life, but, rather a marionette.
>
> KOKORO: Marionette! What is that?
>
> DUHR: You.
>
> KOKORO: What does it mean?
>
> DUHR: It means what you make out a man to be. Do you know what a puppet is?
>
> KOKORO: [*pleased*] Oh, yes. [*indicates with his finger*] So?
>
> DUHR: [*watches the jumping finger*] Yes. Behind the wires are drawn. Cares, emotions, passions pull the wires, and accordingly the puppet dances. Isn't that what you mean?
>
> KOKORO: [*rubs his hands with satisfaction*] Exactly . . . just exactly.
>
> DUHR: And who knows? Perhaps it is a tragic mistake not to be a puppet.
>
> KOKORO: Aren't we mortals better off for it? . . . To feel a power above us . . . beyond us . . . that pushes and pulls and drives . . . and we must do what it wants . . . we cannot help ourselves . . . It is stronger than we. [*hesitates; looks self-consciously down as if he is ashamed of what he is about to say*] Master, don't try . . . any longer . . . to cut the wires with the scissors of your reason. [*Looks up, sees that Duhr is no longer listening; stops talking, steps cautiously away, looks back at him again, then starts to go softly to the door.*]

DUHR: [*coming out of a reverie, during which he wipes his moist eyes with his hand*] Little doctor! [*turns to look at Kokoro, then settles back peacefully*] Don't go away. [*Kokoro comes back*] Stay here. I'd rather not be alone today. Isn't it stupid? Tomorrow—tomorrow I shall have myself in hand again.

KOKORO: [*cowers down at Duhr's feet like a faithful dog*] Dear master!

DUHR: [*reaches down; pulls Kokoro's ear; smiles wistfully*] Puppet! [*stares thoughtfully into the glowing end of his cigarette.*]

CURTAIN[25]

Dr. Kokoro performs a powerful gesture of submission, and Duhr performs a powerful, if patronizing, gesture of melancholy affection. This tableau belies the painful truth that Duhr would rather deny but knows too well: Kokoro's wisdom has prevailed, proving Duhr wrong. He is not "master" at all.

At the same time (and one can imagine, to Murayama's chagrin) this final tableau satisfies conventional cultural expectations by placing the Japanese character in a subordinate, even feminized, position while displaying the older German "master" Duhr's paternalistic authority. The impact of the resulting tableau thus derives from a contradictory aspect, as finally and for the first time, Duhr expresses need and vulnerability, creating a sudden, surprising intimacy between the two men. Their racial difference is already expressed as a type of hierarchical relation, reinforcing the differences between their personalities as "cultural" rather than individual. Markers of gender, and of authority and subordination, help facilitate the unexpected slide into this intensely intimate moment at the end of the play. This intimacy emerges from a sudden condensation of racial difference, cultural difference, and gendered difference into an eroticized figure of domination and submission. This condensation of relations is made possible in the first place by the projection of gender difference onto the cultural binary of East-West. The tableau preserves hierarchal distinctions (the masculine West and the feminine East) and cultural stereotypes (Western reason and Eastern spiritualism). Dr. Kokoro prostrates himself at Duhr's feet, and Duhr tugs at Dr. Kokoro's ear, as if he were petting an animal.

And yet at this point in the play, such a configuration can only be read as a parody of Duhr's empty performance of mastery. Kokoro's slavish gesture of submission and Duhr's stoic expression of affection—even within Duhr's world, these strange postures can no longer be explained as a plausible expression of Asian weakness and effeminacy, on the one hand, and white European supremacy, on the other. The irony behind these gestures further underscores Duhr's vulnerability while allowing the audience to imagine a new, unthinkable sympathy—and even role reversal—between the characters, thereby producing a critical queer intimacy that is not easily explained away by the stereotyped gendering of racial difference and power relations.

Whether or not Murayama was thinking of *Der Meister* when he misremembered *La Ronde*, his account of the scene with the Japanese lover shows a keen awareness of the novelty of his racial difference for the German audience. As many of Murayama's European anecdotes show, this difference implicated his gender and his sexuality, as well as his race. In a similar manner, the textual structures of *Der Meister* provide a clear example of the imbrication of gender, sexuality, and race within the perception of identity in the European imagination. It is therefore not difficult to imagine that Murayama may have conflated his discomfort being a conspicuous audience member at a candid play about sex (*La Ronde*) with his discomfort as a conspicuous audience member at a play with such bald stereotypes of East Asian cultures.

If we compare *La Ronde* and *Der Meister* at the level of content, we notice that both plays revolve around repressions that result in regrettable behavior. The result is meant to provoke critical awareness, if not a sense of shame, in audience members. These plays may have produced adjunct effects in Murayama due to his heightened self-consciousness as a foreigner. In addition, he could easily relate to *La Ronde*'s theme of repressed sexuality leading to shameful encounters, given his feelings of guilt and embarrassment for having patronized prostitutes and his reluctant involvement in the ignominious civil trial over a young woman's sexual violation. In fact, in his autobiography, Murayama's account of viewing *La Ronde* follows directly on his recollections of losing his virginity to a prostitute in Berlin and visiting prostitutes in Hamburg and Leipzig: "filthy, dark, miserable, shameful experiences."[26] Following his descriptions of these miserable experiences, he writes, "What I have just written brings to mind yet another play, my experience viewing Schnitzler's *La Ronde*."[27] Perhaps Murayama felt implicated by *Der Meister*'s racial and ethnic stereotypes, which imputed that Asians are more in touch with their emotions because they are less rational than Europeans, just as he felt implicated by the sexuality on display in *La Ronde*. Murayama's autobiography ties *La Ronde*—and by extension, *Der Meister*—to his self-consciousness of his race and his feelings of shame toward his sexuality. Finally, it is important that the disturbance these works created in Murayama was connected to a heightened sense of viewing and being viewed.

Ultimately, it does not matter whether Murayama confused *Der Meister* and *La Ronde*. What is more important for my discussion is that his writings demonstrate how race, gender, and sexuality were constellated in interwar European culture, providing a matrix for such a *possible* confusion. What interests me is Murayama's sensitivity to these constellations and how they became a central part of his art and identity—repeated again and again in the content, structures, and themes of his paintings, stories, plays, essays, and memoirs, as well as the performance of his public persona.

These formative experiences in Germany form the background of Murayama's early works. After returning to Japan, Murayama turned his life in the spotlight into a kind of performance art, drawing on his experiences of conspicuity, sexual transgression, and alienation in Europe to craft a sensational image of himself as an eccentric avant-garde artist.

A Linked Heart Comedy, Life of an Artist

The *La Ronde* incident and Murayama's early writings and performance aesthetic highlight what Eve Kosofsky Sedgwick has described as the "double movement" of shame "toward painful individuation, toward uncontrollable relationality."[28] According to Sedgwick, shame is activated when one's sense of self is endangered in relation to one's connection with others. I may experience shame when I attempt to connect with someone else and my appeal for recognition is abruptly broken off. Shame can also involve helpless identification with someone with whom one does *not* want to identify. In both cases, shame reveals the circuit of identification with which we are bound to others, a circuit that moves outward and inward, and as such "is both peculiarly contagious and peculiarly individuating."[29] Shame affirms that we are social beings, to the extent that we may feel helplessly implicated by others' failures and embarrassments, wish to escape exposure and judgment, cannot detach ourselves from what others think of us, or feel deeply wounded when we are rebuked. Because "shame both derives from and aims toward sociability," Sedgwick draws a strong link between shame, visibility, spectacle, and theatricality.[30] She writes, "Shame floods into being as a moment, a disruptive moment, in a circuit of identity-constituting identificatory communication. Indeed, like a stigma, shame is itself a form of communication. Blazons of shame, the 'fallen face' with eyes down and head averted—and, to a lesser extent, the blush—are semaphores of trouble and at the same time of a desire to reconstitute the interpersonal bridge."[31] Sedgwick suggests that any experience of shame brings us back to infantile shame-humiliation and its role in constituting identity and our relation to the social. Shame is not just a form of communication; shame is performance:

> So that whenever the actor, or the performance artist, or, I could add, the activist in an identity politics, proffers the spectacle of her or his "infantile" narcissism to a spectating eye, the stage is set (so to speak) for either a newly dramatized flooding of the subject by the shame of refused return, or the successful pulsation of the mirroring regard through a narcissistic circuit rendered elliptical (which is to say: necessarily distorted) by the hyperbole of its original cast. As best described by [Silvan] Tomkins, shame effaces itself; shame points and projects; shame turns itself skin side out; shame and pride, shame and dignity, shame and self-display, shame and exhibitionism are different interlinings of the same give. Shame, it might finally be said, transformational shame, *is performance*. I mean theatrical performance. Performance interlines shame as more than just its result or a way of warding it off, though importantly it is those things. Shame is the affect that mantles the threshold between introversion and extroversion, between absorption and theatricality, between performativity and—performativity.[32]

This double movement of shame, which Sedgwick also refers to as a "narcissistic circuit," can be said to be a major theme in Murayama's interwar output, from highly personal autobiographical works that dwell on feelings of shame and exposure to his provocative, exhibitionist media persona.[33] Murayama's libretto for a multimedia opera entitled *Life of an Artist* demonstrates the centrality of shame, as described by Sedgwick, to the artist's early aesthetic.

As I discuss in more detail later in this chapter, affect is more useful than "emotion" for understanding Murayama's works. Rather than joy, despair, or desire per se, Murayama was interested in the frisson of mixed feelings and the creation of "resonances" and feedback loops.[34] After his formative experiences in Europe, he found this frisson in the new forms of intimacy and alienation in capitalist consumer culture that reconfigured the boundaries of public and private. He approached celebrity and art-making as role play, using them as expressive mediums. In constructing a personal mythology and public persona, Murayama turned his shameful experiences into goods for mass consumption. By writing about very personal, often painful experiences, he was able to self-consciously fashion these episodes of nonbelonging into an avant-garde artist's biography.

The libretto for *A Linked Heart Comedy, Life of an Artist (Or, An Operetta, Life and Heart of an Artist)* was completed the year after Murayama's return from Europe. It is dated November 25, 1923, and was published in the February 1924 debut issue of the journal *Shinkō*.[35] This issue was blocked by censorship, meaning it never circulated. *Shinkō* subsequently folded, and the play was never staged. For these reasons, scholars have only recently begun to situate this work in relation to Murayama's larger oeuvre. Different facets of contemporary media culture are reflected in the themes and structure of the operetta, making it a useful text for examining Murayama's interest in the changing media landscape. Since he planned to include film sequences in *Life of an Artist*, it is also an important work for tracing Murayama's long-held fascination with cinema and, in particular, forms that combined theater and film such as *rensageki* (chain drama) and total theater. In addition, the narrative of *Life of an Artist* revolves around male sexual anxieties and includes musical numbers about female actors, dancers, and sex workers who put their sexuality on display. These songs convey Murayama's fascination with female performers and suggest how the commercialization of sexuality and persona creates new forms of intimacy that can alternately be empowering or unmastering, estranging or affirming, for audiences and performers.

In the operetta, two young artists compete for the affections of a café cello player's niece, a girl named Hertha. The Small Youth is a painter who thinks of himself as a budding Kandinsky and describes his works as "new art" (*iwayuru "atarashii geijutsu"*). His rival is the Big Youth, a sullen and brutish musician whose career prospects look more favorable. Considering the family's future, the aunt and uncle encourage a match with the Big Youth, attempting to remove the Small Youth from the picture by plying him with their own daughter, a sexually precocious thirteen-year-old named Michiko. The Big Youth and Hertha live together for a year before he suddenly breaks their engagement. Hertha's family sues for damages for the loss of her virginity. The Big Youth perjures himself in court, lying that Hertha was actually not a virgin when he took up with her. He persuades the Small Youth, who has since broken up with Michiko, to corroborate his lies by testifying that he was previously involved with Hertha and that she wasn't a virgin then, either. The Big Youth tells the Small Youth that this lie—that they both slept with her, and that the Small Youth had her first—will make the rivals even.

Within this overarching plot structure, Murayama inserts songs, film sequences, and fantastic occurrences that create absurdist digressions from the main plot. For example, when the artists argue over Hertha, the Big Youth is shocked by the Small Youth's hysterical tributes in this "Song of Love":

> An insect is running over a photograph of my lover
> Well my lover is also like an insect
> Her cheeks are rouged and her lips are also red
> When I grasp the thick bun of her swept-back hair in both hands and pull
> Those cunning fruits shake back and forth
> Part your lips, let our tongues touch
> She tastes like an insect
> An insect! An insect! My lover is an insect![36]

In the next scene, the Big Youth dons a mask that makes him look old, frail, and shriveled. As he bemoans his wasted state, a cupid comes down from a single white rope dangling above the stage and shoots arrows in every direction. The play alternates between straightforward exposition and surreal intrusions of symbolic imagery, song, and antirealist performances.

Life of an Artist is one of the works that Murayama based on real-life experiences that he described as humiliating, yet which he wrote about again and again. In his autobiography, he vaguely describes "the most shameful" event in his travels as an incident in which his friend H, who had come to Europe to study piano, was charged with sexually assaulting a German girl.[37] A very violent man, H intimidated Murayama into somehow becoming involved in the trial, but Murayama provides very few details about this event. In *Engekiteki jijoden* (A theatrical autobiography) he writes, "Even when I am determined to make an honest confession, I find that I am utterly unable to write a straightforward account. There is no hope for forgiveness for as long as I hide my head and tiptoe around this event."[38] Again, it is notable that Murayama's account of these events follows closely on his descriptions of sleeping with prostitutes and viewing *La Ronde*, in a section of his autobiography that dwells on his regrettable, embarrassing, or uncomfortable early experiences with sex.

The libretto for *Life of an Artist* is also important because it shows Murayama attempting to create new transversal relationships between different forms of media. It is one of his earliest aesthetic projects that depends on borrowing, repurposing, superimposing, or linking heterogeneous materials and forms. The influence of Wassily Kandinsky, whose works provided a very important model for Murayama, is especially evident in Murayama's attempt to create a rich synesthetic experience in which various elements, appealing to different senses, resonate with one another and produce cumulative effects. *Life of an Artist* includes the expressive use of color, and it may have been influenced by color-tone dramas by Kandinsky, such as *The Yellow Sound* (1909). The "linked hearts" referred to in the full title of *Life of an Artist* are displayed on the outside of characters' costumes and change color with their emotional and mental states.

Life of an Artist can be understood as an attempt to resuscitate *rensageki*, Japanese stage plays that reached the height of their popularity in the 1910s. *Rensageki* invigorated conventional melodrama plots by incorporating short filmed scenes. This combination of theater and cinema was harshly criticized by the pure film movement. Highly conscious of developments in foreign film art and industry that had not yet taken root in Japan, pure film critics treated *rensageki* as one of many irregular, transitional forms (such as film with live narration and musical accompaniment) that they hoped would disappear as cinema became "purified" and developed standard practices based on medium-specific properties.[39]

In a 1926 article "Rensageki," Murayama shows little regard for medium-specific arguments, instead emphasizing how combinations of film and theater can overcome the limitations of each medium. He notes that film lacks many of the advantages of theater:

> It goes without saying that however advanced films may become, films are films, and they do not feature actual people or seem real. Moreover, at least at the moment, color is impossible (today's tinted films are hideous, so these can't be taken into consideration); words and natural sound are impossible; the atmosphere produced by the existence of real space and use of artificial lighting is impossible . . . film lacks the *merit* of theater's "limited perspective," the *visceral* exchange between what happens on stage and with the audience, and the *ephemerality* of theater, in which it is absolutely impossible for the same thing to happen twice.[40]

Similarly, Murayama argues, film creates effects that cannot be found in theater. He concludes that to obtain the most powerful effects and greatest range of expressivity, the forms should be combined. He argues that *rensageki* is the most promising form of agitprop theater (*sendengeki*), implying a genealogical connection between 1910s *rensageki* and 1920s political avant-garde theater,[41] and wraps up the essay by promoting an experimental staging of *William Tell* at the Kokoroza, where Murayama later directed a version of Vsevolod Meyerhold's *Trust D. E.* featuring film projection as part of the scenography. According to Murayama, *rensageki* is the "highest form of theater art" and the art of the future.[42]

Murayama's plan to use film projection in *Life of an Artist* several years before he wrote "Rensageki" indicates his early interest in using modern technology and media to create links between different aesthetic forms. At several points in the libretto for *Life of an Artist*, stage directions call for projecting brief film montage sequences that give poetic expression to characters' desires and emotions and foreshadow later developments. For example, during the prologue, a tenor sings directly to the audience, asking their hearts to rise up and drift in the theater, link together, embrace one another, and commune in experience. After describing wandering hearts gathering in the theater and forming a chorus, the tenor sings, "I will launch myself onstage with a cry—*uraa*—oh, I will launch myself, so please don't forsake me." He then describes a chance meeting with his beloved on the city street:

> Oh, should I happen to see a little green carriage drifting about the streets
> I had better step up and look inside through the window to see if thou art mistress
> No, I will open the door, and this is what I should say
> "You are spring at the height of spring. You are a bride in all white.
> "Walk out into a picture. Step out of your little shoes into a picture.
> "Over the blue vast space of the city
> "Bells ring out. Bells ring out.—"

According to the stage directions, "At this time, from behind the spectator seats, a ray of light shoots onto the stage, and a motion picture is projected on a screen." The directions do not provide specific information regarding how many shots appear in the sequence, how long the sequence lasts, or what shot lengths or camera angles should be used. There is no description of lighting, tinting, or transitions between the shots. The directions only state: "A vast and beautiful modern city boulevard. As a small carriage comes driving up, a gentleman runs up and opens the door, bowing with delight. A bride and groom in wedding dress appear from inside the carriage and slowly step out." Low reverberations of a gong are heard, and a bass begins to sing about the bride and groom. The chorus becomes more frenzied, more voices join in, and the man in the film passionately embraces the couple. Then the film ends, and the auditorium goes dark.[43]

Another cinematic interlude occurs later in the play when, after a fifteen-minute intermission, a bell rings and the lights slowly dim. The stage directions call for wooden percussion instruments and the sound of a trumpet becoming fainter and fainter before fifteen bars of a "pleasant" melody is heard. The Small Youth's song emanates from the back of the stage. He sings about stumbling out of a bar, in a song I discuss in greater detail later in this section. After this song, directions call for a film to be projected onto a screen on the stage, "piercing the darkness." Images appear: "A sloping road, an upside-down road, a circular road, a spiraling road—standing upright and stiff, as if he has rigor mortis, the

Small Youth spins around these and finally ducks into the entrance of a building, which is labeled 'Café Mouse.'" Again, the stage directions do not include information about how the images should be filmed or edited together. However, the description of the Small Youth "spinning around" the different locations, which include "an upside-down road," as he stands "upright and stiff," suggests that the scene was to include inverted images and that superimposition would create the effect of the drunk youth spinning—or the world spinning around him—as he remained perfectly still.[44]

Finally, new forms of celebrity are on display in *Life of an Artist*, in which Murayama places fictional accounts of sensational events from his life alongside songs and commentary on female performers and sex workers who live firsthand the commodification of bodies, intimacy, and desire. It even includes a suite of songs for these performers: "Song of the Actress," "Song of the Prostitute," "Song of the Dancer," and "Song of the Singer." This interleaving of autobiographical confession with songs about the commercialization of female sexuality creates a complex commentary on modern celebrity culture. While Murayama is sensitive to the exploitation that performers face, his imagery makes apparent the strong allure of commercial sex and commercialized sex appeal—and even the excitement of the shame associated with these transactions.

Murayama lost his virginity to a prostitute in Europe and visited prostitutes several more times while abroad. After returning to Japan, he wrote about these experiences in *Bungei jidai* (The literary age). These accounts later appeared in his autobiography, and references to sex workers and female sexuality can be found throughout his works. It has been noted that prostitutes are especially common in Murayama's works about Berlin and are often conflated with other kinds of female performers, such as dancers he encountered during that time. Takizawa Kyōji and Nomoto Satoshi argue that Murayama felt a strong identification with these women. Nomoto has even suggested that Murayama allowed himself to be photographed dancing nude in his studio as a way of inhabiting the position of the sexualized female bodies he incorporated into his work (fig. 5.1).[45] Takizawa writes that the prostitute was emblematic of Murayama's feelings of estrangement from his body and contends that Murayama used depictions of prostitutes to confront his painful, personal experiences of alienation.[46]

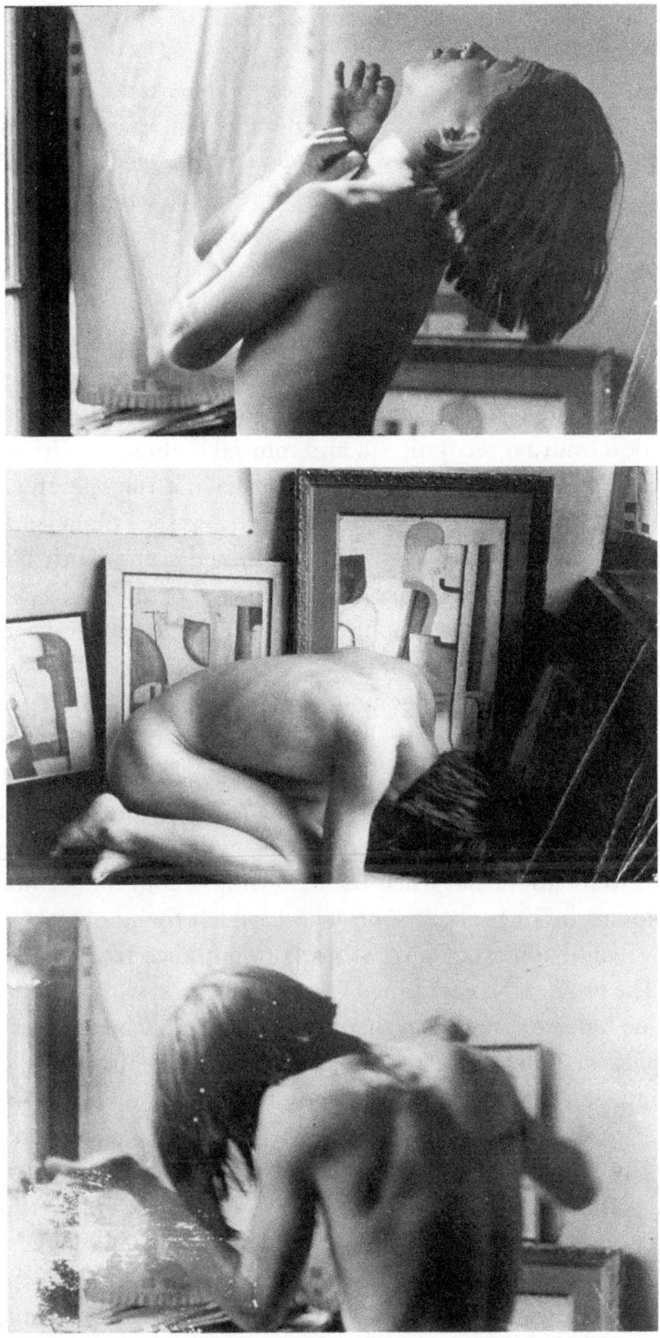

FIGURE 5.1 Photographs of Murayama dancing nude in his home studio.

With the rise of mass-circulated lifestyle magazines, star culture, and movie fandom, the domestic and the private became part of popular entertainment and public discourse. Murayama encouraged the public's fascination with his private life by appearing with his wife in the lifestyle pages, writing confessional accounts of previous sexual experiences, and playing with how his gender and sexuality were perceived. He was notorious for wearing his hair long, cross-dressing, baring his body for photographs, and performing sensual dances. *Life of an Artist* similarly appeals to the reader's voyeurism by fictionalizing intimate details from Murayama's life.

Masaki Yoshikatsu has noted that *Life of an Artist* thematizes linkage, connection, mutual recognition, and mutual embrace.[47] This is broadly true and applies to Murayama's use of media and the operetta's themes: the *rensa* or "link" of the play's title is the same as the "chain" in *rensageki*, so named because of the alternation of filmed scenes with live action. Linkage is also a theme in the operetta's dialogue, song lyrics, and imagery. However, it should be emphasized that in this play "linkage" is usually figured ambivalently if not negatively, much as in *La Ronde*. We find this in descriptions of the agony of romantic yearning, in depictions of frustrated or self-destructive sexual desire, in confessions of sexual shame, and in scenes of bitter betrayals. If *Life of an Artist* foregrounds linkage, it does so by dwelling on moments of rupture and disjunction. It works through shame as understood by Sedgwick. For instance, Masaki fails to mention that when the tenor sings about souls embracing in the prologue, he sings about souls who have left their homes, set loose to wander. The tenor exhorts these souls to embrace in mutual "shame" (*haji*). The prologue is performed in total darkness, with the house lights off and no lights on stage. But shame does not simply break connection—if shame is the cause or the result of uncomfortable, unwanted, or regretted intimacies, it also has a contagious and confessional quality. Shame in *Life of an Artist* is intersubjective, or wants to be intersubjective, and is never fully separated from erotic pleasure. This is evidenced by the repetitive confession or performance of shame in the operetta, typically in conjunction with sexual longing—for example, when a male singer relates his experience of seeing a prostitute or when Hertha sings about her sexual awakening and self-consciousness. In "Song of the Prostitute," the male singer describes how, in the yellow light of morning, he feels shame for the first time as he looks around a prostitute's rented room and senses that she is genuinely proud of her dwelling. Describing this awkward and painful interaction the morning after their transaction, the singer expresses surprise that it is he, and not the prostitute, who feels dirty and ashamed. A moment of potential connection is blocked as the singer realizes they do not feel the same and could not possibly explain themselves to one another.

Throughout the operetta, sex is compared to intoxication, alternately exhilarating and sickening. According to the Small Youth, all that remains of pleasure afterward is an unreliable memory, and everything seems dirty and shameful in the next morning's light. Repeatedly throughout the play, pleasure at its apex becomes its opposite as sensual excess gives way to a sense of revulsion or shame. In the prologue, a chorus of voices represents shamed individuals who congregate in the theater and cry out in a frenzy, over and over, that they are "crazed with pleasure." When he is most enraptured, the painter compares himself and Hertha to insects. In her song of sexual awakening, Hertha sings of spying a dead body in the sewers. She hides in the sewer to avoid the townspeople, overcome by shame because of the way her sexually maturing body is used to lure customers at the tobacconist's shop where she works. Drunk with desire for her, the Small Youth sings a song about stumbling out of a bar:

A bar at night.
A bar on a night where, as soon as I stumble outside, I threw up.
The clinking beer mugs had the mark of your house.
That bar.
Tilting, tumbling down the slope, forgive me for soiling the door of your house.
There's a fountain drawn on the bottom of the bottle, for what purpose I wonder,
As I'm thinking I'll ask, I'll ask
My pleasure reaches its summit,
Heaven and earth become most intimately revolting [*shitashige ni kimiwaruku nari*]
The dyes of the striped signboard become a symbol of my pleasure
Moon and sun and stars clasp each other's hands and slip under your door,
Exchange intimate greetings with me, as well as sideways glances.[48]

In this song, antipodes of heaven/earth, intimacy/revulsion, and pleasure/sickness are presented as linked to one another as in a striped pattern, which becomes a symbol for the Small Youth's euphoria and the stark oppositions it contains.

This theme of alienating pleasure and pleasure in alienation contributes to a critical commentary on how sex and sensuality are priced, advertised, and circulated like commodities in modern culture. Despite its scathing portrayal of male hypocrisy and the exploitation of female sexuality, *Life of an Artist* also suggests that there is something particularly powerful about pleasure that is mixed with disgust or shame. Weaving portraits of female performers, sex workers, and exploited lovers into an autobiographical tale of past humiliations, Murayama's *Life of an Artist* is an act of identification with female performers. It builds emotional intensity through foregrounding the theme of (dis)connection and by linking different media forms. *Life of an Artist* suggests that shame can be powerful and transformative. It can be grounds for some form of mutual recognition, even if fleeting, where no understanding seems possible.

Actress

Murayama wrote the film scenario *Joyū*, or *Actress*, to be serialized in *Eiga jidai* (Film age) from August through November 1926. *Actress* is a fascinating instance of Murayama addressing the issue of stardom in a medium he frequently used to shape his public persona—the mass-circulated magazine. In one sense, *Actress* is an ambitious "film" that could only be mass-produced and mass-circulated on the printed page. Were it not for the genre of published film scenarios, the film may have never been conceived.

The venue for *Actress* was a monthly film magazine that began publication in 1926. *Eiga jidai* was founded by writer and businessman Kikuchi Kan, owner and president of the publishing house Bungei Shunjū, established in 1923. Kikuchi was one of the first *bundan* writers to embrace commercial literature and court a popular readership. He not only defended the newspaper novel against its savage *bundan* critics, he took the extra step of creating his own mass-oriented literary magazines and, in so doing, revolutionized literary journalism. His magazine *Bungei shunjū* (Literary seasons) was meant to appeal to white-collar readers, thus addressing a very different readership than the coterie journals published by the *bundan*. Its target reader was an urban middle-class office worker who needed entertainment for his train commute.[49] Similarly, *Eiga jidai* was to be an accessible middle-brow magazine that brought together the worlds of film and literature. Kikuchi was a right-leaning intellectual and later used populist arguments to support the use of literature and film in wartime mobilization. He also helped pave the way for media personalities and public intellectuals with mass appeal, such as Murayama.

Actress chronicles the two-year rise and fall of a *shōgekijō*, or "little theater," established by a young, ambitious drama troupe. The troupe is eventually undermined by a mechanical actress and her frenzied acolytes. The real-life model for the fantastic troupe is clearly the Tsukiji Shōgekijō (Tsukiji Little Theater), which was founded by *shingeki* (new drama) leader Osanai Kaoru and experimental dramaturge Hijikata Yoshi in 1924, where Murayama was a frequent collaborator. Tsukiji Shōgekijō was still very much active when *Actress* appeared, although just like the troupe in the scenario, it had just celebrated its two-year anniversary and the period of its greatest achievements was already past.[50] During the height of the theater's success, the period of 1924–26, Murayama contributed numerous set designs to Tsukiji Shōgekijō productions, including Soviet constructivist–style sets for Georg Kaiser's *Von Morgens bis Mitternachts* (December 1924).

Another important influence on *Actress* is interwar discourse on the film actress. In Murayama's scenario, young men supervising the construction of a theater come to the worrisome realization that the sole actress in their troupe is fat and plain. The troupe auditions aspiring actresses, subjecting the women to a physical evaluation and a mental test consisting of questions such as "Why is ballet boring?" "What is the effect of a revolving stage?" and "What qualifications do you lack for becoming an actress?" When the applicants are dumbstruck, the men hurl insults: "Hey, what's wrong? Haven't you any sense? Isn't anything going on inside that exquisite brain of yours?" "Impressive as you are on the outside, there's nothing upstairs!" Dismayed by the applicant pool, the company debates whether they really need "human puppets," only to finally agree that the women will be attractive as set dressing even if they fail to pass muster as human beings!

To discourage individualism, each troupe member is given a number. Several members still stick out, such as the poster artist who suffers from advertising mania, and the ambitious, tortured artist director who has bright red hair. When one of the recruited actresses becomes a star, her cult of personality tears the company apart. Her movements are so strange that it is rumored that parts of her body are actually made of glass, wood, or steel. Her performances trigger memories of past loves and humiliations, causing audience members to weep uncontrollably. Her fanatic public forms a sect whose members lash themselves with whips and cut themselves with knives. Her popularity eclipses that of the troupe, overshadowing its increasingly politically tendentious performances. Finally, resolution comes when the director assassinates the actress and commits suicide. After these events, the company puts on one last performance before inexplicably discovering a route to the planet Mars. The performance is just a boorish comedy but, unbeknownst to the audience, the theater has been outfitted with a wild animal pit beneath the audience seats. During the performance, the sounds of fighting lions, leopards, and wolves mix in with the laughter of the crowd. As the performance nears its end, with a single stomp a trapdoor opens, and the audience falls in the pit and is devoured.

Two aspects of Murayama's aesthetic program—his commitment to experimental theater and his cultivation of popular notoriety—can be observed in *Actress*. First, the film scenario gives expression to theater's utopian visions. Throughout his career, Murayama maintained an enduring enthusiasm for intermedial theater. Following his experiments at Tsukiji Shōgekijō, he expounded on intermedial theater in the book *Kōseiha kenkyū* (Constructivist research), which was published in 1926. In it, Murayama carefully describes designs by Walter Gropius, Erwin Piscator, and Vsevolod Meyerhold that incorporate film projection within fully mechanized theaters. Murayama hoped that similar theater practices would take root in Japan, but experiments with film projection in modernist Japanese productions received mixed reviews.[51] In any case, it seems that Murayama did not feel limited by what was actually possible on the stage. He was inspired by El Lissitzky's and Walter Gropius's visionary plans for technological modern theaters that employed different forms of media and movable architecture, integrating performance space and audience space in carefully designed machines. It did not concern him that neither Lissitzky's nor Gropius's designs could be practically executed. These visionary—which is to say impossible—theaters inspired ambitious Murayama works such as *Life of an Artist* and *Actress*, which were too technically advanced to actually be staged.

Second, *Life of an Artist* and *Actress* reflect Murayama's expanded notion of performance, which was extremely aware of contemporary discourse on celebrity as self-commodification. By publishing in a literary journal and a film magazine, Murayama was able to enlarge his audience. By aligning himself with cinema, he advertised his affinities with popular culture as well as the avant-garde. As Miriam Hansen has argued, cinema—and American cinema in particular—

> was perceived, not just in the United States but in modernizing capitals all over the world, as an incarnation of *the modern*, an aesthetic medium up-to-date with Fordist-Taylorist methods of industrial production and the promises of mass consumption, with drastic changes in social, gender, and generational relations, and with the restructuration of experience and subjectivity. Again and again, writings of the 1920s and 30s celebrate American cinema for its distinctly new, contemporary sensibility, its sense of youth, vitality, and spontaneity, its democratic ethos and claim to gender equality (attacked by opponents as a "new matriarchy").[52]

In *Life of an Artist* and *Actress*, Murayama displays an avid, even fiendish, fascination with the disorienting effects of cinema and modern consumer culture. *Life of an Artist* and *Actress* draw attention to new forms of longing and estrangement engendered by modern media and commercial entertainment. As Murayama demonstrates, media celebrity—especially female stardom with its commercialized sex appeal—is rooted in the buying and selling of pleasure. In his works, he examines transactions between audience and performer, buyer and seller, fan and celebrity, beloved and suitor, prostitute and john, and shopgirl and customer, showing how these interactions are amplified with the emergence of a highly sexualized modern consumer culture. Thinly disguised autobiographical incidents appear alongside depictions of female performers and sex workers who commodify their bodies, emotions, and sexuality. These works give us insight into how Murayama understood his own celebrity and mystique. Murayama is alert to the ways that media shapes sexuality, fantasy, and sexual expression. He is sensitive to the exploitation that performers face, even though his imagery also makes apparent the strong allure of commodified sex and intimacy. The scenario of *Actress* may seem deeply misogynistic—especially the audition scene—but here Murayama references widespread concerns that would have been familiar to readers of contemporary magazines, which I examined in the previous chapter on the aspiring actress. For instance, in an issue of *Eiga jidai* that appeared before Murayama published *Actress* in its pages, Kikuchi Kan wrote about film companies having trouble finding good actresses because good families forbid their daughters from applying to these jobs.

Finally, *Actress* shows that Murayama was extremely conscious of the magazine reader as the target audience. In a preface published with the first installment of the scenario, he emphasized his interest in creating a new form of scenario writing that would incorporate poetry, the essay, color, sounds, smells, and long dialogues. He stated that he did not want to be a typical writer who, knowing nothing about cinema, ignores all the means at the disposal of a film director and simply writes a good story, nor did he want to write a technical shooting script that would be boring for the reader of a popular magazine. Accordingly, we can understand *Actress* not so much as a scenario for an experimental film as an experiment in writing. It is a satire of avant-garde theater and the preoccupations of film magazines, written in film scenario form. If we concede that the film it describes is impossible—a film that was never intended to be made—in a strict sense, *Actress* is not a scenario at all.

An Artist's Biography

As I have argued, many of the themes and strategies found in *Life of an Artist* and *Actress* can be traced to Murayama's time in Berlin. His experiences there were crucial to shaping his interest in modernism, mass culture, and celebrity. There he experienced firsthand the use of sensationalism and shock tactics in a variety of artworks. He attended performances by modern dance innovators such as Mary Wigman and Niddy Impekoven, and he witnessed spectacular representations of the volatile masses in theater productions by Max Reinhardt. As a Japanese youth in Europe, Murayama experienced uncomfortable attention from strangers. He coped with loneliness, desire, and confusion in ways that awakened great ambivalence if not shame. These were formative and exciting experiences for him, which he repeatedly returned to in his writing and artwork. I have argued that Murayama's experience of racial difference in Europe was intensified by how he felt it implicated his gender and sexuality. This inflected his well-documented fetishistic interest in European dancers' legs, feet, and hair and his visits to European prostitutes, which became major themes in his early works. Murayama's writings on performers and prostitutes express sympathy for women who must treat their bodies as objects, practicing self-estrangement, and who learn to use their vulnerability as a marketing tool. Voyeurism and exhibitionism figure strongly in his early works, reflecting his own painful experiences of self-estrangement, as well as his fascination with the commodification of the body in art and sexual commerce (fig. 5.2).

The links that Murayama makes between race, sexuality, and gender in his autobiography and his work can be related to affect. His works often start from familiar constructs or materials that, placed into new configurations, require a new appraisal from the viewer. He explores the strange feelings that can be generated with the use of multiple media and the interstices between forms. Although many scholars have already examined Murayama's use of materials and forms, I am particularly interested in how intermediality might be related to new forms of relationality and estrangement. Thinking about Murayama's aesthetic in terms of "defamiliarization" and "decontextualization" tends to place emphasis on his use of everyday objects and formal abstraction alone. More recent scholarship on Murayama moves us closer to seeing these works in terms of stimulus and response.

For instance, Takizawa Kyōji has argued that Murayama's mixed-media constructions should be understood as an attempt to bring disparate materials together in a "mixture" or "fusion" with the expectation that through these unexpected juxtapositions, the specific values of disparate materials will be amplified. He suggests that by combining different materials, Murayama sought to "activate the various inclusive uses and meanings that these materials already have, and use the associations these

FIGURE 5.2 Murayama (right) and Okada Tatsuo perform "Dance That Cannot Be Named" ("Na no tsukerarenai odori"), June 28, 1924, at the Tokyo Imperial University Christian Youth Hall. *Chūō shinbun*, June 29, 1924.

give rise to, in order to give rise to an expression."[53] Takizawa identifies the idea behind Murayama's conscious constructivism as the principle of "linked response" (*rensa hanno*).[54]

Similarly, I argue that Murayama's use of shameful autobiographical incidents as source material was not simply a strategy for enhancing his notoriety. For Murayama, "connection and disconnection" was not simply a theme but also an aesthetic principle that guided his promiscuous use of diverse materials and media forms. Closer examination of *Life of an Artist* and *Actress* shows how the thematics of shame and ambivalent media celebrity allowed Murayama to grapple with the strange circuit of intimacy and alienation that characterizes commodity culture in general. But we must not ignore the fact that in these works he is also exploring radical relationality among different media. *Life of an Artist* and *Actress* deploy cinema as one textual component. These works exemplify how, inspired by experiences of painful individuation and shameful implication in Europe, Murayama developed those experiences of decontextualization, isolation, and unexpected affiliation into a media aesthetic. *Life of an Artist* and *Actress* create category confusion, playing with the boundary between the familiar and the unfamiliar, and cinema and other media.

CHAPTER 6

Expressive Excess

Gendered Bodies and Proletarian Texts

In discussing how the rise of film as a mass medium shaped attitudes toward cinema's persuasive sensory realism, I have paid special attention to representations of overresponsive spectators. It is not possible to understand interwar film discourse on realism and emotion without examining the excessive bodies that gave figuration to cinema's imagined powers. These overreactive spectators were often depicted as female or feminized, due to popular assumptions that women were particularly susceptible to emotional and sensory stimulus. The most excessive responses to cinema were embodied in the stereotype of the aspiring actress, who helplessly and narcissistically identified with screen images and felt compelled to act out her screen fantasies. This notion of the aspiring actress was deployed by commentators who wanted to criticize naive or improper fascination with the cinematic image. These critics included film journalists and film studios that wanted to draw strong distinctions between legitimate and illegitimate viewing practices. For others, such as Murayama Tomoyoshi, what was at issue was not so much women's enthrallment with commercial mass culture so much as the commodification of women's bodies and sexuality, which signaled the emergence of new forms of estrangement, intimacy, and pleasure.

The aim of this chapter is to think more carefully about how ideas regarding women's interests and experiences—especially notions of female pleasure and pain—were used to authorize certain forms of media engagement and invalidate others. We have already seen how aspiring actress discourse cautioned against unreasonable identification with, and wanton pleasure in, the cinematic image. As a moral panic, this discourse expressed anxieties about the growing visibility of sexually and economically independent women. It reflected new appraisals of cinema as a powerful mass medium that expanded the reach of urban culture and contributed to a remapping of social geographies. Stories about suffering women were used to allegorize the vast transformations accompanying modernization and to suggest the pain and peril these changes brought.[1] Lest we mistake this mobilization of female pain as a feminist gesture, it is important to realize that many writers and intellectuals who deployed images of female suffering were also deeply ambivalent about the new prominence of female tastes and pleasures in popular culture. Aspiring actress tales that warned against women's sexual and economic exploitation ultimately placed culpability with the aspiring actress, blaming her narcissism and gullibility for an unhealthy obsession with the movies. Accordingly, any attempt to analyze representations of spectatorial desire and identification in interwar Japan must carefully examine this paradoxical rhetoric of female pleasure and pain, in which mass culture's superficial and materialistic pleasures were imagined as "feminine," but the challenges and evils of modernization were dramatized through female suffering.[2] Socially critical texts used women's victimization to create moral legibility, generate empathy for the victimized, and amplify rhetorical impact. Yet in the same intellectual circles, women's investments in media were denigrated as self-absorbed, and undesirable forms of commercial culture were disparaged through association with "femininity."

In Japan, as in many parts of the world, consumer culture and modernity were strongly associated with the changing status of women and the formation of new women's identities. During the interwar period, magazines, department stores, and consumer advertising targeted women as an important new demographic that was essential for the expansion of consumer capitalism. Hirabayashi Hatsunosuke, an interwar leftist critic, was the first to refer to these developments in terms of a "feminization of culture."[3] Many commentators similarly identified mass culture with the commodification of women's tastes, activities, and desires, but Hirabayashi was one of the few male intellectuals to seriously consider the progressive potential of consumer culture in relation to women's empowerment. Ōya Sōichi, for instance, observed that new magazine titles for women and rising circulations of magazines for a female readership played a central role in propelling the rapid development of the commercial publishing industry. He compared this conquest of a previously untapped market for women's magazines to the "discovery of a vast new colonial territory."[4] Similarly, looking back on the 1920s, writer Aono Suekichi commented in 1933:

> Broadly speaking, no class of magazines has so drastically pushed the advancement of capitalist production within Japanese magazine culture as women's magazines. One might even say that magazine culture has been taken to an utterly unexpected juncture by women's magazines. . . . If this age of commodification advances any further, women's magazines may even become adjuncts to the department store, or none other than miniature *depāto* themselves.[5]

Beyond the literary sphere, the rampant commodification of Japanese culture was personified by the materialistic *moga* or "modern girl," with her socially disruptive sexuality and extravagant self-fashioning. Cultural historians such as Miriam Silverberg have sometimes described the flapper-esque *moga*, with her bobbed hair, energetic physicality, and love for jazz and fashion, as a rebel who overturned social norms. In actuality, only a few intellectuals and reformers—female activists included—were willing to embrace the *moga* and celebrate consumer culture as a progressive force that challenged the status quo. Many among the cultural elite regarded the rise of consumer culture with animosity and alarm, especially as popular tastes and market forces began to threaten cultural hierarchies.[6] Historian Barbara Sato describes intellectuals' rejection of commercial women's culture as a form of misogyny, arguing that elite male "intellectuals' voluble critiques of consumerism sometimes reflected an inability to accept their own alienation from the new process of constructing culture."[7] She points out that this apprehension and dismissal of women's commercial culture was not limited to conservative critics. Whereas conservatives linked consumer culture with moral corruption and decadence, leftists saw popular commercial culture as a distraction standing in the way of revolution, and they too attacked its materialism. Many leftists (male and female) chose to emphasize political and economic issues over questions of gender, disregarding (or attacking) the potential for consumption to be used as a means of self-fashioning and community-building.[8]

The point here is not to argue for or against the subject positions extended by women's consumer culture in interwar Japan. Rather, I wish to show that the debates on mass culture and its affects constituted a politics of emotion that was used to define the very terrain of the political (e.g., public versus private), as well as what bodies, behaviors, and responses "counted" as political and how. This is especially clear when we examine the literature and film associated with the interwar proletarian arts movement, for their works often used sensational images of women to mobilize sentiment toward political ends. Attention to these texts enables us to examine the similarities and differences between avowedly proletarian and unauthorized proletarian works, complicating clear distinctions between political, popular, and modernist modes of representation, while allowing us to consider the charge carried by representations of female bodies and desires in both popular commercial and political texts. In this chapter, I analyze two "proletarian" texts, one authorized and one unauthorized, one literary and one cinematic, that provide a deeper understanding of how works mobilized genre, gender, and medium to create very different experiences of female pain, although these representations feature a similar affective charge or frisson. The Hayama Yoshiki story "Inbaifu" (The prostitute) is the grotesque tale of a sailor who develops revolutionary consciousness after viewing a corpse-like prostitute, whose plight awakens him to the victimization of the proletariat by capitalism. In contrast, the rollicking film *What Made Her Do It?* (*Nani ga kanojo o sō saseta ka*, 1930), based on a proletarian play by Fujimori Seikichi and directed by Suzuki Shigeyoshi for the commercial film company Teikine, portrays female suffering in the modes of sensational melodrama and gross-out body humor.

These texts allow us to see how charged representations of women function within literary and cinematic works about class struggle that draw on specific genres. The reason these representations are charged is not because women and femininity carried fixed associations, but because it was possible to attach strong feelings of attraction and revulsion to female characters and feminine traits. We have already seen this in the aspiring actress panic and the use of female bodies to adjudicate proper and improper forms of engagement with commercial culture and media texts. In their capacity to be coded with strong associations and emotions, we could say that female characters and feminine traits are what Sara Ahmed calls "sticky objects," while genres (e.g., comedy, melodrama, horror) are collections of "sticky signs."[9] Attention to the stickiness of objects and signs—in this case, the interaction between representations of women and genre conventions mobilized by proletarian texts—allows us to examine "the attachments that implicitly govern ways in which signs work with other signs."[10] It allows us to see how see how women's bodies accrued "meaningfulness" through repetitive deployment in different genre frameworks, even though the specific meanings and emotions generated by genre conventions varied considerably from text to text.[11] Finally, it enables us to understand how women's bodies and feminine attributes were used to amplify emotional impact, invite strong identifications, and enhance the persuasiveness of political argument—to no small degree because of how female bodies were framed as persons and objects.

This approach casts the representation of women in proletarian works in a new light. When we only emphasize the negative or positive valence shared by different forms of female imagery in proletarian works, we ignore the complexity of how affect works. Historians who focus narrowly on the negative coding of these representations in particular tend to gloss over how negative associations can variously position the viewer and channel emotion in different ways—sometimes invoking tragedy, other times invoking satire.[12] The female body was used to incite anger and derision, but it was also deployed in narratives of victimization to solicit sympathy and identification. Such effects could be recast once again with the introduction of irony or comedy. Proletarian works use representations of women's bodies in extremis and extreme affects—including anguish, disgust, despair, humiliation, alienation, and anger—to attract and entertain, as well as repel. By analyzing the treatment of female bodies as both persons and objects, we gain insight into textual strategies of producing the disidentification that Marxists and modernists believed to be generative of critical consciousness. While this critical consciousness could be described in terms of what Bertolt Brecht called "alienation effect," I think it is more productive to turn to Georg Lukács and his description of the role of alienation in producing revolutionary consciousness. Examining the mechanics of texts in which readers are asked to regard female characters as both subjects and objects, and with a self-alienating mixture of attraction and repulsion, we come to a better understanding of how emotion and identification were harnessed for political ends. Again, it is perhaps more useful in this context to think of these dynamics in terms of affect rather than emotion. Affect is a measure of sensory intensity and a form of orientation. As I have argued throughout this book, it can also be imagined as a circuit, an economy of pushing and pulling. In contrast, when we speak of emotion, we tend to fall back on the ideational content (happiness, sadness, anger, disappointment) that we ascribe to what we feel. Therefore, affect is more useful for thinking about alienation, identification, and frisson.

Proletarian Realism and the Politics of Representation

Before turning to the texts, it is useful to have some background on the interwar proletarian arts movement. The proletarian arts movement was a broad-based movement of artists, activists, writers, and intellectuals on the leftist spectrum (including liberal thinkers and members of the Japanese Communist Party or JCP) and primarily centered on literature and drama. The movement emerged out of the journal *Tanemakuhito* (The sower, 1921–23) founded by Komaki Ōmi, the son of a politician, who studied in France and participated in the French internationalist Clarté movement. Clarté formed as a response to the horrors of World War I, and it aimed to create international solidarity among progressive, pacifist intellectuals. It began as a coalition of writers and intellectuals in 1919, with an original steering committee that included Henri Barbusse, Anatole France, Thomas Hardy, Upton Sinclair, H. G. Wells, and Stefan Zweig. During the first two years of its existence, Clarté gradually moved toward communism, with Barbusse championing the Communist International (also known as the Third International or Comintern), which was established in 1919. The communist faction of the magazine took over editorial leadership in 1921, but Barbusse increasingly distanced himself from Clarté, as he hoped it would remain independent from political organizations.

As a forum for leftist intellectuals that contributed to the early activities of the French Communist Party, Clarté provided an important model for *Tanemakuhito* and the activities of the early proletarian movement in Japan. When Komaki Ōmi returned to Japan, he founded *Tanemakuhito* with the aim of creating a literary forum for leftist writers and intellectuals that would operate in solidarity with the international communist movement. He devoted a significant amount of space in the first three issues of the journal to publicizing Comintern. However, *Tanemakuhito* was dealt a devastating blow by the Great Kanto Earthquake. Its last full issue appeared after the disaster in September 1923, followed by a small supplement called *Tanemaki zakki* (The sower's miscellany) in January 1924. *Tanemakuhito* writers reorganized and went on to establish the literary magazine *Bungei sensen* (Literary front) in June 1924. *Bungei sensen* became the main publication of the first proletarian writers' organization in Japan, the Japan Proletarian Literary Arts League (Nihon Puroretaria Bungei Renmei, also known as Puroren or JPLAL; established 1925). In 1928, after repeated disagreements that led to different factions within the movement, which resulted in continuing splintering and reorganization, an umbrella organization called the Japan Proletarian Arts League (Nippona Artista Proleta Federacio, NAPF) was formed on May 25, 1928. NAPF was created in part as a response to Soviet criticism that the Japanese movement was weakened by factionalism and ought to move "closer to the masses." These criticisms were conveyed in Comintern's 1927 "Theses on Japan," which were translated by proletarian writer and theorist Kurahara Korehito and published in the October 1927 issue of *Bungei sensen*.

The "Theses on Japan" intensified factional debates within the movement and arguments as to how to achieve the so-called massification (*taishūka*; "moving closer to the masses" or "popularization") called for by Comintern. The two main positions in this debate—which centered around a series of essays exchanged by Kurahara and Nakano Shigeharu in journals such as *Zen'ei* (Vanguard), *Puroretaria geijutsu* (Proletarian art), *Senki* (Battle flag), and *Bungei sensen*—reflected persistent differences between the different factions of politically minded artists that NAPF had absorbed, the Vanguard Artists League (Zen'ei Geijutsuka Dōmei, also known as Zengei or VAL, led by Kurahara) and the Japan Proletarian

Arts League (Puroretaria Geijutsu Renmei, also known as Progei or JPAL, led by Nakano). Kurahara took the orthodox position represented by Comintern, arguing that the vanguard movement must establish greater contact with the masses, which meant creating works imbued with love and understanding for the people. Nakano argued that the only way to rid the masses of their sorrows and give them genuine happiness was through politics. In most historians' accounts, Nakano is portrayed as taking a one-dimensional "Fukumoto-ist" position, which held that "true" Marxists act from a correct understanding of revolutionary philosophy.[13]

In part, the massification debates revolved around the function of art within the movement and the relationship between art and "current objective conditions," the political consciousness of the proletariat, and revolutionary culture. Nakano argued that no true proletarian art could exist in the place of bourgeois culture until revolution had been achieved. He asserted that the movement should focus on the goal of revolution and prioritize agitation and propaganda. Kurahara argued instead for a two-pronged approach. In addition to "subjective" art for instilling revolutionary consciousness (e.g., agitprop), he advocated "objective" art that would convey the actual current conditions of workers and farmers in concrete detail. These positions entailed two different understandings of the relationship between politics and art, and the movement and the masses, and involved different emphases on subjectivity and objectivity.

NAPF and its successor KOPF, the Japan Proletarian Culture Federation (Federacio de Proletaj Kultur-organizoj Japanaj), used different tactics to manage divisions in the movement. Under NAPF, separate and semi-autonomous organizational units were created for activities in theater, literature, art, and music. NAPF was reorganized as KOPF in 1931, and the new organization put greater emphasis on political organizing and facilitated stronger, central, top-down control over its constituent groups. The creation of KOPF was spearheaded by Kurahara after his return from the Soviet Union. As before, there were units dedicated to theater, art, literature, cinema, music, photography, and other fields. However, these various units were now tasked with coordinating their activities and working toward common goals. In addition, the relationship between the umbrella organization and the JCP was made more explicit than before. As a result of KOPF's ties to Comintern and the (outlawed)

JCP, proletarian artists faced increasing persecution in the early 1930s, including arrest and torture, culminating with the shocking death of writer Kobayashi Takiji in 1933. The movement quickly fell apart after many leaders were forced to commit *tenkō* (apostasy), publicly renouncing their political activities and/or beliefs. The movement collapsed in 1934.

During the time the movement was active, debates concerning massification, as well as the subject matter and style of presentation appropriate to the cultural activities of the movement, played out in leftist film journals. For Prokino, the Proletarian Film League of Japan (Nihon Puroretaria Eiga Dōmei), which was established under NAPF, a key question was whether it was possible to reach a wide audience using an alternative (i.e., noncommercial) distribution system and primarily showing small-gauge films (35mm was prohibitively expensive) while shunning the ideologically tainted conventions of mainstream entertainment cinema. This problem became more pressing with the appearance of mainstream commercial films based on or influenced by proletarian works. Film theorists such as Iwasaki Akira drew a strong distinction between popular commercial studio films that adapted proletarian works and the movement's own use of cinema for energizing the masses against landlords and capitalists.[14]

Attempts to distinguish the proletarian arts from decadent modernist and bourgeois capitalist forms of expression entailed a rejection of cheap sensationalism and formalist experimentation. For instance, proletarian writers Nakamoto Takako and Kataoka Teppei distanced themselves from their modernist roots—Nakamoto even denouncing "the style of the petit-bourgeois *shinkankaku* [neoperception] school" with which she was previously associated.[15] Gender bias (or blindness) ruled out subject matter deemed to focus too narrowly on women's concerns. The condescension of student activists, intellectuals, and JCP members toward women is palpable in stories such as Hirabayashi Eiko's "The Last Slaves" ("Saigo no dorei"), in which male activists recognize the female wage labor of bus drivers and factory workers but disparage the café waitresses from whom they exploit sexual favors.[16] Around 1930, several women's magazines that had been established as independent venues for women's writing and feminist discussions became increasingly Marxist in orientation.

This is the period in which the Japanese proletarian movement put greater emphasis on political organizing as it began to adhere more strictly to the Third Period policy set by Comintern. As a result of this policy change, editorial board members involved in the proletarian movement pushed their magazines to engage more directly with Marxist theory and class issues. *Nyonin geijutsu* (Women's arts) is as an example of a women's magazine that faced increasing hostility from the male left (as well as within its own female ranks), only to be co-opted by the proletarian movement and eventually destroyed by a shift in editorial policy that undermined the journal's original focus on women's issues and forced the journal to fold under pressure by the authorities.[17] Some historians have suggested that the proletarian movement (more specifically, the Comintern-directed policy shift) could be blamed for undermining coalitions among women from different backgrounds, with different interests, and with different degrees of political commitment.[18] In prewar Japan, feminism could mean very different things to different women, as the famous *bosei hogo ronsō* (debate on the support and protection of motherhood) among Hiratsuka Raichō, Yosano Akiko, and Yamakawa Kikue shows.[19] With the increasing emphasis on Marxist political organizing (propaganda, recruitment, education, etc.) in progressive intellectual circles in the late 1920s and early 1930s, debates on women's issues fell by the wayside, even in women-run women's magazines. This history forms the background for Barbara Sato's defense of a commercial women's culture in which "consumerism created a new set of images by which [women] could better understand who they were, or at least who they might be."[20] Sato readily acknowledges that the urban middle-class women who made up women's magazines' core readership were neither intellectuals nor activists. She emphasizes that these readers did not necessarily desire independence from their families or rebel against mainstream gender roles. Nonetheless, she argues, women's mass-circulated magazines sparked real changes in women's lifestyles and drew attention to their role in society.

Proletarian writers debated what subject matter could properly be considered political, and authors were sometimes discouraged from writing about love, sexuality, and domesticity. In one of the articles in Kurahara Korehito's famous series of essays on what he called "proletarian realism," "Geijutsuteki hōhō ni tsuite no kansō" ("Thoughts on artistic method," 1931), the leading left-wing theorist criticized proletarian literary works that revolved around the "problem of love" (*aijō no mondai*). Problem-of-love stories by Kataoka Teppei, Tokunaga Sunao, Ema Nakashi, and others tried to diversify the subject matter of proletarian literature, in which (as it was frequently observed) there was an overabundance of stories about labor strikes and rural tenancy disputes but a dearth of stories about other topics. In the essay, Kurahara asserted that love could not in itself constitute a central theme in proletarian literature and complained that problem-of-love stories artificially construed love as the most important issue facing humans. In addition, he argued, the stories problematically suggested inevitable conflicts between personal commitments and social commitments, thus recapitulating the hackneyed conflict between *giri* (duty) and *ninjō* (personal desire) in feudal love suicide plays. Not only that, Kurahara found the treatment of love in problem-of-love stories to be abstract and idealizing. This idealist understanding, he complained, suggested that love was a timeless and essential aspect of human nature. However, he argued, the notion that love transcends history and class is tantamount to petit bourgeois sentimentalism.

While Kurahara insightfully criticizes the ideological contradictions of problem-of-love literature, such arguments provided a rationale for the wholesale dismissal of literary treatments of gender inequality, gendered experience, love and emotions, sexuality, relations between men and women, female friendship, and so on, should these representations not adequately reflect the "reality" that the proletarian movement wanted to represent. For instance, Kurahara criticizes the Kataoka Teppei story "Problem of Love" ("Aijō no mondai"), which deals with the pressure on female activists to provide unremunerated domestic, emotional, and even sexual labor for male activists. In Kurahara's essay, "love" is an illegitimate topic of political analysis—except when viewed through the lens of, and only if subordinate to, questions of class and economic justice.[21] This attitude discouraged the examination of sexism and the gendered division of labor in the movement.

Despite Kurahara's criticism of these stories, proletarian artists deployed sensational images of women and signifiers of femininity to dramatize class conflict. Gendering sharpened the moral contrast between the corrupt powers of capitalism and the victimized proletariat, amplifying the emotional appeal of the movement's political arguments. Although it may be tempting to treat these representations as a piece—in other words, simply as negative depictions of women used to generate sympathy for the revolutionary cause—we can think more productively about the particular meanings that female bodies and markers of femininity accrued by examining the specific contexts in which these images were deployed.

"The Prostitute"

Brian Bergstrom has suggested that the depiction of the body in late 1920s proletarian literature was an extension of and reaction against modernist neoperceptionist writing. As he observes, neoperceptionist writers were primarily concerned with capturing the flux of sensations produced by urban modernity and commercial culture. However, these works stopped short of offering a political analysis of capitalist society.[22] For example, although Yokomitsu Ryūichi infused the novel *Shanghai* with disturbing portrayals of human bodies reduced to commodities and human relationships reduced to economic relations, Heather Bowen-Struyk concurs with Bergstrom, arguing, "*Shanghai* does not advocate revolution nor propose the necessity of forming alliances based on class."[23] Nonetheless, neoperceptionists' avant-garde shock tactics informed the graphic representations of abject poverty and dehumanization found in many proletarian works. Such frightening and disturbing depictions of the body led writer Nishikawa Mitsuru to dub some proletarian works as "shit realism," while critic Aramata Hiroshi compares proletarian literature to "splatter horror."[24] To take one example, in the Kataoka Teppei tale "The Linesmen" ("Tsūshin kōshu"), a telephone line repairman witnesses another company employee sever his finger in what is apparently an act of contrition for having joined the Communist Party. The bizarre spectacle, carried out at a company retreat, seems to have been engineered by management to deter labor organizing. "The Linesmen" is saturated with the macabre sensibility of *ero guro nansensu*, which is most apparent in the mysterious and horrific climax. The event is never fully explained; as such, it retains an air of horror and mystery. Kataoka's story shockingly materializes the violence of capitalism, the suffering endured by laboring bodies, and the narrator's feelings of alienation from his fellow workers. Stories such as this drew attention to the exploitation of the proletariat by making it sensible in vivid narratives of horror, absurdity, and victimization. In these narratives, extreme affects and emotions such as shame, abjection, disgust, despair, fear, absurdity, and estrangement played important roles.[25]

In the Hayama Yoshiki short story "The Prostitute" ("Inbaifu"), the spectacle of a corpse-like prostitute's naked body amplifies the story's message and effects. When the narrator, a worker, beholds the wretched condition of the naked woman, he cannot help but regard her with a powerful mixture of revulsion and desire. These mixed feelings produce an acute sense of self-alienation in the narrator, making possible his critical identification with a woman who has been exploited by capitalism. As a result, the narrator gains proletarian consciousness.[26]

Hayama introduces the theme of split subjectivity at the outset of the story, through the use of frame narration. This is crucial for several reasons: it activates the expectation of an unreliable narrator, it invites the reader's skepticism, and it prompts careful scrutiny of the text for possible explanations for what the narrator professes he is unable to explain. Because the frame narration is situated some years after the narrated events, it foregrounds the narrator's distanced, critical self-reflection. Finally, since frame narration is commonly used in tales of the grotesque and the supernatural, this technique immediately produces a set of genre expectations, preparing us for an unsettling tale of extraordinary events. We are cued to focus on the act of narrating and attend to the narrator's subjective (and incomplete) understanding of events now many years past. This opens an imaginative space for the reader to compare their understanding of events to that of the narrator and actively imagine alternative tellings or interpretations. In other words, the frame narration cues the reader to adopt the subjectivity of the narrator while simultaneously imagining another "objective" rendering of events. This is another instance of what Jonathan Flatley has called affective mapping, since it calls for the reader to project themselves into the text even as they intensely imagine the feelings and the experiences of the narrator.

The narrator's story concerns events that took place one sultry evening ten years ago, in July 1912, when he was still a brash and youthful sailor. He was strolling around Yokohama's American wharf when he was roughly accosted by three men who took his money and promised to show him "fun . . . the kind of fun young guys like."[27] They strong-arm the narrator into following them toward Chinatown, through an area that "reeked of the exotic atmosphere one finds in the Chinese districts in Hong Kong or Calcutta."[28] Walking him down a back street, through a narrow courtyard, and to an empty warehouse, they take him up a fire escape and into an enormous dimly lit room.

As the narrator's eyes adjust to the darkness, he realizes that there is something—or someone—lying behind a pile of beer crate lids in the corner. He approaches the unknown thing and is taken aback by a revolting discovery: the thing is a woman. The narrator struggles to maintain composure and disinterest before the spectacle of her naked body, which seems to straddle the boundary between life and death.

> The scene confronting me was an utterly atrocious one. Behind the beer case lids lay faceup a woman of twenty-two or twenty-three; she was completely naked. She lay on top of a rotting tatami mat. Her shoulders heaved with each breath that she seemed to wring out of herself as though it were her very last. Much that she had apparently vomited when she was still able to take food was spattered from shoulder to pillow, intermingled with dark blood stains. Her hair was matted with it. And her ~~XXXXXX~~ was stuck to ~~XXXXXX~~.[29] A sour stench rose from her head, and her limbs gave off the vile smell particular to cancerous growths. This abnormal reek was such that I doubted human lungs could withstand it. Her eyes were wide open and her pupils seemed to fix themselves on me, but they were probably seeing nothing. Of course, she also appeared not to know I was rooted there before her nakedness. I stood at her feet, transfixed by the sight. As I stood there stock-still, competing thoughts, distinct and parallel [*itsu made mo majiwaru koto no nai, heikōshita kangae*], filled my mind:
>
> Here is a human being to be pitied.
>
> There is a woman to be pitied.
>
> With eyes like two mounted projectors [*watashi no me wa suetsukerareta futatsu no purojekutā no yō ni*], I thrust my immobile gaze upon that corpse. And it was fitting to call it a corpse.
>
> I have a confession to make, a truly painful confession. If that which had lain before me had not been a naked woman but a naked man, I doubt I would have stayed where I was quite so long a time or that my soul would have felt such agitation.[30]

The wretched and listless woman speaks without moving, inviting the narrator to do what he likes. Revolted by his own sexual excitation, the narrator confesses to the reader, "Given that she was a woman, I can't deny that I felt an impulse."[31] Ultimately this is an impulse he cannot act on. His moral outrage building, the narrator becomes determined to free the woman and attacks the man standing guard. Surprisingly, both the guard and the woman denounce him and reject his claim that she is being exploited.

Confused but exhausted and willing to leave, the narrator departs. Later that night, he finds himself helplessly drawn back to the mysterious room. There he learns that the men who keep watch over the prostitute are truly her friends. According to their leader, "Slug," the group takes solace in each other's broken bodies. Together they have found the "crazy hope" to keep on living.[32] Astounded, the narrator admits he had "completely misread the situation."[33] He suddenly realizes, "I was looking at a martyr, not a prostitute. She appeared to me to symbolize the fate of the entire exploited class."[34] Eyes filling with tears, he firmly grasps Slug's hand, presses all of his money into the man's palm, and hurriedly leaves.

The theme of split subjectivity that is introduced through frame narration is underscored again in the narrator's description of his divided response to the sordid spectacle of the prostitute's body. Here, the narrator repeatedly emphasizes the sex of the sorry figure before him, confessing his inability to look away and his struggle with unseemly desire. As he squats at her feet and gazes upon her nakedness,

> I was terrified that her eyes would find mine. In fact, to be honest about it, at the time I was a heroic, humane, chaste young man. There was absolutely no discrepancy between my body and soul. So I did not want her to realize that I had fixed her OO in my searing gaze. Why was it only my eyes that I was unable to subdue?
>
> If she were to see where I was looking she would surely have concluded, "In the end, he's just like any other man."[35]

This passage may be compared to the longer passage quoted above, in which the narrator describes himself as having been seized by two "competing thoughts, distinct and parallel," filling his head: "Here is a human being to be pitied. There is a woman to be pitied." These competing thoughts are immediately given emphasis by the comparison between "*two* mounted projectors" and the narrator's gaze.[36] In the shorter passage quoted as well, the narrator makes reference to two natures opposed within him. On the one hand, he is "a heroic, humane, chaste young man," who believes that the woman before him is the victim of some atrocious crime. On the other hand, his "searing gaze" at her genitals suggests that he is also "just like any other man" for whom women are sexual objects. Indeed, it is only because the incapacitated body before him is a woman's that the narrator is made aware of the tension between his romantic self-image and his undeniable but suppressed "impulse" to exploit someone more helpless than himself. Moreover, only because she is a woman can the narrator treat the prostitute as both more and less than a man. Because she is a woman, her suffering solicits greater sadness and sympathy. At the same time, because she is a woman, it is easier for the narrator to view the prostitute instrumentally, as an object.

This split subjectivity produces proletarian consciousness in the narrator, even though he is initially unable to fully grasp the transformation that has taken place. As the narrator understands it, it is only when Slug and his comrades convince him that they have nothing but the best of intentions that he finally understands the woman as a symbol of the suffering proletariat. Hayama's narration is more sophisticated than the narrator. It shows that the narrator undergoes an experience of intense self-alienation that allows him to acquire a self-reflective distance, which he did not originally possess as a brash, carefree sailor strutting around the wharf. We might describe this process in Lukácsian terms: the narrator continues to identify with himself, as a heroic subject, while experiencing extreme self-dislocation as he comes to identify powerfully with the woman as an exploited object. This dual identification is made explicit in a passage emphasizing the narrator's paralyzing physical empathy with the woman, just after he has left the warehouse:

> I had a moment for some introspection. At which point I began to feel an intense heat. It was the humid heat of bad lungs, the breath of which congealed when exhaled, to be immediately inhaled at the next breath. The stench of vomit and secretions surely from the cancer continued to assail my nostrils. My body felt unbearably weary. Perhaps I had exhausted my

> emotions [*kokoro o tsukaisugita*] in this bizarre affair. Having to say anything or observing any more of it was somehow just too much trouble now. I was ready to lie down anywhere and sleep like a baby.[37]

Here, the narrator does not simply remember the smell of the woman and the sound of her breath. She does not merely occupy his thoughts. Rather, the narrator's entire body acts, senses, and feels like hers. His breathing is labored, his nostrils sting, and his body is exhausted. He feels the impulse to lie down.

Although Georg Lukács's *History and Class Consciousness* (1923) was not translated into Japanese until 1927, Hayama's narration mirrors Lukács's description of the role of alienation in producing revolutionary consciousness. In "Reification and the Consciousness of the Proletariat," Lukács argues that only the proletariat's practical class consciousness can overthrow the social and material relations under capitalism, which, although historical, have come to appear rigid and unchangeable. Lukács's argument assumes that the "commodity structure" is the basis of the objective and subjective experience of material and social relations under capitalism, and that workers have direct access to a practical understanding of the commodity structure in ways that other social classes do not. Lukács builds on Marx's definition of the commodity as a form that envelops the product of labor and obscures the processes of its manufacture. According to Lukács, the commodity structure is not only germane to capitalist production but is reiterated at the level of ideology, where it produces reification (*Verdinglichung*), the apparent "thingliness" of social and cultural processes under capitalism. To the reified mind, relations that are mediated by historical and economic processes seem given or take on the appearance of natural law, whereas in fact these processes and reification are themselves historical phenomena. According to Lukács, the increasingly structural concealment of process under the seemingly universal, impenetrable, and undeniable solidity of things is possible because the commodity structure has become universal form.[38]

The worker's physical role in the process of production is central to Lukács's argument, for this role consolidates a subjective stance and an objective stance in relation to the material basis of capitalism through practical activity. Because the worker perceives his labor objectified in the commodity that, although he has produced it, does not belong to him, he feels alienated from his own activity. The worker's relation to the commodity structure is more immediate than that of the bourgeoisie, because the worker experiences this relation both actively as a subject and passively (helplessly) as an object. Bourgeois intellectuals, on the other hand, experience reification as something already alien to them, removed as they are from the relations between labor and capital. The self-understanding of the proletariat and his role in reproducing the social structures dictated by capitalism simultaneously give rise to an object-like comprehension of the nature of those structures. The worker comes to understand himself as the subject-object of history when his immediate, subjective experience becomes fully known to encompass "*the structural principles and the real tendencies of the objects themselves.*"[39]

Whereas in Lukács the worker's realization takes place vis-à-vis his identification with the machine as both an object to be worked on as well as itself an agent of production, Hayama's narrator arrives at this realization through his encounter with the prostitute. Identifying with the woman (as a subject-object), as well as with himself (as a man), the narrator suddenly understands the relationship between workers and capitalists in immediate experiential terms:

> Wild thoughts spun round in my head like blades of a fan. Hadn't I been starved for sex? And hadn't I become excited? Yet I triumphed over myself. Humph! What a fine piece of work I, Minpei, was! But wait a minute! I was damn near thinking like a capitalist! I hadn't made the woman what she was. But I was strong. But I was weak. Weird. Either way is okay.[40]

On the one hand, this epiphany vis-à-vis the female subject-object gives the narrator's revolutionary consciousness a feminist inflection. The commodity structure given here is not simply that of the relationship between worker-machine-product at the site of production. Instead, in "The Prostitute," the commodity structure is illustrated by the exploitation of female sexuality. And yet Hayama's prostitute remains a commodity. Her sexuality remains the site of economic exchange. She is robbed of her individuality, abstracted into a symbol in a way that mystifies and obscures the sexual exploitation still taking place.

So, as Bergstrom has asked, where exactly *is* the feminism of this story? Bergstrom argues that, as represented by Hayama, the woman's body can only symbolize the condition of the entire proletarian class "insofar as its femininity, rendered legible as the fine web of distinctions that spell out the essential difference between prostitute and martyr, can be made to imply and amplify the extremity of that degradation. Why else would the woman end up as the representative martyr in the story and not the man who compares the degradation of his own body with hers?"[41] Given the strong genre inscription of the text, this indeed disturbing use of the woman's body seems deliberate. Slug and the corpse-like prostitute are monsters—they are the return of capitalism's repressed. Hayama's story produces a sense of the uncanny by having these monsters perform a sickening parody of capitalism in which the horror and violence of capitalist exploitation cannot be ignored. Frame narration, unreliable narrator, liminal or "exotic" space—these features firmly situate "The Prostitute" within the genre of horror. If the narrator achieves proletarian consciousness, it comes as the result of witnessing "the discarded dregs" of capitalist society, "livin' like maggots in a crypt," enacting exploitation as a gruesome theatrical spectacle.[42]

"The Prostitute" uses a brutalized female body to shock and disturb. It attempts to foster Lukácsian revolutionary consciousness by modeling a profoundly self-alienating identification with a person who is first mistaken for a thing and treated as an object as much as (if not more than) a subject. This tactic suggests a fundamentally misogynistic attitude toward women as both more than and less than men, even though the preponderance of genre elements in the story demonstrates that Hayama is consciously drawing on the disturbing violence and exploitation of the horror genre to guide the reader's response. In effect, what we have here is what Ackbar Abbas has called "critical proximity" in distinction to "critical distance."[43] Genre is being mobilized without parody and without irony to accomplish the objectives of the author. Hayama relies heavily on genre conventions to script and intensify the reader's response, but this strategy implicates the author as much as it implicates the narrator, Slug, and his gang in the exploitation of female suffering—even if this spectacle serves a worthy political purpose. Slug's presentation of the prostitute, the narrator's presentation of his bizarre experience, and Hayama's presentation of the narrator's story form a mise-en-abyme of frames with the prostitute's body at their center. To borrow from Abbas, the story is stuck in what "we might call a position of critical proximity, where one is always a part of what one is criticizing."[44]

What Made Her Do It?

Cinema provided new ways of registering the subjective experience of suffering, mobilizing sentiment, and prompting identification from its viewers. From 1927 to 1931, commercial studios influenced by the success of proletarian literature produced the politically informed social dramas that became known as "tendency films" (*keikō eiga*). These films featured rousing stories of oppression and rebellion. They pushed the envelope of what could pass censorship and used sensational, politically charged subject matter as an excuse for stylistic flourishes, such as whip pans, canted camera angles, and flash montage, to express the violence of capitalist oppression and the passion of revolutionary revolt. Critic Fujita Motohiko situates tendency films within a longer genealogy of cinematic responses to economic instability and social unrest, which includes postearthquake ballad films (*kouta eiga*) and rebellious period films (*hangyaku jidaigeki*) by screenwriter Susukita Rokuhei starring Bandō Tsumasaburō.[45] Fujita argues that *keikō eiga* were the most progressive studio films to appear in Japan until the end of World War II, and that they helped raise Japanese cinema out of its pervasive "empty sentimentalism, pessimism, and nihilism."[46] Although the proletarian movement did not officially sanction tendency films, Fujita argues that these films helped foster a deeper understanding of capitalist society in both filmmakers and audiences. In addition, tendency films seem to have been instrumental in stimulating the proletarian arts movement's film activities. As Fujita points out, the Proletarian Film League of Japan (Prokino) did not begin film production and screening activities in earnest until 1930. (Until then, the organization devoted most of its energies to publishing film criticism and film theory.)[47]

The best known tendency films included *A Living Doll* (*Ikeru ningyō*, dir. Uchida Tomu, Nikkatsu, 1929), *Metropolitan Symphony* (*Tokai kōkyōgaku*, dir. Mizoguchi Kenji, Nikkatsu, 1929), *The Sword That Slays One Saves Many* (*Issatsu tashōken*, dir. Itō Daisuke, Ichikawa Utaemon Productions, 1929), *The Sword That Slashes Man and Horse* (*Zanjin zanbaken*, dir. Itō, Shōchiku, 1929), *The Umbrella Maker's Swordsmanship* (*Kasahari kenpō*, dir. Tsuji Kichirō, Nikkatsu, 1929), and the biggest commercial success of them all, *What Made Her Do It?* (*Nani ga kanojo o sō saseta ka*, dir. Suzuki Shigeyoshi, Teikine, 1930).[48] Tendency films that adapted proletarian works included *A Living Doll* (1929, based on a story by Kataoka Teppei), *In Praise of Women* (*Joseisan*, dir. Abe Yutaka, 1930, also based on a story by Kataoka), and *Urban Hyperbola* (*Tokai sōkyokusen*, dir. Ide Kinnosuke for Tōa and Takumi Sadae for Teikine in 1930, based on a story by Hayashi Fusao). Other tendency films were not direct adaptations but drew on proletarian literature's stock characters and situations, such as corrupt landowners, labor disputes, ruthless industrialists, downtrodden tenant farmers, and industrial espionage. In any case, tendency films were criticized by the proletarian movement proper as profit-motivated productions that exploited the entertainment value of provocative subjects such as class struggle and revolution.

Leading Prokino film critic Iwasaki Akira attributed the appearance of the tendency film to the success of proletarian literature, as well as increased awareness of class-related issues among the general public. At the same time, he disparaged the films as attempts by major commercial studios to capitalize on, commodify, and even undermine the proletarian movement. For Iwasaki, the tendency film confronted proletarian filmmakers with the same thorny issues of "massification" that had been raised by Comintern and quickly became central to Japanese proletarian literary debates. In his article "The Massification of Proletarian Art and Its Relation to Actuality" ("Puroretaria eiga no taishūka to sono genjitsusei"), Iwasaki used the tendency films *What Made Her Do It?*, *The Sword That Slashes Man and Horse*, and *The Umbrella Maker's Swordsmanship* to think about the proper form and address of the proletarian film, arguing that the "mass" Prokino served was distinct from the *taishū* targeted by popular literature and film.[49] In the essay "The Tendency Film Problem" ("Keikō eiga no mondai"), Iwasaki complained that tendency films were "served up" as proletarian works when, in fact, they were only "flavored" with ".001 grams or .0001 grams" of ideology.[50] For Iwasaki, the personality of the artist and their level of political commitment was far less determining than structural material and economic factors. In fact, he reserved his most pointed criticism for supposed supporters of the movement who worked at commercial studios. He singled out Kimura Kazuma, studio chief of Shōchiku Shimogamo and advocate for the tendency film, for "optimistically" believing it was possible to make authentically leftist but commercially profitable films.[51] Iwasaki did not bother to discuss the political beliefs of tendency film directors Suzuki Shigeyoshi, Itō Daisuke, and Uchida Tomu. For him, the fact that these directors worked at commercial film companies rendered their personal political beliefs irrelevant. He believed that tendency films affirmed the existence of a mass audience for socially critical films, but he stressed that these commercial productions diluted and distorted the politics of the movement, diminishing the potential audience for more serious proletarian works. In the end, he argued, commercial studios were bourgeois institutions that made tendency films for profit, even if filmmakers were sympathetic to the cause. Iwasaki predicted that if tendency films became unprofitable or invited the wrath of the state, or if the proletarian movement gained momentum and threatened the existence of commercial filmmaking, tendency films would disappear—and he was right.

In the end, strict film censorship killed the tendency film. Censorship hampered filmmakers' ability to create overtly critical representations of class struggle and led to increased financial risk. It cost valuable time and money to respond to censors' objections. Revisions were expensive, and many cuts could easily render a film incomprehensible. According to Gregory Kasza, during the years that tendency films were popular, the number of films censored due to representations of class conflict rose significantly, peaking in 1930. That year, there were a total of seventy-nine cuts under the censorship category "class conflict" compared to only seven in 1929 and nineteen in 1931.[52] Kasza also suggests that the decline of the tendency film can be linked to the Manchurian Incident of 1931, a military skirmish that drew attention away from the economy and contributed to the popularity of continental romance films.[53]

What Made Her Do It? was a commercial hit with an enthusiastic reception from mainstream critics, but it was harshly criticized by Iwasaki and other Prokino affiliates. The film is the story of an orphan girl driven mad by poverty and exploitation. In addition to winning top place in the 1930 *Kinema junpō* Best Ten, the film spawned a sequel called *What Killed*

Her? that took seventh place in the *Kinema junpō* poll the following year. *What Made Her Do It?* ran for five straight weeks in Asakusa where, according to Joseph Anderson and Donald Richie, "audiences rioted in support of its anti-capitalist sentiments, being excited to the point of loud cries of 'Down with Capitalism!' and the like."[54] Suzuki Jūzaburō enthusiastically endorsed the film in *Kinema junpō:*

> This is a faithful film adaptation of a work of new literature (*shinkō bungaku*). The spirit of the original author Fujimori Seikichi breathes in this film. It overflows with the voices of the oppressed proletariat. It cries out to spectators in a loud voice, allowing them to properly recognize the contradictions of the social order laid bare. The title *What Made Her Do It?* survived strict censors' cuts and was marvelously utilized to carry out this mission. Screenwriter and director Suzuki Shigeyoshi should be eternally praised for making this piece of poetry.[55]

Sasaki Norio wrote similarly in *Eiga hyōron* (Film criticism):

> In terms of its deep artistic impact, the power of its verisimilitude, and the new tendency it bodes within the development of the so-called proletarian film, this film far surpasses works of a similar tendency [*onaji keikō no sakuhin*] made in 1929, of which *A Living Doll* and *Metropolitan Symphony* are representative examples.[56]

However, a "joint criticism" of the film in the March 1930 issue *Shinkō eiga* (New film)—featuring Murayama Tomoyoshi, Iwasaki Akira, Sasa Genjū, Kishi Matsuo, and other members of Prokino (nineteen participants in all)—harshly criticized *What Made Her Do It?* for its petit bourgeois perspective and its failure to link the orphan Sumiko's predicament to the plight of the proletarian class.[57] Moreover, the film was a romping comedy and electrifying melodrama with strong modernist elements—a far cry from the concrete, accessible, and analytical realist style pushed by Kurahara Korehito. Compared with the original Fujimori Seikichi play, the film version of *What Made Her Do It?* further sensationalizes the main character Sumiko's suffering, increasing the shock value of her story. Not only that, much of the play's cruelty is played for comedy in the film, turning its bleak social melodrama into *ero guro nansensu*—so much so that the grotesque female bodies on display seem to parody the excessive female bodies of proletarian art and literature.

Fujimori's original play *What Made Her Do It?* chronicles a young woman's descent into delinquency and madness.[58] The protagonist, an orphan named Sumie (Sumiko in the film), endures an endless string of hardships while being shuttled between different charitable institutions, all of which ultimately fail her. She is abused and exploited by relatives, guardians, employers, teachers, and confessors; even her attempted love suicide with an irresolute partner fails. After surviving the suicide attempt, Sumie is "born again" at a Christian women's reformatory. Although she wants to repent and obey her betters, a fellow inmate pressures her to reach out to her former lover by letter. For this infraction, Sumie and the instigator are severely punished by the headmistress. Sumie submits to the headmistress's abuse but balks at confessing her "sins" in front of the entire congregation, which is more humiliation than she can bear. The headmistress refuses to relent, so Sumie stands before the congregation and in a torrential outburst, denounces the home, the headmistress, and even God as "full of lies." In the famous final scene, having lost faith in humanity and all hope for salvation, Sumie goes mad and burns down the reformatory. She dances and laughs hysterically in front of raging flames before being led away to jail.

The film version roughly follows the plot of Fujimori's play and survives in incomplete form. Unfortunately, the very last scene, in which Sumiko burns down the reformatory, is missing. Most of the play's events are dramatized in the film, but the film abandons the play's linear narrative and instead uses a flashback structure. In addition, in the film Sumiko's predicament is heightened through the use of perilous melodramatic situations, actors' grotesque facial expressions and bodily poses, and gross-out comedy, all of which cast the female body in different postures of extremis. These bodily extremes are further accentuated by formalist film techniques. Sumiko's experiences come to life as a frenzied barrage of images through director Suzuki Shigeyoshi's use of avant-garde film devices. Skewed camera angles, swish pans, and rapid-fire montage are used to punctuate the abuse Sumiko suffers at the hands of family members and employers, giving vivid expression to the violent emotions triggered by these experiences, so that the "body" of the film itself appears to be in the throes of hysteria.

Just prior to directing *What Made Her Do It?*, Suzuki took a study trip to Europe, where he viewed many avant-garde films. He returned with several prints, including a copy of Man Ray's poetic surrealist short *L'Étoile de mer* (1928), based on an enigmatic text by poet Robert Desnos.[59] Suzuki's assistant director, Kimura Sotoji, has said that the techniques in *What Made Her Do It?* were taken from the modernist films he and Suzuki had seen, as well as avant-garde films that they had only read about but still wanted to emulate.[60] It appears that some of the references in *What Made Her Do It?* are direct allusions to Soviet montage films. In a scene where Sumiko is tormented by her spoiled young mistress, a montage of three shots animates a laughing Buddha figure, seemingly referencing a similar sequence of shots in Sergei Eisenstein's *Battleship Potemkin* (1925) (fig. 6.1). In *Battleship Potemkin*, shots of three stone lions in different positions are shown in quick succession, making it seem as if the statues are rising to protest the 1905 Odessa massacre shown in the previous scene. Sumiko tosses a plate through a *shoji* screen in defiance of the young mistress's mother, who feeds the maids scraps like dogs. This could likewise be a reference to the sailors' mutiny over rations and the famous plate-breaking sequence in *Battleship Potemkin*. Food is used repeatedly in the film to emphasize Sumiko's deprivation and her shameful treatment by authority, giving *What Made Her Do It?* the same visceral attention to the physical body that one finds in Eisenstein's films. Montage, rapid cuts, and extreme camera angles create shuddering images that amplify the message of *What Made Her Do It?*, conveying Sumiko's torment, the absurd cruelty of her tormenters, and her crescendoing desire to revolt.

The use of modernist film techniques to accentuate Sumiko's physical and emotional distress draws attention to the construction of the film as an apparatus for experience. The inscription of Sumiko's suffering can be read as a kind of mimesis that bestows the film with a body. As film theorist Jennifer Barker points out, we do not have to identify the camera with a specific body within the world of the film to recognize "the relationship of mutual, reciprocal significance" that connects our bodies (as spectators) to the world of the film via the camera's mediation.[61] It is impossible not to notice a correspondence between Suzuki's use of style and Sumiko's physical and emotional predicament. Our encounter with her world is thus shaped by her subjectivity and even her physical engage-

FIGURE 6.1 The "moving" statuary montage sequences in *Battleship Potemkin* (1925) and *What Made Her Do It?* (1930).

ment with her environment, even though the camera does not literally adopt her first-person perspective.

In addition, Suzuki's film emphasizes the psychological contours of Sumiko's world by restructuring the original narrative of the play. The film presents Sumiko's experiences as a series of flashbacks, as opposed to the successive string of episodes found in Fujimori's original drama. Fujimori's play unfolds chronologically like a sensational newspaper novel, one miserable episode after another. In contrast, the film emphasizes memory and association, heightening our sense of Sumiko as the subject of proletarian consciousness and the object of capitalist exploitation. The film's flashback construction further aligns the spectator with Sumiko, allowing the viewer to feel how the sting of injustice can become the spark of revolt. Whereas Suzuki offers images that are inscribed with overwhelming physical and emotional experiences, Fujimori tends to distribute action between onstage and offstage space. As a result, the film has a very distinct, excessive physicality that the stage play lacks.

This physicality is grotesque and excessive. It is exemplified by a scene in which young female servants (Sumiko among them) react to their tyrannical mistress's shrill discipline. The comically screwed-up faces of the reprimanded women create a mix of pleasing and displeasing effects, an aesthetic mixture that is typically associated with the grotesque. This mugging conveys the monstrosity of their bourgeois mistress and the servants' own dehumanization. At the same time, one cannot help but notice that there is also something perversely erotic about these twitching, distorted expressions that slyly manifests melodrama's delight in female suffering (fig. 6.2). Many examples of such bodily excess appear throughout the film. For instance, after her aunt and uncle sell her to a traveling circus, Sumiko is forced to play the target in a knife-throwing routine. In this episode, Sumiko is falsely accused of stealing a fellow performer's money and is barely saved from her drunken handler's whip. It is worth noting that this circus scene is not in Fujimori's original work. The costuming, props, and situation are reminiscent of the exoticism and violence in D. W. Griffith's *Broken Blossoms* (1919). In this sequence, too, extreme low and high camera angles, off-center framing, fast cutting, and chiaroscuro lighting emphasize the physical threat to Sumiko, her powerlessness, and her frenzied emotional and psychological state (fig. 6.3).

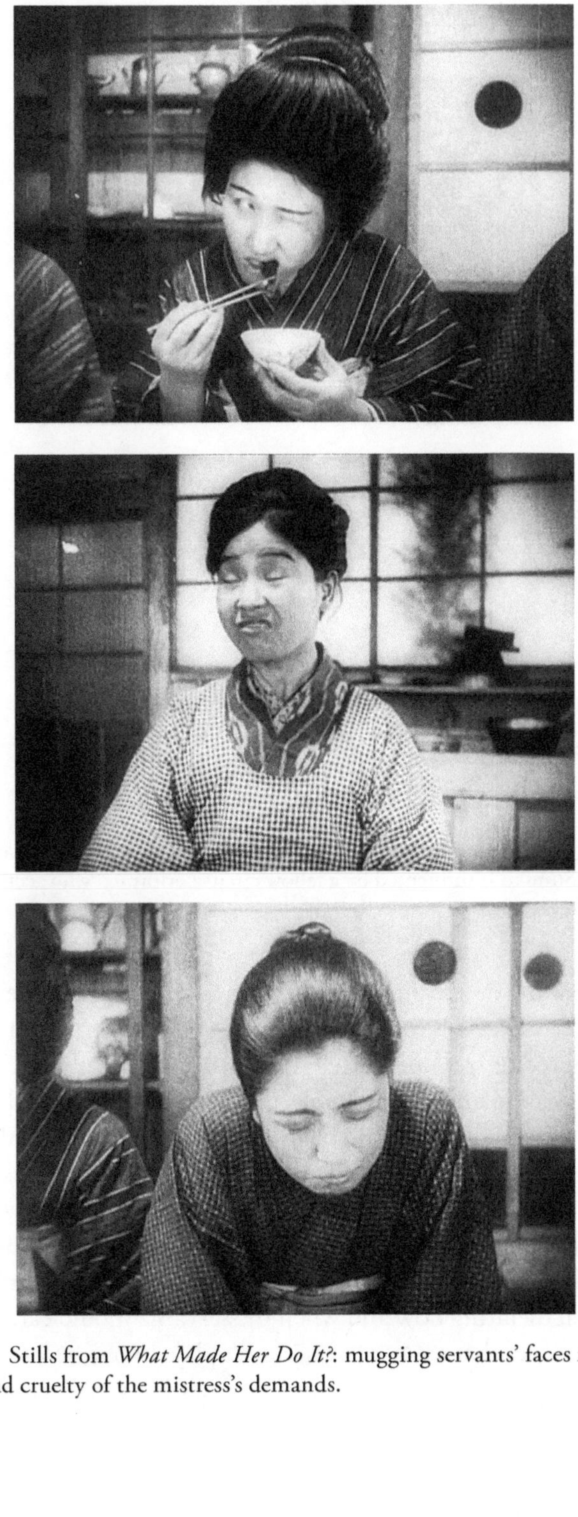

FIGURE 6.2 Stills from *What Made Her Do It?*: mugging servants' faces register the absurdity and cruelty of the mistress's demands.

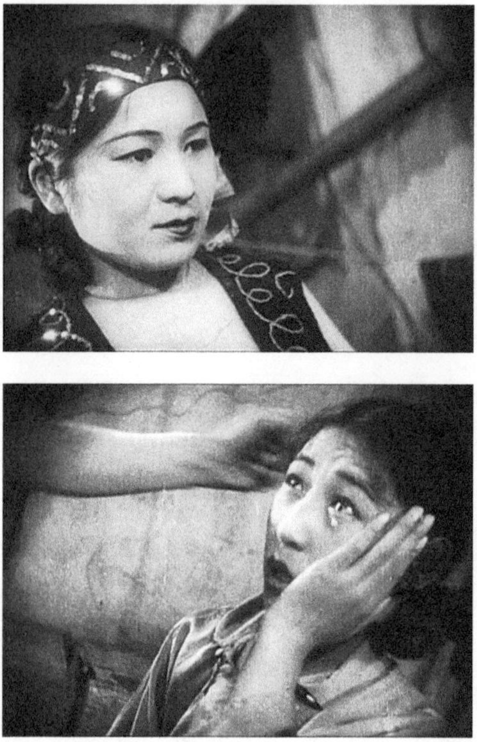

FIGURE 6.3 Stills from *What Made Her Do It?*: canted camera angles are used in the scene where Sumiko is tormented by a fellow circus performer, who accuses her of stealing money.

As mentioned, another element that Suzuki adds to the film to emphasize bodily excess is food. In *What Made Her Do It?* food is conspicuously devoured or spit up, scattered, and thrown. Its ubiquitous presence contributes to the film's highly polarized display of need and abundance, desire and disgust. To a certain degree, these thematics can also be found in the original play, in which several scenes portray how desperately the poor want for food: Sumie's last piece of bread is stolen by a wicked uncle; a baby cries in hunger at his starving mother's shriveled breast; and a wealthy daughter and mother abuse servants who prepare, serve, and clear a meal, even dictating how and when the servants should eat. Suzuki adds even more scenes that are not in Fujimori's play. In one new scene, Sumiko is rescued by a rickshaw driver and devours his gruel. There is also an

FIGURE 6.4 Still from *What Made Her Do It?*: at her uncle's house, Sumiko is not allowed to eat until everyone else is finished. The other children's faces are covered with rice, and they dangle food from bowl to bowl.

original scene in which Sumiko is forced to wait until her cousins have finished eating, and only then is she allowed to pick scraps from their dirty bowls (fig. 6.4). Both the film and the play include the scene of the rich young mistress choking on a fish bone in the house where Sumiko works, but it is difficult to imagine that she choked as explosively on stage as she does in the film (figs. 6.5–6.7).

The use of modernist filmmaking techniques in popular films such as *What Made Her Do It?* attests to the widespread influence of Soviet filmmakers and the European avant-garde. Scholars such as David Bordwell, Aaron Gerow, and Satō Tadao have pointed out that the use of avant-garde techniques—such as flash montage, swish pans, extreme camera angles, and extremely mobile cameras—was not limited to tendency films; nor were such techniques necessarily understood as "avant-garde," let alone politically radical, in interwar Japan. Thanks to the narration of the *benshi*, extreme visual stylization did not have to challenge narrative

FIGURE 6.5 Stills from *What Made Her Do It?*: the young mistress sprays food while choking on a bone.

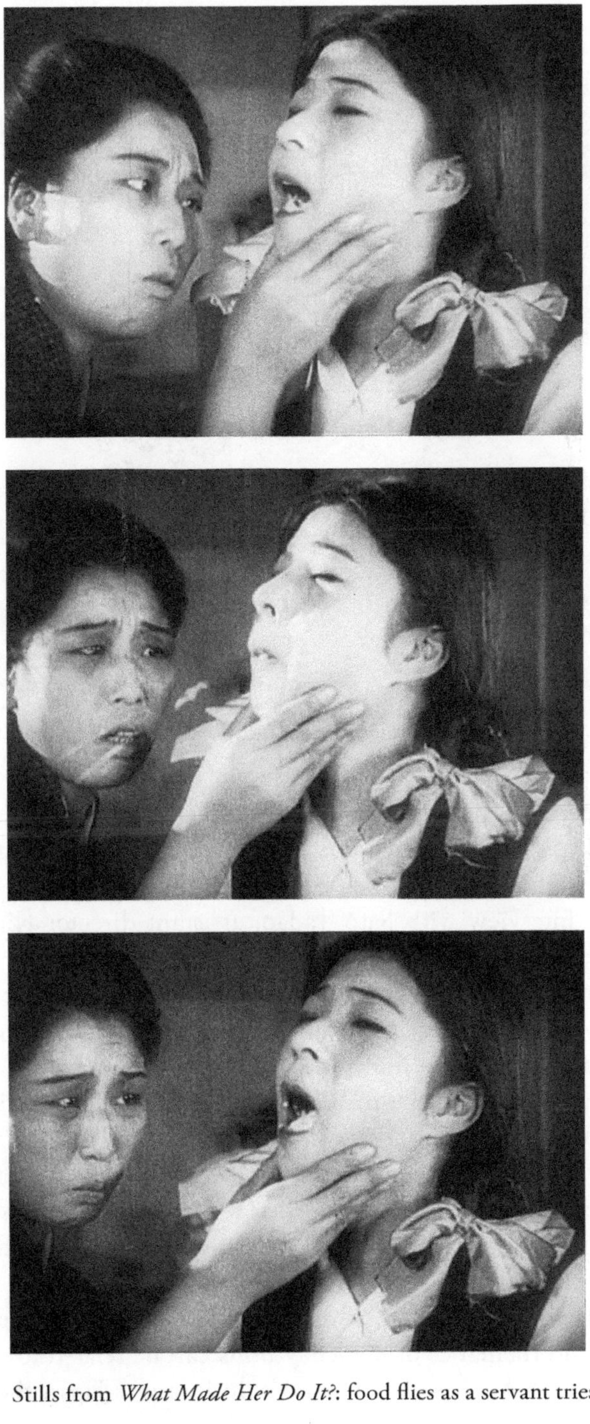

FIGURE 6.6 Stills from *What Made Her Do It?*: food flies as a servant tries to help.

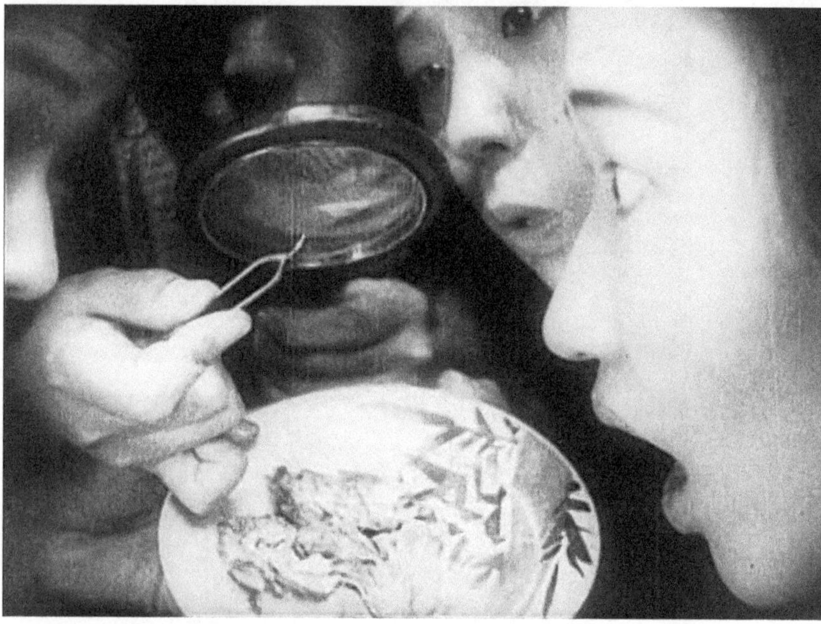

FIGURE 6.7 Still from *What Made Her Do It?*: the offending bone is found.

comprehension. The impact of overt stylization also depended on genre markers (e.g., settings, situations, and character types) and audience expectations, which could be shaped by marketing and critical discourse.[62] In a 1984 interview with Satō Tadao, assistant director Kimura Sotoji rejected characterizations of the politics of *What Made Her Do It?* that rested simply on the use of form. Kimura says he sympathized with the left-wing movement, but political and financial concerns meant he was unable to engage with proletarian ideas in any substantive way. He stresses that his innovations in *What Made Her Do It?* were strictly limited to film form.[63] Still, Kimura was active on the fringes of Prokino, and Suzuki was a contributing member of the Prokino Friends fundraising group. Perhaps Kimura chose to downplay the film's politics in accordance with the widely held position that tendency films were made for profit and entertainment, and as such they were not truly political films.

Scholars such as Miriam Silverberg and Chika Kinoshita propose that the style and thematics of tendency films can be related to the "culture of montage."[64] As these scholars note, in interwar Japan the modernist aesthetic of montage proliferated across a wide range of mass cultural forms—including films, ads, illustrated magazines, popular song lyrics, and more—blurring the boundaries between high art and mass culture. In tendency films, montage was deliberately used to create sharp contrasts between the bourgeoisie and the proletariat and thus give representation to the contradictions of capitalist modernity. Accordingly, Kinoshita writes, "even though the principles of montage and their revolutionary potentials were enslaved to and exploited by [the] culture industry for profits, as long as [popular uses of montage] still carry the message of class struggle in sensationalized form, the message always retains the possibility of manifesting."[65] She argues that many critics have ignored the use of montage in tendency films to highlight class conflict, resulting in an untenable separation of form and content, and politics and aesthetics, in analyses of popular uses of montage.

However, the harshest criticism of tendency films came from Prokino, and this may be why only a handful of scholars, including Fujita and Kinoshita, have given tendency films serious consideration as left-wing films. The commercial success of *keikō eiga* was a source of pride and anxiety for proletarian artists, who felt that their struggles had created the conditions of possibility for tendency films, although they themselves could never gain access to the funds, equipment, means of distribution, and exhibition venues available to commercial filmmakers. This is why Iwasaki viewed tendency films as diluting and distorting the politics of the movement while hijacking the potential audience for more serious proletarian works.

Throughout this book, I have examined how cinema's address to a mass audience and its influence over spectators was perceived during the 1920s, the decade said to have inaugurated the "age of the mass society" in Japan.[66] Unsurprisingly, the rise of mass culture in a time of national crisis drew intense scrutiny to the affects and emotions associated with a burgeoning commercial culture. Considering the proletarian debates on art, politics, and representation, I would argue that we cannot fully understand why these affects and emotions were derisively marked as "feminine" unless we understand how gender intersected with class in both left-wing and right-wing discussions of mass culture. Mass culture could be coded "feminine" because of the important role that female consumers, women workers, and women's culture played in the development of

Japanese industry and the expansion of the consumer economy. In addition, the Japanese proletarian movement used gender markers to embellish an antagonistic rhetoric of labor versus capital. Female consumers represented the excesses and waste of consumer culture, while proletarian women represented capitalism's most vulnerable victims.

My comparison of two texts shows how representations of women—in particular, representations of the female body—could be used quite fluidly to express different ideas and attitudes toward capitalist culture. These representations of women and femininity were "sticky": repeatedly loaded with significance and always coupled with other markers of identity and value. The stickiness of women's bodies and signifiers of femininity allowed representations of women to take on class connotations and other attributes, often with (as Angela Coutts notes) a negative coloring.[67] However, as analysis of "The Prostitute" and *What Made Her Do It?* shows, within the culture wars surrounding capitalist modernity and consumer culture, "gender" was not simply an expression of identity but a shifting frame of reference, a mobile signifier. We can observe its stickiness at work by comparing representations of women across different genres and forms deployed by the proletarian arts movement—including magazine illustrations, short stories, plays and films, and horror, melodrama, and comedy. As Sara Ahmed suggests, we need an emphasis on genre and rhetoric, as opposed to too narrow a focus on objects, to illuminate the mechanisms by which particular emotions and affects get stuck to certain bodies.

In the works I have discussed, women's bodies in extremis are used to attract and repel. The thingliness of women's bodies emphasizes the violence of capitalism against bodies and minds. In particular, women's pitiable suffering is used to prompt a political consciousness that emerges from identification with the victims of capitalism. This troubling identification produces self-alienation in the reader/viewer and thus an ability to see oneself as both a subject and an object. Disidentification with subject-objects is what produces the Lukácsian epiphany necessary for revolutionary consciousness. But this instrumental use of women's bodies consigns these works to a place of critical proximity, making both texts complicit with the structures of capitalist exploitation they illuminate.

Whereas in "The Prostitute" identification is narrated to us, in *What Made Her Do It?* the sensory-affective medium of cinema allows the viewer to experience the violence of Sumiko's oppression and her hysterical response via contortions of the image. The texts do not operate in identical fashion, but despite Prokino's criticism, nor are they radically opposed. The proletarian arts movement had to disavow its use of popular literary genres and deny the similarities between authorized and unauthorized texts in order to assert a critical distance between commercial culture and its own textual practices. Still, one of the objectives of the proletarian arts movement was to produce something like a "feminine" response in readers/viewers with works that attempted to foster emotional identification and mimesis. In "The Prostitute," this identification is even described with an analogy to film, with the narrator's eyes compared to "two mounted projectors."[68] The comparison emphasizes the distance between the narrator and the prostitute, his immobility, and the objectivity of his gaze. It is as if the terrible spectacle of the corpse-like prostitute momentarily causes the narrator to lose his humanity. He freezes into something resembling an object, mirroring the prostitute's death-like state. The sensory dynamism of *What Made Her Do It?* could not be further from the machine-like coldness described in "The Prostitute," but both make cinema the site of a radical act of identification with suffering women.

AFTERWORD

The central aim of this book has been to examine how cinema's address to a mass audience and its connections to commercial culture elicited popular understandings of realism in relation to female bodies and character traits. This approach allows us to think about realism in terms of spectatorial pleasure and identification—in other words, in terms of the imputed emotional, sensual, and psychological persuasiveness of the cinematic diegesis—rather than in terms of formal and textual operations more narrowly conceived or the indexicality of the photographic image. I have avoided writing an intellectual history of Japanese film theories or an industrial history about technological and aesthetic developments, even though the standardization of narrative film practices, the expanding reach of film distribution, and the development of the star system are crucial to how cinema was imagined as a medium of fantasy with powerful mass appeal. Instead, I have tried to situate cinema within a broader media context that allows us to perceive the interplay between cinema and other forms. This overlap and interplay is evident in media representations of the Great Kanto Earthquake, in newspaper coverage of aspiring actresses, in the mixed-media works of Murayama Tomoyoshi, and in the dialogue between the tendency film and sensational proletarian literature. Situating cinema in this wider context allows us to perceive an important discursive field where representations of women and feminine markers were used to define and evaluate the new forms of sensuality, identification, and desire operating within commercial mass culture. This frame for understanding realism in terms of what film theory will later describe as, for instance, cathexis or diegetic suture, is easily overlooked in histories that adopt a more gender-neutral perspective. Moreover, although fraught images of female passions may offer no concise articulation of "realism," they can be analyzed to reveal the cultural politics of cinema and identification. The usefulness of this approach is that it allows us to raise questions not only about the nature of the cinematic medium but also about how the cinematic imaginary was used to express ideas about social and political change.

In closing, I offer a few concluding remarks about the protean nature of Japanese cinema in this period and the role the earthquake played in shaping the cinematic imagination.

First, the 1910s and 1920s was a period of significant film stylistic and industrial transformation. Many film scholars have examined these developments, but Aaron Gerow's pioneering book *Visions of Japanese Modernity: Articulations of Cinema, Nation, and Spectatorship, 1895–1925* has been particularly foundational for my work here, as it draws attention to the mutually constitutive relation between constructions of cinema and constructions of the film spectator in 1910s–1920s Japan. In many respects, Gerow's study is reminiscent of Jonathan Crary's *Techniques of the Observer: On Vision and Modernity in the Nineteenth Century*, which uses a Foucauldian approach to trace the emergence of a modern observer as "an *effect* of an irreducibly heterogeneous system of discursive, social, technological, and institutional relations." As Crary also puts it, "There is no observing subject prior to this continually shifting field."[1] Like Crary's *Techniques of the Observer*, Gerow's *Visions of Japanese Modernity* may be called a media archaeological study in that it examines the larger discursive frameworks—social, political, juridical, technological, theoretical—through which its object (in Gerow's case, *eiga*, or "cinema") first became available to definition, study, and regulation. According to Gerow, *eiga*, modern film, was not only postulated as the goal of Japanese film reform; this concept of cinema as a distinct medium with special properties made it possible for authorities to grasp cinema as a unique social problem. In *Visions of Japanese Modernity*, Gerow is not simply interested in "the things discourse describes but also the historically grounded sets of rules and practices that, never reducible to things or words, do not simply name an already present reality but work to mold and create objects of understanding and knowledge."[2] Much like Crary, Gerow finds that the cumulative effect of new ideas and practices specific to "cinema" was the emergence of a newly conceived spectator, a "transcendental spectator" or "abstract citizen" in whom the meaning of the film was received and reactions to cinema could be studied.[3] This "subject with an inside"[4] was partly the result of "a reconceptualizing of the process of cinematic signification [that] emphasized its universality and location in the sphere of production (privileging that over reception in the space of exhibition) [as well as] transformations in exhibition practice, often geared to appeal to high-class customers," for these developments made possible "the downplaying of benshi as independent stars and the rise of actors as cinematic stars" in a process that increasingly located the subject of narrative enunciation "within" the film text.[5] With the internalization of narrative enunciation within the film text, it became possible to conceive of a parallel internalization of meaning within the film spectator. However, as Gerow is careful to point out, this concept of an interiorized subject who could be controlled raised the specter of other unruly and unmanageable subjectivities who, being resistant and other-directed, might derail the process of proper subjectification. Gerow suggests that these unruly subjectivities were ultimately the basis for the idea of a "modern citizenry uniformly in need of management by the modern imperial state," because according to this conceptual model, all viewers are "equally in danger of succumbing to problematic modes of reception."[6] Thus, Gerow argues, "The opposition, then, was not always between the new, modern subject and the spectator of old, but also between two different versions of a modern subject, one defined by the hierarchical rule of universal intellectual standards, the other by the less stratified combinations of thoughts, perceptions, and bodily impulses."[7] In his conclusion, Gerow notes the difficulty of researching these resistant subjects without homogenizing the multiplicity and mixture for which they stand. In addition, he argues, one should not overlook the very role that ideas about insubordinate and unruly subjectivities played in justifying the notion of an interiorized subject to be systematically studied and controlled.[8]

What does this imply about the images of female/feminized subjectivities and desires that I have examined in this book? As Gerow's research suggests, these figures cannot automatically be understood as counterhegemonic.[9] For instance, the allegorical use of women's suffering in interwar proletarian texts suggests a masculinist understanding of indignity and humiliation rather than a feminist worldview: these are gynophobic texts. Likewise, the image of the aspiring actress concatenated weaknesses and impulses that were imagined as inherently feminine, allowing this representation to be used to illustrate an undisciplined, self-absorbed relation to cinematic images. At the risk of collapsing such disparate examples under one rubric, I have attempted to provide various examples of gendered tropes that showed concern with the emotions, desires, and identifications stimulated by modern media—especially forms of narcissistic involvement and projection, visual fascination and pleasure, and materialistic desire. Notably, these are also among the sensory-affective structures imagined to undergird the diegetic force of classical narrative cinema.

I return to Gerow to reflect on what my study might contribute to our understanding of Japanese film history. As Gerow demonstrates, popular notions of unruly and impressionable spectators—namely, women, children, and lower-class film viewers—not only motivated the development of film censorship and other regulatory measures but also, in their disturbing excess and imagined insusceptibility to control, negatively constituted dominant ideas about normal film spectatorship. Obstacles such as an incomplete archive stymie a thorough historical investigation of these purportedly resistant subjectivities—subjectivities that, after all, may have only existed in the cultural imagination. Nevertheless, there is value in further interrogating this discursive field. If we do not interrogate images of female spectatorship and consumption, if we ignore the imputed nature of women's engagement with cinematic images, the female viewer (as a construct if not an empirical fact) is at risk of remaining invisible in film histories and histories of film theory despite being hyperproductive of interwar notions of film realism and spectatorship.[10] In this book, I have tried to go beyond strict definitions of film theory to demonstrate the salience of popular notions of female subjectivity to the powers ascribed to cinema during this important transitional period, which involved the consolidation of classical narrative, the rise of the mass audience, and new links between cinema and consumer culture in Japan. How can we fail to theorize the function of woman within cinema's cultural imaginary in this period? Images and ideas about women played a central role in the vernacular understanding of cinema's powers.

If we ignore the use of gendered tropes to produce popular concepts about film realism, legitimizing some forms of fantasy and identification while delegitimizing others, we risk reinforcing a male-authored theorization of the medium that speaks through and about women while denying women enunciation. Should we ignore the importance of women to 1920s Japanese film discourse, and neutralize the significance of gender to ideas about spectatorship and realism, we once again exclude women from the process of cultural meaning-making despite the importance of sexual difference to the articulation of ideas about cinema as a sensory-affective medium.[11]

In addition to thinking about popular theories of cinema's persuasive sensory realism through a gendered lens, this book has argued that new concepts of realism and spectatorial engagement coalesced around the rise of the mass audience for cinema in 1920s Japan. The Great Kanto Earthquake is a key event in this history. Not since the Russo-Japanese War had any event given rise to such a frenzy of representations across different media, in high art and popular culture, and commercial and state-sponsored forms.[12] The disaster stimulated demand for information, images, and entertainment, inaugurating an age of mass media. The earthquake directed attention to cinema's ability to reach a wide audience and shape public sentiment, and it contributed to new definitions of what cinematic realism might entail. What (if any) representations could possibly be commensurate with the actual experience of the earthquake? Censorship, trauma, and the inexhaustible scope of the disaster placed its full horror beyond what could be said or shown. Earthquake media producers confronted the challenge of conveying the enormity of an event that exceeded representation. Tokyo-based filmmakers grappled with extraordinarily difficult filming conditions in the aftermath of the earthquake, at a time when Japanese cinema was still widely considered to be technically and technologically impoverished compared to American and European cinema.[13] Under these circumstances, how could Japanese filmmakers possibly satisfy the public's demand for realism?

In chapters on the Great Kanto Earthquake films, I argued that these obstacles shifted focus from the visible and the speakable to other registers of sensing and knowing. We might say that these extra dimensions helped flesh out Japanese cinema's transition from a presentational to a representational aesthetic, one that engaged a sense of touch and depth, and was deepened by audiences' behind-the-scenes knowledge of film stars' lives and the filmmaking craft. Like so many other earthquake media producers, filmmakers used the strategy of montage and the popular genre of *jitsuwa* to bolster the insufficient realism of their representations. This encouraged innovative forms of imaginative audience engagement that involved projection, speculation, and abstraction and placed new significance on actors' and spectators' bodies.

If I have avoided comparing the Great Kanto Earthquake to the 2011 Tōhoku earthquake, tsunami, and nuclear disaster; to the bombings of Hiroshima and Nagasaki; or to the 1995 Great Hanshin Earthquake, this is partly due to my specific concerns with early twentieth-century modernity and the emergence of mass-mediated society in Japan. I have tried to situate cinema and the changes it was undergoing in relation to the forms of identification and desire that were most identified with modern commercial culture in the interwar period. Nevertheless, in doing so I have also chosen to approach interwar Japanese media discourse through a set of ideas and questions about media that are also relevant to our contemporary moment. The rise of social media since the early 2000s has led to an explosion of debates on media and connectivity, virtual sex and relationships, personalization, (over)sharing, new publics and their privatization, media users' self-image and life satisfaction, support networks, civic engagement, new forms of enterprise and value creation, and much more. There is a keen sense that social media use has fundamentally altered the nature of our interpersonal relationships, professions (with more emphasis on personal branding and public-facing activities), and politics, from the Arab Spring to the election of Donald Trump. Twitter, Facebook, Instagram, YouTube, Snapchat, and other platforms have engendered new forms of media distribution and consumption and contributed to new ways of thinking about intimacy, community, activism, identity, labor, and reality in media studies.

The March 11, 2011, triple disaster led to an increase in SNS (social networking service) usage, new appraisals of social media technology, and changes in how governmental agencies use social media.[14] A full consideration of the use of social media platforms, email, mobile devices, carrier messaging services, and other internet-enabled networks and telecommunications in the aftermath of 3/11 is beyond the scope of my discussion here. However, social media and other digital platforms proved central to how the general public experienced and learned about the disaster; even today, these technologies shape how the disaster is being remembered, represented, and tracked. Much discussion of social media and disaster has focused on social media technologies' usefulness for disseminating information within areas where normal communication is disrupted, particularly where mainstream media do not have access to, or are not reporting on, local conditions.[15] As a result of widespread public distrust of mainstream media outlets in the aftermath of the meltdown at the Fukushima Daiichi Nuclear Power Plant, some reported that Japanese increasingly embraced SNS as an alternative news source.[16] The importance of digital media to disaster response, recovery, and reflection has spurred researchers and institutions in and beyond Japan to collaborate on the Japan Disasters Digital Archive (JDA, launched July 2012) with the intention of preserving "first-hand information and primary documentation of the events of March 11, 2011 and their aftermath."[17] Notably, this archive is described as "an interactive space encouraging, and indeed thriving on, user participation," bringing together "public and private actors" and serving "as a site of shared memory for those most affected by these events and most concerned about their consequences."[18] These statements reflect a strong consciousness of the everyday ways that users engage with digital platforms, including those the archive draws on. Rather than simply appropriating images, messages, information, and other ephemera related to 3/11 from various sources (including Twitter), JDA positions itself as connecting archives of materials and facilitating the already existing ways in which people engage with digital platforms. This pragmatic media consciousness is a conscientiousness that respects the singularity of individual relations to the disaster and the multiple roles that networks (public and private) play in people's lives. The carefully worded description of JDA's mission reflects a conventional understanding of digital technology as both public and intimate, capable of connecting individuals and potentially exposing them to risks, such as the possibility that their personal information, private thoughts, and images could be circulated much further than intended or in ways beyond their control. As scholars have shown in recent work on 3/11 and its impact on television, film, and news media, even conventional media cannot be understood outside the frame of media convergence and the increasingly important role that social media play in people's lives.[19] These are just a few examples of how 3/11 has drawn greater attention to the affordances of social media technologies and the function of digital platforms in today's media environment.

Accordingly, it could be argued that both the Great Kanto Earthquake and the triple disaster of 3/11 helped consolidate understandings and practical applications of specific media technologies at a time when attention to the affordances of these technologies and their social functions was still relatively new. My analysis of interwar cinema and its media context draws implicitly on questions raised by the current phenomena of social media and media convergence, particularly discussions of media usage and precarity, virtual realities and sexualities, and capitalism, feminization, and affect.[20] If image capitalism and the internet have affected how we imagine the sociotechnological mediation of sex, love, and identity, as well as the claims of imaginary or virtual experiences to be material or "real," why not use a similar optic to examine media in an earlier stage of consumer capitalism on the same terms?

The realism of the image, its relation to public sentiment, the mobilization of sentiment in political projects—concern with such issues is always renewed during times of crisis. The purpose of this book has been less to think about the direct connection between the Great Kanto Earthquake and such concerns than to consider how the catastrophe heightened the stakes for thinking about the persuasive sensory address of cinema, just as the rise of fascism shaped Walter Benjamin and Siegfried Kracauer's concern with cinema and mass culture in the 1920s and 1930s. Historical contingencies draw our attention to the contours of media in ways we might not otherwise have imagined them, before or since. Accordingly, Weihong Bao has called for a "relativization of cinema's medium specificity" that takes into account historical and local specificity, though always with attention to a larger, global frame. She argues that a "displacement of cinema's medium specificity from its aesthetic and material-technological anchors to historically specific politics, often caught in the geopolitical dynamic across the globe, brings us the twin benefits of rethinking cinema vertically and horizontally. Vertically, concerning its own past and future and, horizontally, in relation to other media and as a global medium with its varied histories and identities."[21] The interwar period is one such rich and complicated time of media transition in Japan, through which it is possible to trace multiple histories of cinema and perceive many definitions of the medium. This has been my aim as a historian: to engage imaginatively with the medium as a perceptual apparatus that can reveal historical audiences' ways of being in the world.

Notes

Introduction

1. "Katsudō o mite, hōkakyō ni natta, Teidaisei taku no bijin jochū, Fukkoku meijoyū ni kaburete" [After watching movies, beautiful maid in Imperial University student's home goes arson crazy, possessed by famous French actress], *Tōkyō asahi shinbun*, March 24, 1921, evening edition, 2.

2. "Meijoyū o yumemite, Kamata e oshiyoseru iede onna," *Tōkyō asahi shinbun*, evening edition, April 28, 1928, 2; "Naraku no dontei e, mizukara shizumu joyū shigansha no mure, sore ni shitagau hanzai no iroiro," *Nikkatsu gahō* (October 1926), 52–55.

3. Matsumoto Yoshirō, "Itamashiki kana, joyū shigansha no mukuro," *Nikkatsu gahō* (August 1926), 16.

4. Matsumoto, "Itamashiki kana," 16.

5. Matsumoto, "Itamashiki kana," 17.

6. Matsumoto, "Itamashiki kana," 17.

7. For a discussion of Meiji modernization and the limits of liberal philosophy and democratic thinking in Japan, see Mackie, *Creating Socialist Women*, 24–30.

8. For examples, see Maeda, "Development of Popular Fiction"; Sato, *New Japanese Woman*, especially chap. 3; and Aso, *Public Properties*, chap. 5.

9. See Harootunian, *Overcome by Modernity*, especially 11–13. Sato's *New Japanese Woman* includes extensive discussion of Hirabayashi and other intellectuals' perceptions of female consumers and mass culture.

10. Silverberg, *Erotic Grotesque Nonsense*.

11. Silverberg, *Erotic Grotesque Nonsense*, 29.

12. For example, the decline of photochemical celluloid cinema and the rise of the digital has occasioned a resurgence of interest in cinematic realism and a reevaluation of the work of film theorists who framed realism in terms of cinema's analog relationship to the profilmic. Since the digital turn, the field has witnessed a revival of interest in key concepts inherited from classical film theory, such as the notion of the photographic image as an indexical sign. See, for instance, Bazin, *What Is Cinema?*; Andrew

and Joubert-Laurencin, *Opening Bazin*; Rodowick, *Virtual Life of Film*; Morgan, "Rethinking Bazin"; and Andrew, *What Cinema Is!*

13. See Rosen, *Narrative, Apparatus, Ideology.*

14. For example, Studlar, "Visual Pleasure and the Masochistic Aesthetic."

15. See, for instance, Doane, *Desire to Desire*; Bruno, *Streetwalking on a Ruined Map*; or Hansen, *Babel and Babylon*. For a general consideration of the importance of theories of spectatorship and subjectification for "New Film History," see Parikka, "Media Archaeology of the Senses: Audiovisual, Affective, Algorithmic," chapter 2 in *What Is Media Archaeology?*

16. See Bao, *Fiery Cinema*, as an example.

17. Berlant, *Female Complaint*, x.

18. Although I sometimes use the word *affect* to distinguish general states of arousal and inchoate feeling from "emotions," which are more easily identified with particular psychological states and concepts, I use these terms interchangeably unless indicated otherwise. Important touchstones for my approach to affect and emotion include Deleuze, *Francis Bacon*; Massumi, *Parables for the Virtual*; and the work of Silvan Tomkins and Eve Kosofsky Sedgwick in Tomkins, *Shame and Its Sisters*, as well as Sedgwick, *Touching Feeling.*

19. Ahmed, *Cultural Politics of Emotion*, 45.

20. Metz, *Imaginary Signifier*, 66–67.

21. Hansen, "Fallen Women, Rising Stars," 13, 12, 12.

22. Bao, *Fiery Cinema*, 16.

23. See Gunning, *D. W. Griffith*, and Gerow, *Visions of Japanese Modernity*, 153.

24. Ahmed, *Cultural Politics of Emotion*.

1. Great Kanto Earthquake Documentary Films and the State

1. Hansen, "Mass Production of the Senses," 60.

2. On the use of conventional narrative patterns to create moral clarity in melodramas about the Great Kanto Earthquake, see Bates, *Culture of the Quake*, chap. 4. Weisenfeld's *Imaging Disaster* provides extended analysis of how Japanese and Western image-making traditions shaped representations of the Great Kanto Earthquake.

3. See Schencking, *Great Kantō Earthquake*, chap. 3. For an analysis of postearthquake issues of mass-circulated women's magazines and their emotive address, see Kitahara, "'Kanjō' no media."

4. Ōsawa, "Kantō Daishinsai kiroku eigagun," 48.

5. Schencking, *Great Kantō Earthquake*, 86.

6. See, for instance, the discussion in Weisenfeld, *Imaging Disaster*, 60–61.

7. In "Kantō Daishinsai kiroku eigagun," Ōsawa offers the most comprehensive study of existing film prints, accompanied by thoughtful discussion of issues pertaining to the identification of earthquake documentary films. Ōsawa examines the percentage of overlapping footage among eight extant earthquake documentary films in the National Film Archive of Japan collection. The percentage is taken as the number of shots out of the total number of shots in the existing print that match footage found in one or more

films. Only one surviving print, which is unidentified and may be incomplete, does not contain any overlapping footage. Three prints contain between 86 and 88 percent overlapping shots, including the footage shot by Kōsaka Toshimitsu and Isayama Saburō for Nikkatsu Mukōjima studio, believed to be the source for the most widely reproduced footage (54).

8. The film I focus on in the last section of this chapter is the Ministry of Education and Tokyo Shinema Shōkai film *Actuality of the Great Kanto Earthquake and Conflagration* (*Kanto Daishin taika jikkyō*, 1923). Although it does not survive in its entirety, the extant film likely reflects the carefully constructed documentary. Only 3 percent of the shots in the existing film print overlap with other surviving earthquake documentary films, suggesting that this documentary does not contain the most commonly included footage, but it was one of the most widely screened and best known earthquake films.

9. Noda, *Nihon dokyumentarī eiga zenshi*, 11. For more on Japanese documentary film, see Nornes, *Japanese Documentary Film*.

10. Kamiya, "'Kōtaishi toōeiga' to Onoe Matsunosuke," 35.

11. See Kamiya, "'Kōtaishi toōeiga' to Onoe Matsunosuke," 42.

12. Kamiya, "'Kōtaishi toōeiga' to Onoe Matsunosuke," 36 and 52.

13. For a list of known screenings of fifteen films related to Hirohito's travels that were screened from June to December in Japan, see Kamiya, "'Kōtaishi toōeiga' to Onoe Matsunosuke," 40. It is not known how many unique films were made. Announcements of these screenings did not always list the manufacturer, and it is possible that the same footage was screened under different titles. It also appears that in some cases Japanese film companies exhibited footage they had purchased from foreign film companies (39).

14. Kamiya, "'Kōtaishi toōeiga' to Onoe Matsunosuke," 38.

15. In "'Kōtaishi toōeiga' to Onoe Matsunosuke," Kamiya describes a softening of filming restrictions after Hirohito's trip. For instance, after his return it became permissible to film the prince walking, which had previously been forbidden. She notes that non-Japanese cameramen in England were seemingly less inhibited than Japanese cameramen, encouraging the prince to smile and take off his glasses. Still, she notes, the location and number of cameras filming his "welcome" event was specified by the government—seven cameras on the wharf, seven cameras in front of Numazu Station, and three cameras on the water—indicating an ongoing desire to control filming conditions, including the angles from which the prince regent was seen (38).

16. In the Edo period, Yushima was an important site for *bussankai*, or academic exhibitions where scholars and collectors displayed their specimens. The site was absorbed by the Ministry of Education when the ministry was founded in 1871. The establishment of the central state museum can be traced to the ministry's first exhibition, the Ministry of Education Exposition (Monbushō Hakurankai), at Yushima in 1872. Items from this exposition remained on display for viewing on a limited basis after the exposition had officially closed. In 1900, the museum was renamed the Tokyo Imperial Household Museum and came under the control of the Imperial Household Ministry, where it remained until its transfer during the US Occupation in 1952. As Aso notes in *Public Properties*, this change of hands from the Ministry of Education to the Imperial Household Ministry was accompanied by "a series of structural as well as surface changes that promoted the interests of the imperial family as a distinct entity" and public institution

(73). In fact, she writes, "It would be more precise to say that the national museum system was honed and repurposed beginning in the late 1880s to serve a different set of state goals, which required promoting the prestige of the imperial family and its role as public benefactor" (83). These goals clearly drive the state's incursions into film production in the early 1920s, when much of this activity involves both the Ministry of Education and the Imperial Household Ministry and pertains to the prince regent.

17. These films were usually shown together, and their footage may have been combined and screened as a single film. For more on these films, see Itakura, "*Shigeki Nankō ketsubetsu*."

18. In "'Kōtaishi toōeiga' to Onoe Matsunosuke," Kamiya observes that this could also be considered a reenactment of the Matsunosuke film *Shigeki Nankō ichidaiki*, released by Nikkatsu on June 19, 1921 (45). However, it should be noted that even though Nikkatsu cameramen were dispatched to Tokyo for the Motion Picture Exhibit, Taikatsu was given sole permission to film this portion of the prince regent's inspection. See Itakura, "*Shigeki Nankō ketsubetsu*," 47.

19. For analysis of the significance of Hirohito's copresence with Matsunosuke in this film, see Itakura, "*Shigeki Nankō ketsubetsu*"; Kamiya, "'Kōtaishi toōeiga' to Onoe Matsunosuke," 44–46; and Fujiki, *Making Personas*, 81–86.

20. The titles and content of these films are unclear. See Murayama, "Mō hitotsu no Shōwa eiga," 179–80. On Taishō-era films about the imperial family, see also Nornes, *Japanese Documentary Film*, 12–14.

21. Murayama, "Mō hitotsu no Shōwa eiga," 178; Nishimoto, "Eiga to Monbushō," 271. For more on the Committee for Social Education and its film activities, see Fujiki, *Making Personas*, 80.

22. As Schencking points out, most estimates of the earthquake's magnitude range from as low as 7.9 up to 8.2. "Catastrophe, Opportunism, Contestation," 833.

23. Schencking, "Great Kanto Earthquake," 296. As many as 134 separate fires were recorded. See Borland, "Capitalising on Catastrophe," 880.

24. These approximate figures are taken from the statistics in Matsuo, *Kantō Daishinsai to kaigenrei*, 1.

25. Schencking, "Catastrophe, Opportunism, Contestation," 833. For more on the state of the Japanese economy at the time of the earthquake, see also Harootunian, *Overcome by Modernity*. In *Great Kantō Earthquake*, Schencking notes that in the seven most affected prefectures, 2.5 million became homeless as a result of the earthquake (38).

26. Schencking, "1923 Tokyo," 113.

27. Schencking, "1923 Tokyo," 114–15.

28. Schencking, "Great Kanto Earthquake," 296.

29. See Schencking, *Great Kantō Earthquake*, 59–67, for more on challenges pertaining to food and water distribution after the earthquake.

30. See also Ryang, "Great Kanto Earthquake," and Allen, "Price of Identity."

31. According to Yamada Shōji, rumors began spreading September 1 and the massacres began that night, although the violence was especially frequent from September 2 onward. "Kantō Daishinsai to gendai," 11. According to Matsuo, despite the imposition of martial law, the massacres in Tokyo continued unchecked until September 4, at which point a ban on citizens carrying arms was declared (*Kantō Daishinsai to kaigenrei*, 3).

There is disagreement as to both the number of deaths and the degree to which the Japanese government, press, and military tolerated (and occasionally incited and helped organize) the violence. The Ministry of Justice reported only 243 deaths (and the Police Affairs Bureau only 231), but scholars place the actual figure somewhere between Yoshino Sakuzō's estimate of 2,700 and the official Korean estimate of 6,400, with most contemporary accounts agreeing that the number was probably at least 6,000. For more about the range of estimates, see Gordon, *Modern History of Japan*, 154; Borland, "Capitalising on Catastrophe," 882; Bates, "Authentic Suffering, Anxious Narrator," 359; Ryang, "Great Kanto Earthquake," 745–46.

32. For an examination of the causes and responsibility for the massacres, including discussion of the role played by police and government officials, see Yamada, *Kantō Daishinsai ji*.

33. Mack, *Manufacturing Modern Japanese Literature*, 56.

34. Borland, "Capitalising on Catastrophe," 886; Schencking, "1923 Tokyo," 119.

35. Bates, "Authentic Suffering, Anxious Narrator," 360.

36. Data from Fujisawa Morihiko and Bureau of Social Affairs Home Office, *The Great Earthquake of 1923 in Japan* (Tokyo: Naimushō-Shakaikyoku, 1926), cited in Bates, *Culture of the Quake*, 8.

37. Bates's book *Culture of the Quake* provides a detailed exploration of the divisions in Japanese society at the time of the quake, examining how these inequalities were addressed in postearthquake literature, film, and other forms of narrative. His analysis provides important context for the increasing interest in cinema's mass address, its realism, and its persuasiveness. A basic desire to appeal to the masses and resolve deep societal fissures can be seen in many of Bates's examples. For instance, two imperial rescripts were issued in the months following the quake. These were printed in mass-circulated newspapers and had commentary so that ordinary Japanese could understand their difficult language. Bates argues that the rescripts reflected the state's interest in overcoming social divisions and mobilizing the people for nation-building projects. As he observes, the rescripts referred to the public as *kokumin* (the national people), implying an address to the entirety of the nation rather than just earthquake survivors (12–13). The Ministry of Education's earthquake documentary similarly provided a clear and easy-to-understand narrative of the disaster and reconstruction—one that even illiterate viewers could understand. It also included images of the prince looking at and gesturing toward the camera, creating a direct link between state authority and the people via the medium.

38. Okutani Fumitomo, "Kantō no daisaigai wa ikanaru shin'i ka," in *Michi no tomo*, no. 401 (1923), 15, quoted in Borland, "Capitalising on Catastrophe," 889.

39. Horie Kiichi, "Tōkyō-shi no saigai to keizaiteki fukkōan" [Tokyo's disaster and economic plan for reconstruction], *Chūō kōron* 38, no. 11 (1923), 50–52, quoted in Schencking, "Great Kanto Earthquake," 306.

40. Schencking, "Great Kanto Earthquake," 306.

41. In *Great Kantō Earthquake*, Schencking suggests that *tenbatsu* discourse did not so much fade as transform, since popular mobilization efforts increased and moral rhetoric played an important role in earthquake reconstruction. His argument draws on historian Sheldon Garon's pathbreaking work on moral suasion campaigns in interwar Japan for support. See Garon, *Molding Japanese Minds*.

42. "Hi no kieta 'asobi no sekai,' kanshin na no wa geishōgi no giennetsu" [The fire has gone out in "the world of play," but the charity of geisha and prostitutes impresses], *Ōsaka asahi shinbun,* September 7, 1923, morning edition, 4.

43. Schencking, *Great Kantō Earthquake,* 81.

44. Schencking, *Great Kantō Earthquake,* 83.

45. Schencking, *Great Kantō Earthquake,* 80–81.

46. Schencking, *Great Kantō Earthquake,* 82–83.

47. "Daishinsai katsudō shashin," *Ōsaka asahi shinbun,* September 3, 1923, extra, n.p.

48. Advertisement, *Ōsaka asahi shinbun,* September 7, 1923, morning edition, 2; advertisement, *Ōsaka asahi shinbun,* September 23, 1923, morning edition, 7; "Honsha shinsai eiga, Manshū kakuchi no juneizō tei" [Plans to show our company's earthquake film all around Manchuria], *Ōsaka asahi shinbun,* September 20, 1923, evening edition, 2.

49. Advertisement, *Ōsaka asahi shinbun,* September 9, 1923, evening edition, 3.

50. The Masa Shōkai film *Teito Daishinsai* [Great Earthquake in the Imperial Capital] (1,200 feet) was filmed on September 1 and 2. Advertisement, *Ōsaka asahi shinbun,* September 16, 1923, morning edition, 7. Konishi Film Production Studio and Yagi Yosaburō Shōten made a fifteen-hundred-foot newsreel with plans for a second, advertised in the *Ōsaka asahi shinbun,* September 7, 1923, evening edition, 3. According to censorship records from 1927, the Hayakawa Art Film Production film was 393 feet on two reels (21 minutes at 16 fps). See Tochigi and Tsuneishi, "Jōei eiga kaisetsu," 14.

51. Wang, "Kantō Daishinsai to kōkū shashin," 165.

52. Wang, "Kantō Daishinsai to kōkū shashin," 157.

53. For these and other photographs of the Great Kanto Earthquake, see Kitahara, *Shashinshū: Kantō Daishinsai.*

54. *Nihon eiga nenkan* [Japanese film yearbook], 3. According to the monthly timeline of events published in the yearbook, on November 1, 1923, the Kyōchōkai collected film scripts on "mutual love and cooperation." On November 4, under the sponsorship of Kokugakuin University, a huge event with "comfort films" (*ian eiga*) was held in the Meiji Shrine outer garden. Waseda University sponsored a screening of comfort films at the Asakusa Kannon temple on November 21. The following day there was a screening of comfort films at the Imperial University auditorium, followed by screenings at Aoyama Gakuin and Azabu Middle School on November 23 (4–5).

55. "Eigakai" [Film world], *Tōkyō asahi shinbun,* October 4, 1923, evening edition, 3.

56. "Baka keiki wa kinmotsu de, katsudō ya shibai ga futaake, sokujitsu kaijōshite sashitsukaenai to keishichō no oyurushi ga deta" [Films and plays open but funny business is forbidden, barring unforeseen circumstances, police allow entertainment to resume], *Tōkyō asahi shinbun,* September 30, 1923, evening edition, 2.

57. An earthquake exhibition sponsored by the Tokyo metropolitan government in 1924 and held at the Jichi Kaikan and a nearby hall in Ueno was similarly mobbed by huge crowds that caused chaos. See Weisenfeld, *Imaging Disaster,* 246.

58. "Shinsai eiga wa kinshi, shinai kakukan e totsuzen no gotasshi, jinshin anteisuru made" [Abrupt directive to every theater in the city, *shinsai eiga* are forbidden, until the public settles down], *Tōkyō asahi shinbun,* October 5, 1923, evening edition, 2; and "Shinsai eiga jōjō o yurusaru" [*Shinsai eiga* screenings permitted], *Tōkyō asahi shinbun,* October 9, 1923, evening edition, 3.

59. See Ōsawa, "Kantō Daishinsai kiroku eigagun," 59.

60. Advertisement, *Tōkyō asahi shinbun*, October 12, 1923, morning edition, 3; advertisement, *Tōkyō asahi shinbun*, October 15, 1923, evening edition, 1. In fact, footage shot by Shirai Shigeru for Nikkatsu was partially confiscated by an army officer and later temporarily banned because it would "destabilize the populace." Screenings of this documentary only resumed after footage of troops sent to reinforce martial law was cut from the film. See Bates, "Wrath of Heaven," 41.

61. Advertisement, *Tōkyō asahi shinbun*, October 16, 1923, morning edition, 2.

62. See "Shinsai eiga wa kinshi," and "Baka keiki wa kinmotsu de."

63. "Taishō jūsannendo Nihon eigakai" [The 1924 Japanese Film World], in *Nihon eiga nenkan*, 1.

64. "Taishō jūsannendo Nihon eigakai," in *Nihon eiga nenkan*, 1; see advertisement in *Tōkyō asahi shinbun*, October 3, 1923, evening edition, 3. According to this ad, the Nikkatsu film is eight reels long.

65. See Kirihara, *Patterns of Time*, 41–43, and Fujita, *Gendai eiga no kiten*, 39–49.

66. Tanaka Saburō, "Kinji shikan" [A personal view of recent events], *Kinema junpō* (January 1, 1924), 25.

67. According to statistics from the online Nihon Eiga Database [Japanese film database], http://jmdb.ne.jp. Thanks to Michael Raine for aggregating this data.

68. There is some discrepancy among accounts. For instance, in a postwar memoir, Tanaka Eizō says that the Mukōjima glass stage "collapsed violently" in the earthquake. "Nikkatsu Mukōjima jidai (yon)" [The age of Nikkatsu Mukōjima (Four)], *Shinario* [Scenario] 11, no. 5 (May 1955), 36.

69. Kozono Suenori, "Daishinsai to Mukōjima satsueijo," *Nikkatsu gahō* (November 1923), 6.

70. *Nikkatsu shijūnenshi*, 47. See also "Baka keiki wa kinmotsu de," 2.

71. Negishi Kōichi, "Daishinsai kyōkō no hōshin ni tsuite" [Regarding future policy after the Great Earthquake], *Nikkatsu gahō* (November 1923), 2.

72. *Nikkatsu shijūnenshi*, 47.

73. *Nikkatsu shijūnenshi*, 47.

74. Ōsawa, "Kantō Daishinsai kiroku eigagun," 59. The surviving print is sixty-four minutes long.

75. Murayama, "Mō hitotsu no Shōwa eiga," 180.

76. Ōsawa, "Kantō Daishinsai kiroku eigagun," 59.

77. Ōsawa, "Kantō Daishinsai kiroku eigagun," 59. According to Murayama in "Mō hitotsu no Shōwa eiga," *Actuality of the Great Kanto Earthquake and Conflagration* was shown at ninety venues (180).

78. Tochigi and Tsuneishi, "Jōei eiga kaisetsu," 11. For more on Shirai's footage of the Great Kanto Earthquake, see Bates, "Wrath of Heaven," 41.

79. Shirai's original film is nonextant, but his footage was purchased by the Ministry of Education. See Bates, "Wrath of Heaven," 41.

80. It is worth noting that many earthquake documentary films compiled footage from other earthquake documentary films. It was not uncommon for films to reproduce footage from other earthquake films without permission. See Ōsawa, "Kantō Daishinsai kiroku eigagun," on the complexity of properly identifying these documentary

films. Tsuneishi points out that many documentary film prints were later cut up, and the footage was reused in other documentaries or fiction films or sold as keepsakes. In addition to film prints, the National Film Archive of Japan holds fragments of earthquake documentaries in its collection, many from unidentified sources. See Tsuneishi, "1923-nen no 'gekishin.'" As of late March 2013, ten earthquake documentary films that are not identical have been discovered. The National Film Archive of Japan holds eight of these films, three of which have not yet been positively identified (Ōsawa, "Kantō Daishinsai kiroku eigagun," 49).

81. Tsuneishi, "1923-nen no 'gekishin,'" 204. There is some question as to whether Ina's film was released publicly at the time of the earthquake because of the extreme nature of its imagery. According to Ōsawa in "Kantō Daishinsai kiroku eigagun," the existing print shares many shots in common with other surviving earthquake documentaries (forty-eight out of ninety-six). Judging from this and the design of the film's intertitles, Ōsawa believes it is very likely the film was screened in 1923 (54).

82. Advertisement, *Ōsaka asahi shinbun*, September 8, 1923, evening edition, 2.

83. See Crary, *Techniques of the Observer*. For the relationship between the railroad, early cinema, and traveling shots, see Schivelbusch, *Railway Journey*; Kirby, *Parallel Tracks*; and Gunning, "Before Documentary" and "'Whole World Within Reach.'" On the moving panorama, see Huhtamo, "Peristrephic Pleasures."

84. Burch, *Theory of Film Practice*. For an elaboration on Burch's concept of presentational film style with reference to Japanese cinema and its difference from Western mainstream film, see Burch, *To the Distant Observer*.

85. Gunning, *D. W. Griffith*, 66, 67. See also Gunning, "The Cinema of Attractions."

86. Gunning, *D. W. Griffith*, 67. For more on the *benshi* and Japanese silent film narration, see Dym, *Japanese Silent Film Narrators*.

87. It is unclear whether these are deputized police. The intertitle refers to these men as *jikeidan* or "vigilantes."

88. In "'Kōtaishi toōeiga' to Onoe Matsunosuke," Kamiya suggests that this strategy is also apparent in *Shigeki Nankō ketsubetsu*, in which the presentation of the prince's viewing of Matsunosuke's performance automatically aligns the spectator with Hirohito's point of view (46).

89. Hori, *Promiscuous Media*, 53.

90. Bruno, *Streetwalking on a Ruined Map*, 59. This aspect of earthquake representations is also explored by Weisenfeld in *Imaging Disaster*. For Bruno, this lurid fascination with looking, with establishing knowledge of and wielding power over bodies, reveals film as one "instantiation of a discourse on sexuality and sexual difference" (64).

91. Sedgwick, *Touching Feeling*, 16.

92. Actors at Nikkatsu's Mukōjima film studio, located across the Sumida River from Asakusa in the eastern part of the city, described Tokyo's churning ruins as "warped and contorted like expressionist stage sets." See Koizumi Kasuke, "Ichi nichi osokattara inochi ga nai" [One day later and I would have perished], *Nikkatsu gahō* (November 1923), 21, and Kitō Shigeru, "Sono hi no omoide: Kyōfu ni ononoku Sakai no Mei-chan" [My memory of that day: Sakai Mei-chan trembling in terror], *Nikkatsu gahō* (November 1923), 30. Painter and poet Takehisa Yumeji, who before the earthquake had published a series of drawings from his viewings of the German expressionist film *The*

Cabinet of Dr. Caligari, made sketches of Tokyo's wrecked cityscape and called them *hyōgenha no e*, or "expressionist pictures." Nakazawa, "Bunshin to hyōi," 113.

93. Sedgwick, *Touching Feeling*, 17.
94. Sedgwick, *Touching Feeling*, 15.
95. Sedgwick, *Touching Feeling*, 16.
96. Schencking, *Great Kantō Earthquake*, 87.
97. Schencking, *Great Kantō Earthquake*, 88–89.

2. *The Testimony of the Body*

1. Kozono Suenori, "Daishinsai to Mukōjima satsueijo" [The Great Earthquake and Mukōjima studio], *Nikkatsu gahō* (November 1923), 7.
2. Negishi Kōichi, "Daishinsai kyōkō no hōshin ni tsuite" [Regarding future policy after the Great Earthquake], *Nikkatsu gahō* (November 1923), 5.
3. Flatley, *Affective Mapping*, 7.
4. Flatley, *Affective Mapping*, 7.
5. Kozono, "Daishinsai to Mukōjima satsueijo," 8.
6. *Nihon eiga nenkan*, 2–3.
7. *Nihon eiga nenkan*, 2.
8. *Nikkatsu shijūnenshi*, 47. See also *Nikkatsu gojūnenshi* for more on the establishment of the company and its first fifty years.
9. Kurume Miyoji, "Nyūrakugo no Mukōjima sakuhin ni nozomu" [Hopes for Mukōjima films after the transfer to Kyoto], *Nikkatsu gahō* (May 1924), 65.
10. For more on Kyoto's modernization and the early history its film industry, see Tomita, "Eiga toshi Kyōto," and Lewis, "Kyoto—The 'Hollywood of Japan.'"
11. Yamamoto Rokuha, "Shishin" [Personal message], *Kinema junpō* (April 11, 1924), 4.
12. Tanaka Saburō, "Kinji shikan" [A personal view on recent events], *Kinema junpō* (January 1, 1924), 25.
13. Yamamoto Rokuha, "Shimogamo yori" [News from Shimogamo], *Kamata* (October 1923), 47.
14. *Nihon eiga nenkan*, 4. At least eleven fictional films were made about the earthquake, but none survive today. See Bates, *Culture of the Quake*, 81. Bates provides detailed plot descriptions of many of these films in "Wrath of Heaven."
15. Bates, *Culture of the Quake*, 3.
16. "Shinsai eiga: *Daichi wa yuragu*" [Earthquake film: *The Earth Shakes*], *Nikkatsu gahō* (November 1923), 40–42. See also Bates's discussion of *The Earth Shakes* in *Culture of the Quake*, which analyzes the plot as an example of *tenken* or *tenbatsu* discourse, 133–35. In "Wrath of Heaven," Bates offers a reading of the films' melodramatic structures that differs from what I argue here. According to Bates, the narratives shifted blame away from frivolous leisure culture and onto the excesses of the wealthy in an attempt to alter the terms of *tenken* discourse, which was critical of cinema and consumer culture, and win greater legitimacy for the film industry. In contrast, I am primarily interested in how melodramatic narratives provide a structure for identification and rememoration, allowing audiences to read their own—and others'—experiences into the templates provided by the films.

17. "Shinsai eiga: *Daichi wa yuragu*," 41.

18. Reviewed by Tanaka Saburō in *Kinema junpō* (November 21, 1923), 11. For further discussion of *In the Face of Death*, see Bates, *Culture of the Quake*, 80–88. Bates's sources describe the father and daughter's tale as the central narrative, the framework for the other characters' stories. This is likely a more accurate reflection of how the film was structured, as opposed to the "compilation" format that Tanaka's review suggests.

19. Advertisement, *Tōkyō asahi shinbun*, October 24, 1923, morning edition, 1.

20. Advertisement, *Tōkyō asahi shinbun*, May 15, 1924, evening edition, 2.

21. Advertisement, *Tōkyō asahi shinbun*, June 5, 1924, evening edition, 2.

22. Two examples of extended melodramatic narratives are the novels *Les Misérables* by Victor Hugo and *The Count of Monte Cristo* by Alexandre Dumas (père), which were made into lengthy, multipart films by Henri Fescourt in 1925 and 1929, respectively. In this chapter, I am generally thinking about melodrama in the terms described by Peter Brooks in *Melodramatic Imagination*.

23. See Flatley, *Affective Mapping*, 7.

24. See especially Flatley's discussion of Henry James's *The Turn of the Screw* in *Affective Mapping*, 98–99.

25. Flatley, *Affective Mapping*, 88.

26. Flatley, *Affective Mapping*, 89.

27. Flatley, *Affective Mapping*, 89. Giuliana Bruno dramatizes this process in her book *Streetwalking on a Ruined Map*, which examines the lost films of pioneering early Italian filmmaker Elvira Notari. As Bruno notes, one of the results of "feminism as scholarship" has been a "historical change in the authorial scene," which includes the process of attributing authorship as well as its definition. As a result, "women, historically excluded from authorship, have become authors by writing about other women" (235). Anticipating Flatley's arguments, Bruno suggests that the shifting authorial scene and analysis of lost texts foreground the acts of "imagination and imposition" (Flatley, *Affective Mapping*, 89) that are always involved in positing significance and authorial intention. In contrast to the Oedipal scenario described in Roland Barthes's "The Death of the Author," in which reader-son kills author-father in the act of liberating meaning from the tyranny of authorial intention, Bruno describes a "mother/daughter and author/reader" relation that is an "interchangeable relation . . . where alternatively all positions may be occupied by, and shifted between, two female subjects" (*Streetwalking on a Ruined Map*, 24). In other words, her analysis foregrounds the role of intersubjectivity and transference in reading. See also Bruno, *Streetwalking on a Ruined Map*, 234–40.

28. Flatley, *Affective Mapping*, 102.

29. Flatley, *Affective Mapping*, 92–93.

30. Flatley, *Affective Mapping*, 90.

31. The special earthquake issue of *Nikkatsu gahō* was not published until November 15, 1923. Publishing companies and bookstores in Tokyo were hit much harder than were film companies. Most of the September issues of Tokyo-based journals had already been printed and mailed out for distribution by September 1, but fires caused by the earthquake in Kanda, Hongō, Nihonbashi, Kyōbashi, and neighboring areas in the Shitamachi caused most of the publishers and an estimated 80 percent of bookstores to burn down. The *Ōsaka asahi shinbun* raised concerns over whether October issues would

be published and expressed solidarity with the affected companies (while promoting Osaka's newfound advantage): "people in Kansai look to Kanto as the wellspring of all culture, but in the future there must be an effort to create a Kansai base for publishing culture." See "Zasshi ga zenmetsushita, jūgatsu kara wa hotondo demai, insatsu bunka no daidageki" [Magazines wiped out, most will not continue after October, huge blow to publishing culture], *Ōsaka asahi shinbun*, September 8, 1923, morning edition, 2. Like many similar publications, *Nikkatsu gahō* was a relatively young publication. Film journals only began appearing in Japan in the 1910s, beginning with the publication of *Kinema rekōdo* in 1913. Monthly film magazines with space devoted to full-page pictorials, such as *Kamata* and *Nikkatsu gahō*, enabled readers to keep close tabs on the latest releases and studio gossip. They carried reviews of the newest releases and reports on productions in progress. Magazines tied to particular studios published contributions by studios' filmmakers and actors.

32. *Nikkatsu gahō* (November 1923), 38.

33. See also Bates's discussion of this magazine issue in *Culture of the Quake*, 82–84.

34. Bates, *Culture of the Quake*, 74.

35. Bates, *Culture of the Quake*, 76.

36. Studlar, "The Perils of Pleasure?," 273.

37. *Nikkatsu gahō* (November 1923), 28.

38. In *Making Personas*, Fujiki suggests that an emphasis on psychology and technique over bodily realism and raw physical expressivity becomes stronger throughout the decade, with intellectual critics also urging audiences "to keep a certain emotional distance from the performers" (147).

39. Bean, "Technologies of Early Stardom," 417.

40. Bean, "Technologies of Early Stardom," 418–19.

41. Bean, "Technologies of Early Stardom," 423.

42. Kitō Shigeru, "Sono hi no omoide: Kyōfu ni ononoku Sakai no Mei-chan" [My memory of that day: Sakai Mei-chan trembling in terror], *Nikkatsu gahō* (November 1923), 30. Many accounts played up the humor of actresses caught in incongruous costumes or their overdramatics. At Shōchiku's Kamata film studio, the earthquake interrupted the filming of a prison scene with actresses playing inmates in an Ushihara Kiyohiko–directed film. The actresses were in prison uniforms when the wardrobe building collapsed, burying their regular clothing in the rubble. In his memoir, Ushihara recounts, "In the midst of incessant aftershocks, they were in hysterics, tearfully begging to be allowed to go home. With all this confusion and the rolling shockwaves, I was reduced to the single concern of getting my ladies clothed!" Quoted in High, "Japanese Film and the Great Kanto Earthquake," 8.

43. Kitō, "Sono hi no omoide," 31.

44. Koizumi Kasuke, "Ichi nichi osokattara inochi ga nai" [One day later and I would have perished], *Nikkatsu gahō* (November 1923), 21.

45. *Nikkatsu gahō* (November 1923), 36.

46. Tarō [Anonymous], "Aru hi no koto" [What happened that day], *Nikkatsu gahō* (November 1923), 37.

47. Senō Matsuko, "Gojikan o mizu no naka ni" [Five hours in the water], *Nikkatsu gahō* (November 1923), 23.

48. Uesugi Rokurō, "Tsuma to ko to mei no sannin o ushinatte, kataru ni kanashi tsuioku no namida" [I lost my wife, daughter, and niece, tears of memories unbearable to relate], *Nikkatsu gahō* (November 1923), 16–17.

49. For examples, see Kōno, "Shinsai to kōkishin."

50. "Abikyōkan no teito o jūō ni chikushite mawatta honsha Yoshida tokuhain no shisatsuki" [Eyewitness account of our special correspondent Yoshida, who rushed all around the imperial capital as it shrieked in agony], *Ōsaka asahi shinbun*, September 3, 1923, morning edition, 2.

51. LaCapra, "Holocaust Testimonies," in *Writing History, Writing Trauma*. LaCapra points out that these two forms of traumatic memory are never mutually exclusive, although one hopes that traumatic reenactment will eventually give way to working through and reflection: "When the past becomes accessible to recall in memory, and when language functions to provide some measure of conscious control, critical distance, and perspective, one has begun the arduous process of working over and through the trauma in a fashion that may never bring full transcendence of acting out (or being haunted by revenants and reliving the past in its shattering intensity) but which may enable processes of judgment and at least limited liability and ethically responsible agency" (90). These forms of traumatic memory—compulsive repetition and conscious recall—cannot be dichotomized, for they overlap. LaCapra writes, "In memory as an aspect of working through the past, one is both back there and here at the same time, and one is able to distinguish between (not dichotomize) the two. In other words, one remembers—perhaps to some extent still compulsively reliving or being possessed by—what happened then without losing a sense of existing and acting now. This duality (or double inscription) of being is essential for memory as a component of working over and through problems" (90).

3. "Realism" and Modernity

1. See Bowser, *Transformation of Cinema*, and Keil and Stamp, *American Cinema's Transitional Era*.

2. Hansen, *Babel and Babylon*, 79.

3. Aaron Gerow describes a crucial shift occurring in the concept of the spectator in 1920s Japan. Rather than the construction of consumer subjectivity, he focuses on the question as to whether individuals could be held accountable "to the external hierarchies of public consciousness and social surveillance, or to hierarchies internalized in the family-state at home and the self-regulation of desire in the individual" (*Visions of Japanese Modernity*, 219). He argues that the existence of cinema was ultimately useful for positing a subject who could (potentially) process images and information in accordance with internalized values. He calls this concept of subjectivity the "interiorized subject." For Gerow, this involved the emergence of a "transcendental spectator"—in his words, "an abstract citizen—a mass of homogenized film consumers—that would now be the object of protection and correction" (*Visions of Japanese Modernity*, 197). See Gerow, *Visions of Japanese Modernity*, 191–221.

4. Hansen, *Babel and Babylon*, 78.

5. On the rise and fall of the store theater, see Paul, *When Movies Were Theater*.

6. Hansen, *Babel and Babylon*, especially 84–89.

7. See Schencking, chapter 4 in *Great Kantō Earthquake*, "Admonishment: Interpreting Catastrophe as Divine Punishment," and Borland, "Capitalising on Catastrophe," especially 887–91.

8. In *Advertising Tower*, Gardner provides a brief, useful overview of definitions of "the crowds" (*gunshū*), "the people" (*minshū*), and "the mass" (*taishū*) in the 1920s, or what he calls Japan's "new media age" (7). His analysis of subjectivity, the masses, the city, and modern culture in the modernist writings of Hagiwara Kyōjirō and Hayashi Fumiko reminds us that conceptions of the crowd were not only shaped by authorities but also central to the rising avant-garde as well as proletarian literature and arts. As Gardner points out, the events of Great Kanto Earthquake radicalized Tokyo's urban intelligentsia, especially its modernist writers and artists. His analysis of urban modernity and subject formation in modern literature focuses mostly on "the self." Still, his discussions of Hayashi's modernism and mass culture, and Hagiwara's "physiological, proto-cybernetic view of the self and the environment, transplanted onto the relationship between 'self' and 'society,'" suggest a multitude of frameworks for thinking about intersections between subjectivities, bodies, affect, media culture, and urban environments of the 1920s (92). For more on the rise of mass culture after the 1904–05 Russo-Japanese War and the Great Kanto Earthquake as "the moment of emergence of modern Japanese mass society" (29), see also Silverberg, *Erotic Grotesque Nonsense*.

9. For more discussion of the cultural politics of changing film representation practices, see also Lewis, "*Blood and Soul* (1923)."

10. Wakayama Osamu, "Shokan danpen" [Some thoughts], in *Kakushinseru Mukōjima satsueijo*, 5.

11. For an excellent discussion of the increasing emphasis on the actor's physical body in the 1920s, plus ambivalence toward this emphasis on physical sensuality rather than craft, see chapter 6, "Replacing the *Onnagata*," in Fujiki, *Making Personas*.

12. Suzuki Kensaku, "Onnagata ni tsuite" [Regarding the *onnagata*], in *Kakushinseru Mukōjima satsueijo*, 14.

13. For more on this bulletin, see Lewis, "*Blood and Soul* (1923)."

14. Ōi Tadasu, "Mondaigeki to kibungeki" [The problem drama and the mood drama], *Mukōjima* (June 1923), 20.

15. Yamamura Fuyuo, "Randamu inpuresshon" [Random impressions], *Mukōjima* (June 1923), 19.

16. Mikoshiba Morio, "Minshū geijutsu to shite no eiga no kachi" [The value of film as the people's art], *Nikkatsu gahō* (March 1925), 3–4.

17. To raise just two examples: in the November 15, 1923, special earthquake issue of *Nikkatsu gahō*, Negishi's endorsement of cinema: "in order to appreciate other entertainments some amount of cultivation is necessary, but films can be enjoyed without any kind of preparation" (4–5). In "Katsudō shashin no hanashi" [Discussion of motion pictures] in the August 1926 issue of *Nikkatsu gahō*, pioneering director Murata Minoru wrote: "Despite the fact that the essence of cinema remains a very difficult subject, there is nothing so easy to become quickly familiar with as the cinema, and so anyone can easily review films. . . . For this very reason, it is a truly democratic [*demokuratikku na*] *misemono* [attraction]. One could say, 'Until now, I have never seen a film because I

despise the movies, but yesterday I saw one for the first time . . .' and begin a review straight away" (2). Murata goes on to say that the same ease applies to movie-making; it may take as little as a month to become a famous film actor, director, or technician.

18. Mori Iwao, "Geijutsu ka geijutsu de nai ka" [Is it art or not?], *Kinema junpō* (April 1, 1922), 7.

19. Mikoshiba, "Minshū geijutsu to shite," 3.

20. Mikoshiba, "Minshū geijutsu to shite," 3.

21. Mikoshiba, "Minshū geijutsu to shite," 4.

22. Mikoshiba, "Minshū geijutsu to shite," 4.

23. Mikoshiba Morio, "Yakusha shosei tetsugaku" [Philosophy for the actor], *Nikkatsu gahō* (October 1926), 36–37.

24. Mikoshiba, "Yakusha shosei tetsugaku," 36.

25. Ishikawa Hakuchō, "Kamakura kara Kamata e kaette" [Returning to Kamata from Kamakura], *Kamata* (October 1923), 39.

26. Ishikawa, "Kamakura kara Kamata e kaette," 39.

27. Ishikawa, "Kamakura kara Kamata e kaette," 39–40.

28. Ishikawa, "Kamakura kara Kamata e kaette," 40.

29. Schencking, "1923 Tokyo," 115.

30. Bates, "Fractured Communities," 36–37.

31. The 1925 figure is based on research conducted between August and October 1925 for the *Nihon eiga jigyō sōran*, 129. The count from 1922 is taken from Bates, "Fractured Communities," 36–37.

32. Komatsu, "Foundation of Modernism," 364.

33. Publishers were sustained by an enormous demand for books after the earthquake destroyed libraries, private collections, and the standing supplies of Tokyo booksellers. Subject matter expanded in both directions, with increasingly specialized titles catering to niche audiences vying with the newfound popularity of *sōgō zasshi*, or general interest magazines. See Mack, *Manufacturing Modern Japanese Literature*, 64–65. According to Silverberg in *Erotic Grotesque Nonsense*, between 1918 and 1932 the number of current registered periodicals increased from 3,123 to 11,118 (24).

34. Bates, "Wrath of Heaven," 39.

35. For Japanese film releases, see the table "Taishō jūsannendo Nihon eiga fūkirisū ichiran" [Number of Japanese films released in 1924 at a glance], in *Nihon eiga nenkan*, 458. For foreign film releases, see the table "Taishō jūsannendo gaikoku eiga fūkirisū ichiran" [Number of foreign films released in 1924 at a glance], 456–57. In late 1927, *Kinema junpō* estimated the daily number of admissions nationwide at 431,193. This would put admissions at nearly 130 million per month in 1927. See Komatsu, "Foundation of Modernism," 364.

36. See *Kinema junpō* (February 1, 1927), 6.

37. See Gardner, *Advertising Tower*; Driscoll, *Absolute Erotic, Absolute Grotesque*; Silverberg, *Erotic Grotesque Nonsense*; and Mack, *Manufacturing Modern Japanese Literature.*

38. Some date the emergence of Japanese educational filmmaking even earlier. Peter High points out early film entrepreneur Umeya Shōkichi's success with news actualities, hygiene and science films, and travelogues in the period 1906–11. According to High, "In late 1906, Umeya decided the hallmark of his promotion-distribution enterprise [the

company M. Pathé] should be 'public benefit' and he began seriously importing documentary-type features aimed at educating the masses about the principles of modern science" ("Umeya Shokichi," 124). In addition, Umeya created a sensation with footage of Meiji statesman Itō Hirobumi's funeral and an expedition to Antarctica filmed by cameraman Taizumi Yasunao. See High, "Umeya Shokichi."

39. Standish, *New History of Japanese Cinema*, 134.

40. In *Japanese Cinema between Frames*, Laura Lee argues that "tricks such as the substitution splice were introduced as constitutive ingredients of a more modern, Western, and cinematic film practice" (37). Nevertheless, she also points out, "reformers more or less unanimously detested Makino and Matsunosuke for representing everything backward in Japanese cinema" (32–34).

41. Standish, *New History of Japanese Cinema*, 65.

42. Kasza, *State and Mass Media in Japan*, 72.

43. Kasza, *State and Mass Media in Japan*, 56.

44. See Kato, "Taisho Democracy as the Pre-Stage."

45. See Takemura, *Taishō bunka*.

46. For more on wartime film policy, see High, *Imperial Screen*, and Baskett, *Attractive Empire*.

47. Gordon, *Modern History of Japan*, 111.

48. Gordon, *Modern History of Japan*, 118.

49. Gordon, *Modern History of Japan*, 131.

50. Gordon, *Modern History of Japan*, 132. For more on the 1905–18 riots and contradictions at the heart of Japan's imperial democracy, see Gordon, *Labor and Imperial Democracy*.

51. *Tōkyō shinsairoku*, 12.

52. Schencking, "Great Kanto Earthquake," 303.

53. See Schencking, "Great Kanto Earthquake," 297. Schencking's book *Great Kantō Earthquake* is a far-ranging examination of the factors shaping reconstruction.

4. Desire and Identification

1. Matsumoto Yoshirō, "Kyoei jigoku ni akogareru, kanashiki joyū shigansha!" [Miserable aspiring actresses lured by the hell of vanity!], *Nikkatsu gahō* (February 1926), 12–15.

2. On lasting associations between acting and prostitution, see Kano, *Acting Like a Woman*, 24–27 and 42–43; Fujiki, *Making Personas*, 196–200, 202, and 210.

3. This is also noted by Anselmo in the US context in "Made in Movieland," 150. She describes the negative rhetoric surrounding female film fans' imitative behavior as the industry's "equivocal response" to an increasing dependence on teenage girls, as paying customers and as film workers, during a transitional period characterized by the rise of the star system (134).

4. See Lewis, "Kyoto—The 'Hollywood of Japan.'"

5. This is the context in which Stamp discusses *Traffic in Souls*, *The Inside of the White Slave Traffic*, and other films pertaining to the 1910s white slavery craze. She examines how the American movie theater was linked to thrilling forms of spectatorship and

illicit forms of female circulation, such as kidnapping and prostitution. She points out, as debates over "motion picture morals" in the 1910s shifted from the space of the theater to the subjects onscreen, the tabloid sensationalism of these films blurred the line between what was going on in the movies and crimes supposedly transpiring in the theater itself. Sociologists and critics were troubled by the large female audience turnout at white slavery pictures, even as filmmakers and exhibitors used those same audiences to legitimize the films' supposed educational and moral address. Cinema was believed to exert strong powers of suggestion over the young, impressionable, and mentally impaired (e.g., children, women, and spectators with a history of mental illness or severe recent stress), and it was feared that white slavery films would turn cinematic attraction into actual temptation, causing excitable female viewers to develop a taste for real vice. See Stamp, *Movie-Struck Girls*. For more on movie-struck girls in the United States and United Kingdom, see Stamp, "'It's a Long Way to Filmland'"; Kenaga, "Making the 'Studio Girl'"; O'Rourke, "'On the First Rung'"; Anselmo, "Made in Movieland"; and Anselmo-Sequeira, "Screen-Struck."

6. Stamp, *Movie-Struck Girls*, 94.

7. See Kano, *Acting Like a Woman*.

8. The article "Teikoku Joyū Yōseijo setsuritsu" [Establishment of Imperial Actress Training Center] announced that the center would open on September 1, 1908. Trainees would study literature, arts, and proper makeup application, among other subjects. Women who were between the ages of sixteen and twenty-five and who could be vouched for by two persons residing in the city of Tokyo were eligible for admission. Upon graduation, the women would undertake a two-year practicum at the Imperial Theater, although with the school's permission they might be allowed to perform at other theaters. See *Tōkyō asahi shinbun*, August 7, 1908, morning edition, 7. The earliest ad for the school in the *Asahi shinbun* I have seen is July 31, 1909.

9. "Tōkyō no onna, onna yakusha no gakkō" [Women of Tokyo, school for female players], *Tōkyō asahi shinbun*, September 5, 1909, 5. The article "Tōkyō no onna, risōteki shinjoyū" [Women of Tokyo, the ideal new actress] profiled one of the trainees. *Tōkyō asahi shinbun*, August 30, 1909, 5.

10. See "Shinjoyū (1), yakusha ni naritai onna ga shidai ni ōkunaru" [The new actress (1), more women want to become players], *Tōkyō asahi shinbun*, November 13, 1912, morning edition, 6.

11. In the seventh part of the series, the paper compares various actresses who passed Shōchiku's entrance exam and concludes that those from the Tokyo area are preferable to those from Osaka, Kobe, Kyoto, and other Kansai cities: "For the new actress of the new age, girls who live in the city and breathe the Tokyo air are best—maybe it's hereditary." Of the 123 applicants from Osaka, Kyoto, Kobe, Nagoya, Nara, Okayama, and Wakayama, only 20 girls got callbacks. By comparison, more than half of the girls from the Tokyo region got callbacks. "Shinjoyū (7), Kansai chihō no joyūnetsu, Shōchiku Kaisha no shinboshū" [The new actress (7), actress fever in the Kansai region, Shōchiku company's new recruitment], *Tōkyō asahi shinbun*, November 19, 1912, morning edition, 6.

12. "Kyoei no yume kara, ochiyuku onna jigoku, appare sutā ni narisokone ukikusa no yō na onna no mure," *Tōkyō asahi shinbun*, October 3, 1925, morning edition, 7.

13. "Kyoei no yume kara," 7.

14. "Joyūnetsu no futari shōjo, tomete kudasai to kōban e," *Tōkyō asahi shinbun*, August 1, 1927, morning edition, 7.

15. "Joyū shigansha o kankinshite bōkō, Gojō yūbinkyoku no aku shoki, Shōchiku no kippu nukitori kara roken" [Corrupt clerk at Gojō Post Office who trapped and assaulted aspiring actresses exposed by stolen Shōchiku tickets], *Tōkyō asahi shinbun*, October 24, 1923, morning edition, 2.

16. "Joyū shigan no musume, nijūhachi na taburakasaru, Dai Ichi Kokusai Eiga Kaisha to nanori, kyōhakushite wa ryokan e" [Twenty-eight young aspiring actresses swindled, forced to go to inn by so-called First International Film Company], *Tōkyō asahi shinbun*, September 30, 1926, morning edition, 7.

17. "Eiga joyū boshū de onnatachi o tsuru akkan, sanzan na me ni atta onna futari, ma no te o nogarete sa mayō," *Tōkyō asahi shinbun*, May 31, 1929, evening edition, 2.

18. "Kyoei no danjo o tsuridashita, shinema-dan no shōtai, Dairen ni naku joyū Nemoto Midori kara oyamoto ni kita sukui no denpō" [The true nature of cinema troupe that lured vain men and women, parents receive telegram for help from actress Nemoto Midori crying in Dairen], *Tōkyō asahi shinbun*, October 3, 1925, morning edition, 7.

19. "Sashidashinin fumei de, kita shibō denpō, Manmō shisatsu no ue sharei no kōkoku ni tsurareta, Dairen de taoreta Kiyoshi no jikka," *Tōkyō asahi shinbun*, October 3, 1925, morning edition, 7.

20. "Manchō chihō de shirareta ratsu'ude, danchō Kanda Hiderō no sosei, tsuma wa Shōchiku joyū Takakura Kaneko," *Tōkyō asahi shinbun*, October 3, 1925, morning edition, 7.

21. "Eiga no sutā o kokorozashite, mi o horobashita wakai musume, oya ni somuite mudan de jōkyō, umauma satsueijochō ni uritobasaru, me ga samete umi no namida," *Tōkyō asahi shinbun*, December 25, 1925, morning edition, 7.

22. "Takumi na kōkoku de, chihō no onna o tsuru, karera no yariguchi ni chūiseyo (Suzuki hoan buchō no dan)" [Watch out for the methods of those who lure country girls with clever advertisements (a discussion with security chief Suzuki)], *Tōkyō asahi shinbun*, December 25, 1925, morning edition, 7.

23. Matsumoto, "Kyoei jigoku ni akogareru," and Matsumoto, "Naraku no dontei e, mizukara shizumu joyū shigansha no mure, sore ni shitagau hanzai no iroiro," *Nikkatsu gahō* (October 1926), 52–55.

24. Matsumoto, "Kyoei jigoku ni akogareru," 12.

25. Matsumoto, "Kyoei jigoku ni akogareru," 12.

26. Matsumoto, "Kyoei jigoku ni akogareru," 12.

27. Matsumoto, "Kyoei jigoku ni akogareru," 15.

28. Matsumoto, "Naraku no dontei e," 54.

29. Matsumoto, "Naraku no dontei e," 54.

30. Matsumoto, "Kyoei jigoku ni akogareru," 14.

31. Matsumoto, "Kyoei jigoku ni akogareru," 14.

32. Fujiki, *Making Personas*, 142, 149.

33. Fujiki, *Making Personas*, 148.

34. Fujiki, *Making Personas*, 249.

35. Anselmo, "Made in Movieland," 147.

36. "Katsudō o mite, hōkakyō ni natta, Teidaisei taku no bijin jochū, Fukkoku meijoyū ni kaburete," *Tōkyō asahi shinbun*, March 24, 1921, evening edition, 2.

37. "Joyū shigansha no wakaki onna ga Kamata kenbutsu no shuki, sono jōnin ni okutta tegami yori," *Katsudō sekai* (July 1924), 108–11, 116.

38. "Joyū shigansha no wakaki onna," 109.

39. "Joyū shigansha no wakaki onna," 109.

40. Anselmo-Sequeira, "Screen-Struck," 15.

41. Anselmo-Sequeira, "Screen-Struck," 16.

42. Anselmo-Sequeira, "Screen-Struck," 17.

43. For an analysis of American fan magazines and their inscription of a female reader who is at once "distanced, skeptical, and active as well as . . . relational, intimate, and empathetic" (269), see Studlar, "The Perils of Pleasure?"

44. Stamp, "Wages and Sin."

45. Stamp, "Wages and Sin," 99.

46. Bruno, *Streetwalking on a Ruined Map.*

47. Bruno, *Streetwalking on a Ruined Map*, 51.

48. See also Hansen's argument in *Babel and Babylon* that women's participation in mass culture led to the consolidation of Hollywood's textual and industrial practices during the 1910s by promoting the commodity form of spectatorship. She argues that mass consumer culture transformed women's relationship to the public sphere by blurring the demarcations between public and private and dismantling the stark categories of gender, class, and ethnicity that had limited women's social horizons. Yet Hansen points out, "For middle-class women this meant a liberation from the narrow confines of domestic space, but also, in the long run, the surrender of a traditionally female sphere of influence to the corporately organized sphere of mass consumption" (116). Not only that, women's investments in mass culture were often attacked or disparaged.

49. Anselmo-Sequeira, "Screen-Struck," 23.

50. Anselmo-Sequeira, "Screen-Struck," 1.

51. In *Erotic Grotesque Nonsense*, Silverberg argues that the regional unevenness of interwar Japan has been greatly exaggerated, as the growth of the mass media in the 1920s helped foster a shared modern imaginary that overcame regional differences. She contends that film, radio, magazines, and the recording industry created a "marketplace of mass culture" in which images of modernity were equally available to Japanese in country and city alike (27).

52. Ambaras, *Bad Youth*, 2.

53. Ambaras, *Bad Youth*, 2.

54. Ambaras, *Bad Youth*, 49.

55. Ambaras, *Bad Youth*, 5.

56. Ambaras, *Bad Youth*, 63, 190.

57. Ambaras, *Bad Youth*, 31. For more on the relationship between colonial policies and the regulation of deviance in Japan, see Frühstück, *Colonizing Sex.*

58. The term "permanent film theater" is frequently used to describe venues that specialize in film exhibition and feature architectural elements that lend themselves to this specialization, whether or not these spaces were purpose-built to do so. As the name sug-

gests, in contrast to storefront theaters (retail spaces leased or taken over by exhibitors) and vaudeville halls, permanent film theaters were erected or remodeled to accommodate regular film exhibition, they were billed as venues of film exhibition, and they existed as part of a larger system of production, distribution, and exhibition that helped regularize cinema as a form of commercial entertainment. Still, in the 1910s to the 1930s, many film theaters continued to offer other forms of entertainment, such as entr'acte stage shows. In "Movie Attendance of Japanese Children," Salomon notes, "In 1927, for example, there existed 1,436 theatres that alternated movies with variety and stage attractions—often within the same program—in addition to 1,043 actual cinemas" (153). For more on film theater architecture in the United States, as well as the overlap between film and stage practices, see Paul, *When Movies Were Theater.*

59. See Ueda, "Eiga jōsetsukan no shutsugen," and Ueda, *Nihon eiga sōsōki.*

60. Gerow, *Visions of Japanese Modernity*, 55.

61. For more on cinema and children in this period, see Salomon, "Movie Attendance of Japanese Children."

62. Gerow, *Visions of Japanese Modernity*, 54.

63. Gerow, *Visions of Japanese Modernity*, 57–58.

64. "Jigoma (1): Jigoma to wa nanzoya, katsudō shashin no firumu ni arawareta hanzai kosuinetsu" [Zigomar (1): Just what is *Zigomar?* Fervor for criminal genius revealed by motion picture film], *Tōkyō asahi shinbun*, October 5, 1912, morning edition, 5.

65. "Hatabi no hanzai, hito no atsumari wa hanzai o umu" [Weekend crimes, gatherings of people spawn crimes], *Tōkyō asahi shinbun,* November 8, 1911, morning edition, 5; emphasis added.

66. For more on *ryōki*, see Angles, "Seeking the Strange."

67. Ambaras, *Bad Youth*, 50.

68. Ambaras, *Bad Youth*, 67.

69. For more on degenerate schoolgirls and moral panics on the perceived threat of urban culture, see the chapter "The Lure of the Modern: Imagining the Temporal Spaces of City and Countryside," in Karlin, *Gender and Nation in Meiji Japan.*

70. "Onna dōshi jōshi o hakaru, ichinin wa jūsho ichinin wa buji, koko ni mo hisomu darakusei no zaiaku," *Tōkyō asahi shinbun,* May 6, 1909, morning edition, 5.

71. Taking refuge at or wasting time in the cinema is cited as evidence of delinquency in articles such as "Denniku kiri no hannin wa jūrokusai no shōnen, umaretsuki no shikijōkyō" [Criminal who slashes victims' buttocks is a sixteen-year-old boy, natural-born sex maniac], *Tōkyō asahi shinbun*, December 9, 1913, 5. Other articles describe criminals finding their victims at the movies, such as "Manto akushōnen no ōkō (49), Shitaya Asakusa no jitsurei (zoku), kodomosarai no mokuteki" [Juvenile delinquents rampant throughout the entire city (49), real cases from Shitaya Asakusa (continued), intention to kidnap], *Tōkyō asahi shinbun*, April 15, 1910, morning edition, 6, which describes children at the Denkikan and Sanyūkan being tricked out of their money or lured away with sweets. In an earlier installment (part 47), the head of a girls' school discusses the many love letters sent to the school's twenty or thirty students: over 100 love letters in one year. According to the school, eight or nine out of ten of these letters are invitations to meet in the darkness of a movie theater. "Manto akushōnen no ōkō

(47), Shitaya Asakusa no jitsurei, ankoku no hikaisho" [Juvenile delinquents rampant throughout the entire city (part 47), real cases from Shitaya Asakusa, secret meeting places in the dark], *Tōkyō asahi shinbun*, April 13, 1910, morning edition, 6.

72. "Manto akushōnen no ōkō (50), Shitaya Asakusa no jitsurei (zoku), shinkyo Asakusa shochō no dan, katsudō shashin torishimari no konnan" [Juvenile delinquents rampant throughout the entire city (50), real cases from Shitaya Asakusa (continued), new police chief speaks, the difficulty in regulating moving pictures], *Tōkyō asahi shinbun*, April 16, 1910, morning edition, 6.

73. The chief seems to be responding directly to part 41 in the series, which deals with juvenile delinquency in Hongō ward, in which a school principal expresses concern that the majority of victims in movie theater crimes are young girls. The principal demands gender-segregated seating and suggests that children be forbidden from going to the movies. Despite the geographic focus of the article (Hongō ward), the principal gripes about "places like Asakusa" (*Asakusa-tō*). See "Manto akushōnen no ōkō (41), Hongō no jitsurei, katsudō shashin no torishimari" [Juvenile delinquents rampant throughout the entire city (41), real cases from Hongō, regulating motion pictures], *Tōkyō asahi shinbun*, April 7, 1910, morning edition, 5.

74. "Manto akushōnen no ōkō (50)," 6.

75. "Manto akushōnen no ōkō (54), tōkyokusha no dan" [Juvenile delinquents rampant throughout the entire city (54), authorities speak], in *Tōkyō asahi shinbun*, April 22, 1910, morning edition, 5. See the chapter "Civilizing 'Degenerate Students,'" in Ambaras, *Bad Youth*, for a discussion of different types of Meiji-period delinquents, their dress, and their habits as described by contemporary observers and sensationalized in the popular press.

76. Hur, *Prayer and Play*.

77. See, for instance, Yoshimi, *Toshi no doramaturugī* and *Media jidai no bunka shakaigaku*.

78. One of Yoshimi's best examples in *Toshi no doramaturugī* is the *kankōba*, or modern bazaar. He describes the turn of the century as the height of the *kankōba* age. Shopping became a form of spectating when the first *kankōba*, a precursor to the department store, was established in connection with the First National Industrial Exhibition of 1877. In the *kankōba*'s long stalls, goods were placed on view with price tags visible, allowing visitors to browse without assistance and thus encouraging a completely new kind of visually oriented consumption. By 1902, there were nearly thirty *kankōba* in Tokyo, approximately one-quarter of which were in Ginza (149, 151). Other locations included Ginza, Kyōbashi, Jinbōchō, Nihonbashi, and other commercial neighborhoods. The most famous of these, the Teikoku Hakuhinkan, once boasted nearly 70 shops (151). In "Dawn of Cinema in Japan," High offers another perspective on the theater-building boom. According to High, the entrepreneur Tahata Kenzō heard a rumor that Tokyo city officials were going to limit film theaters by restricting permits to one per city district. Tahata quickly formed a company with his uncle in order to buy up property, clear the land, and claim the permits. Each plot was staked with a sign that said "A Fukuhōdō movie theater is being constructed on this spot." Although Tahata planned to sell the land and permits to existing Tokyo film companies for exorbitant prices once the ordinance went into effect, the ordinance never

came to pass, and Fukuhōdō became a legitimate theater construction company. See High, 50.

79. Lippit, *Topographies of Japanese Modernism*, 121.
80. Foucault, "Of Other Spaces," 23.
81. Mulvey, "Notes on Sirk and Melodrama," 76.
82. Neale, "Melodrama and Tears," 12.
83. Neale, "Melodrama and Tears," 11.
84. Neale, "Melodrama and Tears," 12.
85. Neale, "Melodrama and Tears," 20.
86. Neale, "Melodrama and Tears," 22.
87. See, for instance, Brooks, *Melodramatic Imagination*. Yoshimoto Mitsuhiro writes that while "melodrama articulates the conflict between the old and new social structures and modes of production" (34), rather than essentializing melodrama, it is more useful to historicize the genre and remember that "any generic category is neither more nor less than [a] theoretical construct and that the ultimate purpose of generic criticism is to deconstruct the illusion of the completeness of the genre and to analyze the layers of sedimented ideologemes constructed into a seemingly distinct genre" (33–34). Yoshimoto, "Melodrama, Postmodernism, and Japanese Cinema."
88. Russell, *Cinema of Naruse Mikio*.
89. See Yamamoto Kajirō, *Katsudōya suiro*.

5. Intimacy and Alienation

1. Essential references on Mavo include Weisenfeld, *Mavo*; Omuka, *Nihon no avangyarudo geijutsu*; and Omuka, ed., *Taishōki shinkō bijutsu*.
2. For more on Kikuchi and his magazine *Eiga jidai*, see Lewis, "Kyoto—The 'Hollywood of Japan'"; on Gonda and early film study, see Gerow, *Visions of Japanese Modernity*; on Tanizaki and his film activities, see Lamarre, *Shadows on the Screen*.
3. For instance, see the *zadankai* (roundtable discussion) of the twentieth joint review meeting of *Shinchō* and its remarks on *shinshin sakka* (new authors) in the January 1925 issue of the magazine, or the *zadankai* of the twenty-second meeting (March 1925) and its discussion of the popular novel and newspaper literary columns. Other major articles on the new age of popular culture and the *bundan* include a special edited section featuring nine contributors on the theme "Tsūyoku shōsetsu o donna hyōjun de eramu ka" [What is your criterion for the popular novel?] (June 1925) and essays such as "Bungei no tokushuka to tsūzokuka: Tsūzoku shōsetsu to kongo no bundan" [The rarefication and popularization of literature: The popular novel and the future of the *bundan*], by Kawaji Ryūkō (Kawaki Makoto) (June 1925).
4. Takizawa, "Avangyarudo no 'seikatsu' to 'sakuhin,'" 112–13.
5. Takizawa, "Avangyarudo no 'seikatsu' to 'sakuhin,'" 113.
6. Angles, "Seeking the Strange," 101–2.
7. Omuka, *Nihon no avangyarudo geijutsu*, 7.
8. Hagiwara, "Berlin 1922," 44.
9. Jinno, "Murayama Tomoyoshi no dōga," 50.
10. Hagiwara, "Berlin 1922," 24.

11. Hagiwara, "Berlin 1922," 26.

12. For more on the 1922 congress and the debates on constructivism, see Stephen Bann's introduction to *Tradition of Constructivism*, xxv–xlix.

13. Murayama, *Engekiteki jijōden*, 2:101; quoted in Hagiwara, "Berlin 1922," 28.

14. See Hagiwara, "Berlin 1922."

15. Murayama, *Engekiteki jijoden*, 2:116.

16. For an account of the play's initial publication and early performances, see Schinnerer, "History of Schnitzler's *Reigen*."

17. It is unclear where Murayama saw the play, but it was performed by various companies in Bonn and Paris in February, Christiania in March, Neumünster in June, and Dresden in July 1922. In August, the Kammerspiele of Hamburg toured Holland with the play, where it was censored in several Dutch cities. Despite public denunciations, audience disturbances, stink bombs, mobs storming the theater, and arrests at Viennese performances in 1921, the play was staged without incident in Vienna in March 1922. See Schinnerer, "History of Schnitzler's *Reigen*," 850–54 and 856.

18. Murayama, *Engekiteki jijoden*, 2:122.

19. Murayama, *Engekiteki jijoden*, 2:122.

20. Hagiwara, "Berlin 1922," 41.

21. Bahr, *Master*, 27.

22. Bahr, *Master*, 28.

23. Bahr, *Master*, 87–89.

24. Bahr, *Master*, 88. Ellipses in the original.

25. Note: Duhr was called "Arthur" in the American stage adaptation. I am quoting Glazer's translation, which I have checked against Bahr's original text, but using Bahr's original characters' names.

26. Murayama, *Engekiteki jijoden*, 2:121.

27. Murayama, *Engekiteki jijoden*, 2:122.

28. Sedgwick, "Shame, Theatricality, and Queer Performativity," 37.

29. Sedgwick, "Shame, Theatricality, and Queer Performativity," 36.

30. Sedgwick, "Shame, Theatricality, and Queer Performativity," 37.

31. Sedgwick, "Shame, Theatricality, and Queer Performativity," 36.

32. Sedgwick, "Shame, Theatricality, and Queer Performativity," 38.

33. Sedgwick, "Shame, Theatricality, and Queer Performativity," 38.

34. According to Brian Massumi in "Autonomy of Affect," if feelings are personal and biographical, emotions are social and affects are prepersonal. Massumi suggests that affects are experienced as intensities rather than qualities or categorical states (e.g., "happiness" or "anger"). Affects are unformed and unstructured, and they may be (but not always) precognitive and/or prelinguistic (88–89). Several theorists suggest that affect is closer to "the body" than intellection and more like sensation—for example, a certain affect may arise when blood suddenly flushes the skin or when one shudders involuntarily. For instance, see Tomkins, "What Are Affects?" in *Shame and Its Sisters.*

35. Murayama, *Rensa shinzō kigeki.*

36. Murayama, *Rensa shinzō kigeki*, 22.

37. Murayama, *Engekiteki jijoden*, 2:124.

38. Murayama, *Engekiteki jijoden*, 2:124.

39. See Ōya, "Rensageki ni okeru eiga bamen."

40. Murayama, "Rensageki," 46.

41. Iwamoto has examined the links between these forms in his essay "From *Rensageki* to *Kinodrama*."

42. Murayama, "Rensageki," 6.

43. Murayama, *Rensa shinzō kigeki*, 5–6.

44. Murayama, *Rensa shinzō kigeki*, 17–18.

45. Nomoto Satoshi, "Jii to sentan: 'Mavo' to sono shūken" [Masturbation and the avant-garde: 'Mavo' and its contexts], *Ritsumeikan Gengo Bunka Kenkyū* [Ritsumeikan studies in language and culture] 22, no. 3 (January 2011), 60. Cited in Takizawa, "Avangyarudo no 'seikatsu' to 'sakuhin,'" 91.

46. Takizawa, "Avangyarudo no 'seikatsu' to 'sakuhin,'" 88–93.

47. See Masaki, "Tamashii no hōyō."

48. Murayama, *Rensa shinzō kigeki*, 17–18.

49. Kinoshita, "Mise-en-scène of Desire," 120.

50. The company remained intact until 1929, when an internal rift split Tsukiji Shōgekijō permanently into two companies. As theater historian Brian Powell suggests in "Japan's First Modern Theater," 1926 marked the end of the theater's ascendancy and the close of an era.

51. For instance, see Itō Kōichi's criticism of the use of film projection in the plays *R. U. R.* and *Nebeneinander* at Tsukiji Shōgekijō in "Gekijō eiga kō" [A consideration of films for the theatrical stage], *Tsukiji Shōgekijō* 5, no. 3 (1928), 50–52.

52. Hansen, "Fallen Women, Rising Stars," 11–12.

53. Takizawa, "Avangyarudo no 'seikatsu' to 'sakuhin,'" 87.

54. Takizawa, "Avangyarudo no 'seikatsu' to 'sakuhin,'" 87.

6. Expressive Excess

1. For example, see Lewis, "Media Fantasies."

2. See, for instance, Ito, *Age of Melodrama*; Coutts, "Imagining Radical Women"; Karlin, *Gender and Nation*. As Hansen argues in "Fallen Women, Rising Stars," in silent-era Japanese cinema and Shanghai cinema, "As in other silent cinemas (Russian, Scandinavian, German, French), the contradictions of modernity are enacted through the figure of the woman, very often, literally, across the body of the woman who tries to live them but more often than not fails, who has to become a corpse by the end of the film. As in many nineteenth-century literary traditions, women function as metonymies, if not allegories of urban modernity, figuring the city in its allure, instability, anonymity, and illegibility, which is often suggested through juxtapositions of women's face and bodies with the lights of Shanghai, abstracted into hieroglyphics. In more narrative terms, female protagonists serve as the focus of social injustice and oppression; rape, thwarted romantic love, rejection, sacrifice, prostitution function as metaphors of a civilization in crisis" (15). See also Hansen, "Vernacular Modernism."

3. For more on Hirabayashi and the "feminization of culture," see Harootunian, *Overcome by Modernity*, especially 11–13, and Sato, *New Japanese Woman*, especially 22–25, 39–43, 48, 61, 74–75, and 106–7.

4. Quoted in Satō, *"Kingu" no jidai*, 31.

5. Quoted in Satō, *"Kingu" no jidai*, 28.

6. For a more thorough discussion, see Mack, *Manufacturing Modern Japanese Literature.*

7. Sato, *New Japanese Woman*, 34.

8. In *New Japanese Woman*, Sato notes a few exceptions, such as Chiba Kameo, Hirabayashi Hatsunosuke (who popularized the phrase "the feminization of culture"), and Nii Itaru (61).

9. Ahmed, *Cultural Politics of Emotion*, 91.

10. Ahmed, *Cultural Politics of Emotion*, 93.

11. For another approach to the repetitive use and excessive coding of female bodies in Japanese cinematic texts, see Coates, *Making Icons.*

12. For instance, in "Imagining Radical Women," Angela Coutts groups together a variety of visual representations of women in the Japanese proletarian magazines *Bungei sensen* [Literary front], *Senki* [Battle flag], and *Fujin senki* [Women's battle flag] during 1923–31, which she identifies as carrying negative connotations.

13. For more on the massification debates, see for example, Shea, *Leftwing Literature in Japan*; Karlsson, "Kurahara Korehito's Road to Proletarian Realism"; and Sugino, "Nakano Shigeharu (jō)" and "Nakano Shigeharu (ge)." For an excellent introduction to Nakano, see Silverberg, *Changing Song.*

14. For an introduction to Prokino, see Nornes, *Japanese Documentary Film*; Namiki, *Nihon Puroretaria Eiga Dōmei*; and Makino, "Rethinking the Emergence."

15. Quoted in Frederick, *Turning Pages*, 152.

16. For an analysis of this story, see Karlsson, "Thirst for Knowledge," 346–48.

17. Coutts, "Gender and Literary Production," 180–83. For more on *Nyonin geijutsu*, see Coutts, *Nyonin geijutsu.*

18. See, for instance, Mackie's discussion of the "malestream" proletarian movement's belated recognition of women's interests and the subordination of those interests to Comintern policy in *Creating Socialist Women in Japan*, especially chap. 5. Coutts explores this problem in "How Do We Write a Revolution?"

19. Mackie discusses these debates in *Creating Socialist Women*, 86–93.

20. Sato, *New Japanese Woman*, 19.

21. For more on Kurahara Korehito's essay "Geijutsuteki hōhō ni tsuite no kansō" [Thoughts on artistic method] in the context of his 1928 to 1932 essays on proletarian realism, see Karlsson, "Kurahara Korehito's Road to Proletarian Realism."

22. Bergstrom, "Revolutionary Flesh," 332–34, 338.

23. Bowen-Struyk, "W(h)ither the Nation," 390.

24. Bowen-Struyk, "Introduction," 257–58.

25. See Bowen-Struyk's reading of the story in "W(h)ither the Nation," 382.

26. For an alternative reading of this story, see Bowen-Struyk, "Sexing Class." Whereas my interpretation focuses on the narrator's conflicting feelings of identification and desire, which together produce his split-subjectivity, Bowen-Struyk's reading depends on what she argues is the narrator's desire and *misrecognition* of the "prostitute," which she uses as grounds to criticize the gender politics of the text. While I generally agree with Bowen-Struyk's persuasive reading, I am interested in something different: the narra-

tor's experience of self-alienation and his Lukácsian identification with the prostitute as a subject-object.

27. Hayama, "Prostitute," 56.

28. Hayama, "Prostitute," 57.

29. Original editors' note to the Rogers translation published in Bowen-Struyk and Field, *For Dignity, Justice, and Revolution*, 59: "This sentence contains the first of four excisions in the text as first published and the only time the type was simply effaced and not replaced with the customary Xs or Os. For that reason, we have struck through the twelve Xs inserted in postwar editions." As Bowen-Struyk and Field explain, publishers often practiced self-censorship, obscuring potentially objectionable words and phrases by substituting characters with Xs and Os (*fuseiji*). In some cases, the context and the number of *fuseiji* allowed the reader to guess what words had been removed. In the case of this quoted passage, however, the original text was completely redacted, and although many censored publications were published with the redacted text restored in the postwar, elided text in "The Prostitute" was represented by *fuseiji* in postwar editions.

30. Hayama, "Prostitute," 59–60. I have made some modifications to Rogers's translation with reference to the original Japanese text, Hayama, "Inbaifu," 172.

31. Hayama, "Prostitute," 62.

32. Hayama, "Prostitute," 67.

33. Hayama, "Prostitute," 67.

34. Hayama, "Prostitute," 68.

35. Hayama, "Prostitute," 62. I have made some slight modifications to Rogers's translation based on the original Japanese text, Hayama, "Inbaifu," 174.

36. Emphasis added.

37. Hayama, "Prostitute," 64–65. I have modified Rogers's translation with reference to the original Japanese text, Hayama, "Inbaifu," 177.

38. Lukács, "Reification and the Consciousness of the Proletariat."

39. Lukács, "Reification and the Consciousness of the Proletariat," 155. Original emphasis.

40. Hayama, "Prostitute," 65.

41. Bergstrom, "Revolutionary Flesh," 336.

42. Hayama, "Prostitute," 67.

43. Abbas introduces the idea of critical proximity in his discussion of Hong Kong filmmakers who work within commercial genres even as they explore the disorienting effects of the 1984 Joint Declaration that stipulated Hong Kong's return to China in 1997. In "New Hong Kong Cinema" he writes, "From what vantage point can the filmmaker describe this cultural space and sick eros? Certainly not from the outside, from a privileged critical distance. . . . The position of the Hong Kong filmmaker, then, is what we might call a position of critical proximity, where one is always a part of what one is criticizing. . . . Given commercial pressures, it is understandable that even the most independent of filmmakers find themselves working with popular genres like the gangster (or 'hero') film, the ghost story, and the kung fu movie. What is remarkable, however, is that these filmmakers produce some of their best work within these genres (this is an example of what I mean by critical proximity). . . . By no means parodies of their respective genres, these films use the limits of genre as a discipline and a challenge

(somewhat like writing a poem in rhyme)" (68–69). One may similarly recognize in Hayama's story an attempt to imagine a new set of conditions (in this case, brought about by revolution) while still being unable to fully dislocate from the present.

44. Hayama, "Prostitute," 68.

45. See Fujita, *Gendai eiga no kiten.*

46. Fujita, *Gendai eiga no kiten*, 127.

47. Fujita, *Gendai eiga no kiten*, 98. Fujita's account is somewhat misleading. Beginning in 1928, Sasa Genjū, a member of the Sayoku Gekijō (Left-Wing Theater) trunk theater began using a Pathé Baby 9.5mm camera. He made films of events such as the 1927–28 Noda soy sauce company strike and the 1928 May Day. Some of the films he made in 1928 were shot on 16mm. By 1930, in accordance with policy that embraced political organizing and "bringing politics into the everyday" (*nichijōteki mochikomi*), Prokino members traced the origins of the organization to Sasa's film activities (which took place more than two years before Fujita dates Prokino's first public screening), not the leftist criticism and film theory being produced at *Eiga kōjō* [Film factory] and *Eiga kaihō* [Film emancipation]. It is also worth noting that Prokino made a clear distinction between mobile projection unit screenings in farming villages and workers, which Sasa practiced as early as his first films, and "public screenings" for general audiences in theaters or lecture halls.

48. Fujita's *Gendai eiga no kiten* is an excellent reference for information on these and many lesser known productions that critics regarded as tendency films.

49. Iwasaki's article originally appeared in the June 1930 issue of *Sekai no ugoki* [Movement of the world] and was reprinted in the compilation of his writings *Eiga to shihon shugi.*

50. Iwasaki, "Keikō eiga no mondai," 252.

51. Iwasaki, "Keikō eiga no mondai," 258–60.

52. Kasza, *State and Mass Media in Japan*, 62.

53. Kasza, *State and Mass Media in Japan*, 66.

54. Anderson and Richie, *Japanese Film*, 68.

55. Quoted in Fujita, *Gendai eiga no kiten*, 109.

56. Fujita, *Gendai eiga no kiten*, 109.

57. "Gappyō *Nani ga kanojo o sō saseta ka*" [Joint criticism: *What Made Her Do It?*], *Shinkō eiga*, March 1930, 134–43.

58. Fujimori, *Nani ga kanojo o.*

59. Kimura and Satō, "'Keikō eiga' kara Man'ei e," 246.

60. Kimura and Satō, "'Keikō eiga' kara Man'ei e," 246.

61. Barker, *Tactile Eye*, 3.

62. For instance, see Bordwell's characterization of "flamboyant style" in "Visual Style in Japanese Cinema," as well as Gerow's discussion of Kinugasa Teinosuke's neo perceptionist film *Kurutta ichi peiji* (*A Page of Madness*, 1927), its avant-garde construction, its exhibition with *benshi* narration, and its reception as a conventional melodrama in *Page of Madness.*

63. Kimura and Satō, "'Keikō eiga' kara Man'ei e," 247.

64. See Silverberg, *Erotic Grotesque Nonsense*, and Kinoshita, "Mise-en-scene of Desire."

65. Kinoshita, "Mise-en-scene of Desire," 70–71.
66. Silverberg, *Erotic Grotesque Nonsense*, 29.
67. See Coutts, "Imagining Radical Women."
68. Hayama, "Inbaifu," 172.

Afterword

1. Crary, *Techniques of the Observer*, 6; original emphasis.
2. Gerow, *Visions of Japanese Modernity*, 8.
3. Gerow, *Visions of Japanese Modernity*, 197. In some ways Gerow's description of the interiorized subject echoes Christian Metz's definition of the "transcendental spectator," whose interiority, suspension of disbelief, and sense of identity (which makes possible their capacity for subsequent identifications) makes cinematic signification possible:

> "In the cinema the *subject's knowledge* takes a very precise form without which no film would be possible. This knowledge is dual (but unique). I know I am perceiving something imaginary (and this is why its absurdities, even if they are extreme, do not seriously disturb me), and I know that it is I who am perceiving it. This second knowledge divides me in turn: I know that I am really perceiving, that my sense organs are physically affected, that I am not phantasising, that the fourth wall of the auditorium (the screen) is really different from the other three, that there is a projector facing it (and thus it is not I who am projecting, or at least not all alone), and I also know that it is I who am perceiving all this, that this perceived-imaginary material is deposited in me as if on a second screen, that it is in me that it forms up into an organised sequence, that therefore I am myself the place where this really perceived imaginary accedes to the symbolic by it inauguration as the signifier of a certain type of institutionalised social activity called the 'cinema.'
>
> "In other words, the spectator identifies with himself, with himself as a pure act of perception (as wakefulness, alertness): as the condition of possibility of the perceived and hence as a kind of transcendental subject, which comes before everything there is."

Metz, Imaginary Signifier, 48–49; original emphasis.

4. Gerow, *Visions of Japanese Modernity*, 206.
5. Gerow, *Visions of Japanese Modernity*, 160.
6. Gerow, *Visions of Japanese Modernity*, 160.
7. Gerow, *Visions of Japanese Modernity*, 205–6.
8. Gerow, *Visions of Japanese Modernity*, esp. 226–29.
9. See also Christine Marran's caution against reading sensational media representations of rebellious women and their aberrant expressions of gender and sexuality as necessarily transgressive in *Poison Woman*.
10. Rebecca Wanzo's work on both the invisibility and hypervisibility of black women's suffering in *The Suffering Will Not Be Televised* is an important example of a critical exploration of these issues in another context.

11. Here I am paraphrasing Laura Mulvey's classic essay "Visual Pleasure and Narrative Cinema": "Woman then stands in patriarchal culture as signifier for the male other, bound by a symbolic order in which man can live out his fantasies and obsessions through linguistic command by imposing them on the silent image of woman still tied to her place as bearer of meaning, not maker of meaning." In *Narrative, Apparatus, Ideology*, 199.

12. See Weisenfeld's overview of visual representations of the earthquake and reconstruction in *Imaging Disaster*.

13. For one analysis of how Japanese filmmakers' consciousness of these deficits shaped Japanese film aesthetics and critical discourse, see Miyao, *Aesthetics of Shadow*.

14. See Galbraith and Karlin, "Introduction," 2, and Kaigo, "Social Media in Japan."

15. For discussions of social media and 3/11 that focus on information dissemination and social infrastructure, see Kaigo, "Social Media in Japan"; Bestor, "Disasters, Natural and Unnatural"; and Hjorth and Kim, "Good Grief."

16. Kaigo, "Social Media in Japan," 67.

17. "About JDA," http://jdarchive.org/en/about/about-archive, accessed April 1, 2018.

18. "About JDA," http://jdarchive.org/en/about/about-archive, accessed April 1, 2018.

19. See for instance Karlin, "Precarious Consumption After 3.11," and Fujiki, "Networking Citizens through Film Screenings."

20. A short list of works that have influenced my thinking in this regard includes Saitō, *Beautiful Fighting Girl*; Allison, *Millennial Monsters* and *Precarious Japan*; Fujii, "Intimate Alienation"; Azuma, *Otaku*; Zhang, "Fashioning the Feminine Self"; Galbraith and Lamarre, "Otakuology"; and Lukács, *Scripted Affects, Branded Selves*. These texts informed this book as well as the research and writing for two essays on Japanese media, emotional regulation, and immaterial labor in more recent times: "*Shiage* and Women's Flexible Labor" and "From Manga to Film: Gender, Precarity, and the Textual Transformation of *Air Doll*." These essays were written as I completed this book.

21. Bao, "Trouble with Theater," 363.

Bibliography

Periodicals and Trade Journals

Osaka asahi shinbun (Osaka Asahi newspaper)
Tokyo asahi shinbun (Tokyo Asahi newspaper)
Eiga jidai (Film age)
Eiga kenkyū (Film research)
Kamata
Katsudō rekōdo (Film record)
Katsudō sekai (Movie world)
Kinema junpō (Movie times)
Mukōjima
Nikkatsu gahō (Nikkatsu illustrated)
Shinchō (New currents)
Shinkō eiga (New film)

Books and Articles

Abbas, Ackbar. "The New Hong Kong Cinema and the *Déjà Disparu*." *Discourse* 16, no. 3 (Spring 1994): 65–77.

Ahmed, Sara. *The Cultural Politics of Emotion*. 2nd ed. New York: Routledge, 2015.

Allen, Michael J. "The Price of Identity: The 1923 Kantō Earthquake and Its Aftermath." *Korean Studies* 20 (1996): 64–93.

Allison, Anne. *Millennial Monsters: Japanese Toys and the Global Imagination*. Berkeley: University of California Press, 2006.

———. *Precarious Japan*. Durham, NC: Duke University Press, 2013.

Ambaras, David. *Bad Youth: Juvenile Delinquency and the Politics of Everyday Life in Modern Japan*. Berkeley: University of California Press, 2006.

Anderson, Joseph L., and Donald Richie. *The Japanese Film: Art and Industry*. Expanded ed. Princeton, NJ: Princeton University Press, 1982.

Andrew, Dudley. *What Cinema Is!: Bazin's Quest and Its Charge*. Malden, MA: Wiley-Blackwell, 2010.

Andrew, Dudley, and Hervé Joubert-Laurencin. *Opening Bazin: Postwar Film Theory and Its Afterlife*. New York: Oxford University Press, 2011.

Angles, Jeffrey. "Seeking the Strange: *Ryōki* and the Navigation of Normality in Interwar Japan." *Monumenta Nipponica* 63, no. 1 (2008): 101–41.

Anselmo, Diana W. "Made in Movieland: Imitation, Agency, and Girl Movie Fandom in the 1910s." *Camera Obscura* 32, no. 1 (2017): 129–65.

Anselmo-Sequeira, Diana. "Screen-Struck: The Invention of the Movie Girl Fan." *Cinema Journal* 55, no. 1 (Fall 2015): 1–28.

Aso, Noriko. *Public Properties: Museums in Imperial Japan*. Durham, NC: Duke University Press, 2013.

Azuma Hiroki. *Otaku: Japan's Database Animals*. Translated by Jonathan E. Abel and Shion Kono. Minneapolis: University of Minnesota Press, 2009.

Bahr, Hermann. *The Master*. Adapted by Benjamin F. Glazer. Philadelphia: Nicholas L. Brown, 1918.

Bann, Stephen, ed. *The Tradition of Constructivism*. New York: Viking Press, 1974.

Bao, Weihong. *Fiery Cinema: The Emergence of an Affective Medium in China, 1915–1945*. Minneapolis: University of Minnesota Press, 2015.

———. "The Trouble with Theater: Cinema and the Geopolitics of Medium Specificity." *Framework: The Journal of Cinema and Media* 56, no. 2 (Fall 2015): 350–67.

Barker, Jennifer. *The Tactile Eye: Touch and the Cinematic Experience*. Berkeley: University of California Press, 2009.

Barthes, Roland. "The Third Meaning." Translated by Stephen Heath. In *Image, Music, Text*, edited by Stephen Heath, 52–68. New York: Hill and Wang, 1977.

Baskett, Michael. *The Attractive Empire: Transnational Film Culture in Imperial Japan*. Honolulu: University of Hawai'i Press, 2008.

Bates, Peter Alexander. "Authentic Suffering, Anxious Narrator: Survivor Anxiety in Nagata Mikihiko's 'The Wild Dance of the Flames.'" *Japan Forum* 22, no. 3–4 (2010): 357–80.

———. *The Culture of the Quake: The Great Kanto Earthquake and Taishō Japan*. Ann Arbor: Center for Japan Studies, University of Michigan, 2015.

———. "Fractured Communities: Class and Ethnicity in Representations of the Great Kanto Earthquake." PhD diss., University of Michigan, 2006.

———. "The Wrath of Heaven: The Great Kantō Earthquake and Japanese Cinema." In *Film on the Faultline*, edited by Alan Wright, 36–52. Bristol: Intellect, 2015.

Bazin, André. *What Is Cinema?* Translated by Hugh Gray. 2nd ed. 2 vols. Berkeley: University of California Press, 2004.

Bean, Jennifer M. "Technologies of Early Stardom and the Extraordinary Body." In *A Feminist Reader in Early Cinema*, edited by Jennifer M. Bean and Diane Negra, 404–43. Durham, NC: Duke University Press, 2002.

Bergstrom, Brian. "Revolutionary Flesh: Nakamoto Takako's Early Fiction and the Representation of the Body in Japanese Modernist and Proletarian Literature." *positions: east asian cultures critique* 14, no. 2 (Fall 2006): 311–43.

Berlant, Lauren. *The Female Complaint: The Unfinished Business of Sentimentality in American Culture*. Durham, NC: Duke University Press, 2008.

Bestor, Theodore C. "Disasters, Natural and Unnatural: Reflections on March 11, 2011, and Its Aftermath." *Journal of Asian Studies* 72, no. 4 (November 2013): 763–83.

Bordwell, David. "Visual Style in Japanese Cinema, 1925–1945." *Film History* 7, no. 1 (Spring 1995): 5–31.

Borland, Janet. "Capitalising on Catastrophe: Reinvigorating the Japanese State with Moral Values through Education Following the 1923 Great Kantō Earthquake." *Modern Asian Studies* 40, no. 4 (2006): 875–907.

Bowen-Struyk, Heather. "Introduction: Proletarian Arts in East Asia." In "Proletarian Arts in East Asia," edited by Heather Bowen-Struyk, special issue, *positions: east asia cultures critique* 14, no. 2 (Fall 2006): 251–78.

———. "Sexing Class: 'The Prostitute' in Japanese Proletarian Literature." In *Gender and Labour in Korea and Japan: Sexing Class*, edited by Ruth Barraclough and Elyssa Faison, 10–26. New York: Routledge, 2009.

———. "W(h)ither the Nation in Japanese Proletarian Literature? Imagining an International Proletariat." In "Proletarian Arts in East Asia," edited by Heather Bowen-Struyk, special issue, *positions: east asia cultures critique* 14, no. 2 (Fall 2006): 373–404.

Bowen-Struyk, Heather, and Norma Field, eds. *For Dignity, Justice, and Revolution: An Anthology of Japanese Proletarian Literature*. Chicago: University of Chicago Press, 2015.

Bowser, Eileen. *The Transformation of Cinema: 1907–1915*. Berkeley: University of California Press, 1990.

Brooks, Peter. *The Melodramatic Imagination: Balzac, Henry James, Melodrama, and the Mode of Excess*. New Haven, CT: Yale University Press, 1996.

Bruno, Giuliana. *Streetwalking on a Ruined Map: Cultural Theory and the City Films of Elvira Notari*. Princeton, NJ: Princeton University Press, 1993.

Burch, Noël. *Theory of Film Practice*. Translated by Helen Lane. New York: Praeger, 1973.

———. *To the Distant Observer: Form and Meaning in the Japanese Cinema*. Revised and edited by Annette Michelson. Berkeley: University of California Press, 1979.

Coates, Jennifer. *Making Icons: Repetition and the Female Image in Japanese Cinema, 1945–1964*. Hong Kong: Hong Kong University Press, 2016.

Coutts, Angela. "Gender and Literary Production in Modern Japan: The Role of Female-Run Journals in Promoting Writing by Women during the Interwar Years." *Signs: Journal of Women in Culture and Society* 32, no. 1 (2006): 167–95.

———. "How Do We Write a Revolution? Debating the Masses and the Vanguard in the Literary Reviews of *Nyonin geijutsu*." *Japan Forum* 25, no. 3 (2013): 362–78.

———. "Imagining Radical Women in Interwar Japan: Leftist and Feminist Perspectives." *Signs: Journal of Women in Culture and Society* 37, no. 2 (2012): 325–55.

———, ed. *Nyonin geijutsu*. Special issue, *Japan Forum* 25, no. 3 (2013).

Crary, Jonathan. *Techniques of the Observer: On Vision and Modernity in the 19th Century*. Cambridge, MA: MIT Press, 1990.

Deleuze, Gilles. *Francis Bacon: The Logic of Sensation*. Translated by Daniel W. Smith. Minneapolis: University of Minnesota Press, 2005.

Doane, Mary Ann. *The Desire to Desire: The Woman's Film of the 1940s*. Bloomington: Indiana University Press, 1987.

Driscoll, Mark. *Absolute Erotic, Absolute Grotesque: The Living, Dead, and Undead in Japan's Imperialism, 1895–1945*. Durham, NC: Duke University Press, 2010.

Dym, Jeffrey A. Benshi, *Japanese Silent Film Narrators, and Their Forgotten Narrative Art of* Setsumei*: A History of Japanese Silent Film Narration*. Lewiston, NY: Edwin Mellen Press, 2003.

Flatley, Jonathan. *Affective Mapping: Melancholia and the Politics of Modernism*. Cambridge, MA: Harvard University Press, 2008.

Foucault, Michel. "Of Other Spaces." Translated by Jay Miskowiec. *Diacritics* 16, no. 1 (Spring 1988): 22–27.

Frederick, Sarah. *Turning Pages: Reading and Writing Women's Magazines in Interwar Japan*. Honolulu: University of Hawai'i Press, 2006.

Frühstück, Sabine. *Colonizing Sex: Sexology and Social Control in Modern Japan*. Berkeley: University of California Press, 2003.

Fujii, James. "Intimate Alienation: Japanese Urban Rail and the Commodification of Urban Subjects." *Differences: A Journal of Feminist Cultural Studies* 11, no. 2 (Summer 1999): 106–32.

Fujiki, Hideaki. *Making Personas: Transitional Film Stardom in Modern Japan*. Cambridge, MA: Harvard University Asia Center, 2013.

———. "Networking Citizens through Film Screenings: Cinema and Media in Post-3.11 Social Movements." In *Media Convergence in Japan*, edited by Patrick W. Galbraith and Jason G. Karlin, 60–87. N.p.: Kinema Club, 2016.

Fujimori Seikichi. *Nani ga kanojo o sō saseta ka* [What made her do it?]. In *Fujimori Seikichi zenshū* [The complete works of Fujimori Seikichi], 457–83. Tokyo: Kaizōsha, 1932.

Fujita Motohiko. *Gendai eiga no kiten* [The origin of modern cinema]. Tokyo: Kinokuniya Shoten, 1956.

Fujitani, Takashi. *Splendid Monarchy: Power and Pageantry in Modern Japan*. Berkeley: University of California Press, 1998.

Galbraith, Patrick W., and Jason G. Karlin, "Introduction: At the Crossroads of Media Convergence in Japan." In *Media Convergence in Japan*, edited by Patrick W. Galbraith and Jason G. Karlin, 1–28. N.p.: Kinema Club, 2016.

Galbraith, Patrick W., and Thomas Lamarre. "Otakuology: A Dialogue." In "Fanthropologies," edited by Frenchy Lunning, special issue, *Mechademia* 5 (2010): 360–74.

Gardner, William O. *Advertising Tower: Japanese Modernism and Modernity in the 1920s*. Cambridge, MA: Harvard University Asia Center, 2006.

Garon, Sheldon. *Molding Japanese Minds: The State in Everyday Life*. Princeton, NJ: Princeton University Press, 1998.

Gerow, Aaron A. *A Page of Madness: Cinema and Modernity in 1920s Japan*. Ann Arbor: Center for Japanese Studies, University of Michigan, 2008.

———. *Visions of Japanese Modernity: Articulations of Cinema, Nation, and Spectatorship, 1895–1925*. Berkeley: University of California Press, 2010.

Gordon, Andrew. *Labor and Imperial Democracy in Prewar Japan*. Berkeley: University of California Press, 1991.

———. *A Modern History of Japan: From Tokugawa Times to the Present*. New York: Oxford University Press, 2003.

Gunning, Tom. "Before Documentary: Early Nonfiction Films and the 'View' Aesthetic." In *Uncharted Territory: Essays on Early Nonfiction Film*, edited by Daan Hertogs and Nico De Klerk, 9–24. Amsterdam: Stichting Nederlands Filmmuseum, 1997.

———. "The Cinema of Attractions: Early Film, Its Spectators, and the Avant-Garde." In *Early Cinema: Space, Frame, Narrative*, edited by Thomas Elsaesser and Adam Baker, 56–62. London: British Film Institute, 1990.

———. *D. W. Griffith and the Origins of the American Narrative Film: The Early Years at Biograph*. Urbana: University of Illinois Press, 1991.

———. "'The Whole World Within Reach': Travel Images Without Borders." In *Virtual Voyages: Cinema and Travel*, edited by Jeffrey Ruoff, 25–41. Durham, NC: Duke University Press, 2006.

Hagiwara Ken. "Berlin 1922: Yūgakuchū no kangeki taiken ni miru, genfūkei to shite no konton" [Berlin, 1922: Formative memories of chaos, viewed from the perspective of a spectator abroad]. In *Murayama Tomoyoshi: Gekiteki sentan* [Murayama Tomoyoshi: The theatrical cutting edge], edited by Iwamoto Kenji, 23–52. Tokyo: Shinwasha, 2012.

Hansen, Miriam Bratu. *Babel and Babylon: Spectatorship and American Silent Film*. Cambridge, MA: Harvard University Press, 1991.

———. "Fallen Women, Rising Stars, New Horizons: Shanghai Silent Film as Vernacular Modernism." *Film Quarterly* 54, no. 1 (2000): 10–22.

———. "The Mass Production of the Senses: Classical Cinema as Vernacular Modernism." *Modernism/Modernity* 6, no. 2 (April 1999): 59–77.

———. "Vernacular Modernism: Tracking Cinema on a Global Scale." In *World Cinemas, Transnational Perspectives*, edited by Nataša Ďurovičová and Kathleen Newman, 287–314. New York: Routledge, 2010.

Harootunian, H. D. *Overcome by Modernity: History, Culture, and Community in Interwar Japan*. Princeton, NJ: Princeton University Press, 2000.

Hayama Yoshiki. "Inbaifu" [The prostitute]. In *Nihon no bungaku* [Japanese literature], vol. 39, 167–80. Tokyo: Chūō Kōronsha, 1970.

———. "The Prostitute." Translated by Lawrence Rogers. In *For Dignity, Justice, and Revolution: An Anthology of Japanese Proletarian Literature*, edited by Heather Bowen-Struyk and Norma Field, 53–67. Chicago: University of Chicago Press, 2015.

High, Peter. "The Dawn of Cinema in Japan." *Journal of Contemporary History* 19, no. 1 (January 1984): 23–57.

———. *The Imperial Screen: Japanese Film Culture in the Fifteen Years' War, 1931–1945*. Madison: University of Wisconsin Press, 2003.

———. "Japanese Film and the Great Kanto Earthquake of 1923." *Kokusai Kankei Gakubu kiyō* [Journal of College of International Studies] 1, no. 3 (1985): 1–14.

———. "Umeya Shokichi: The Revolutionist as Impresario." In *Tagen bunka to mirai shakai* [Multiculturalism and future society], 105–34. N.p.: Nagoya University, 2004.

Hjorth, Larissa, and Kyoung-hwa Yonnie Kim. "Good Grief: The Role of Social Mobile Media in the 3.11 Earthquake Disaster in Japan." *Digital Creativity* 22, no. 3 (2011): 187–99.

Hori, Hikari. *Promiscuous Media: Film and Visual Culture in Imperial Japan, 1926–1945.* Ithaca, NY: Cornell University Press, 2017.

Huhtamo, Erkki. "Peristrephic Pleasures: On the Origins of the Moving Panorama." In *Allegories of Communication: Intermedial Concerns from Cinema to the Digital*, edited by Jan Olsson and John Fullerton, 215–48. Bloomington: Indiana University Press, 2004.

Hur, Nam-lin. *Prayer and Play in Late Tokugawa Japan: Asakusa Sensōji and Edo Society.* Cambridge, MA: Harvard University Asia Center Press, 2000.

Itakura Fumiaki. "*Shigeki: Nankō ketsubetsu* (1921-nen) no kanensei negafirumu o dōteisuru" / "Identifying the Nitrate Negative Film of *Shigeki Nanko Ketsubetsu* (1921)." *Kenkyū kiyō / Bulletin of the National Museum of Modern Art, Tokyo* no. 14 (2010): 45–55.

Ito, Ken K. *An Age of Melodrama: Family, Gender, and Social Hierarchy in the Turn-of-the-Century Japanese Novel.* Stanford, CA: Stanford University Press, 2008.

Iwamoto Kenji. "From *Rensageki* to *Kinodrama.*" *Review of Japanese Culture and Society* (December 1998): 1–13.

Iwasaki Akira. *Eiga to shihon shugi* [Film and capitalism]. Tokyo: Oraisha, 1931.

———. "Keikō eiga no mondai." [The tendency film problem]. In Iwasaki Akira, *Eiga to shihon shugi*, 264–76. Tokyo: Oraisha, 1931.

Jinno Yuki. "Murayama Tomoyoshi no dōga ni okeru modanizumu to kodomo sekai: Kindai Nihon ni okeru kodomo no tame no irasutorēshon hyōgen" [Modernism and the world of children in Murayama Tomoyoshi's children's illustrations: Illustrated art for children in modern Japan]. *Design riron* [Design theory] (2009): 47–61.

Kaigo, Muneo. "Social Media in Japan and the Great Eastern Japan Earthquake." In *Social Media and Civil Society in Japan*, edited by Muneo Kaigo, 37–71. Singapore: Palgrave Macmillan, 2017.

Kakushinseru Mukōjima satsueijo [Reforming Mukōjima studio]. Tokyo: Nippon Katsudō Kabushiki Kaisha, 1923.

Kamiya Makiko. "'Kōtaishi toōeiga' to Onoe Matsunosuke: NFC shozō firumu ni miru Taishō kara Shōwa ni kakete no kōtei o meguru media senryaku" / "Film and the Imperial Household in the 1920s Japan: Analyzing Footage of Crown Prince Hirohito Visiting Europe and Onoe Matsunosuke Films in the NFC Collection as Publicity." *Kenkyū kiyō / Bulletin of the National Museum of Modern Art, Tokyo* no. 20 (2016): 35–54.

Kano, Ayako. *Acting Like a Woman in Modern Japan: Theatre, Gender, and Nationalism.* New York: Palgrave, 2001.

Kantō Daishinsai to kiroku eiga: Toshi no shi to saisei [The Great Kanto Earthquake and documentary film: The death of a city and its rebirth]. Edited by Tōkyō Daigaku

21-seiki COE Puroguramu and Tōkyō Kokuritsu Kindai Bijutsukan Firumu Sentā. Tokyo: Tōkyō Daigaku Daigakuin Jinbun Shakaikei Kenkyūka, 2004.

Karlin, Jason. *Gender and Nation in Meiji Japan: Modernity, Loss, and the Doing of History*. Honolulu: University of Hawai'i Press, 2014.

———. "Precarious Consumption After 3.11: Television Advertising in Risk Society." In *Media Convergence in Japan*, edited by Patrick W. Galbraith and Jason G. Karlin, 30–69. N.p.: Kinema Club, 2016.

Karlsson, Mats. "Kurahara Korehito's Road to Proletarian Realism." *Japan Review* 20 (2008): 231–73.

———. "Thirst for Knowledge: Women's Proletarian Literature in *Nyonin geijutsu*." In *Nyonin geijutsu*, edited by Angela Coutts, special issue, *Japan Forum* 25, no. 3 (2013): 346–61.

Kasza, Gregory. *The State and the Mass Media in Japan, 1918–1945*. Berkeley: University of California Press, 1988.

Kataoka Teppei. "The Linesmen." Translated by Gregory Golley. In *For Dignity, Justice, and Revolution: An Anthology of Japanese Proletarian Literature*, edited by Heather Bowen-Struyk and Norma Field, 159–71. Chicago: University of Chicago Press, 2015.

Kato Shūichi. "Taisho Democracy as the Pre-Stage for Japanese Militarism." In *Japan in Crisis: Essays on Taisho Democracy*, edited by Bernard S. Silberman and H. D. Harootunian, 217–36. Princeton, NJ: Princeton University Press, 1974.

Keil, Charlie, and Shelley Stamp, eds. *American Cinema's Transitional Era: Audiences, Institutions, Practices*. Berkeley: University of California Press, 2004.

Kenaga, Heidi. "Making the 'Studio Girl': The Hollywood Studio Club and Industry Regulation of Female Labour." *Film History* 18, no. 2 (2006): 129–39.

Kimura Matsuo and Ishii Toshio, eds. *Ehagaki ga kataru Kantō Daishinsai: Ishii Toshio korekushon* [The Great Kanto Earthquake told through postcards: The Ishii Toshio collection]. Tokyo: Tsuge Shobō, 1990.

Kimura Sotoji and Satō Tadao. "'Keikō eiga' kara Man'ei e" [From the "tendency film" to Man'ei]. In *Musei eiga no kansei* [The formation of the silent film], vol. 2 of *Kōza Nihon eiga* [A course in Japanese cinema], edited by Imamura Shōhei, Satō Tadao, Shindō Kaneto, Tsurumi Shunsuke, and Yamada Yōji, 242–59. Tokyo: Iwanami Shoten, 1986.

Kinoshita, Chika. "Mise-en-scene of Desire: The Films of Mizoguchi Kenji." Ph.D. diss., University of Chicago, 2007.

Kirby, Lynne. *Parallel Tracks: The Railroad and Silent Cinema*. Durham, NC: Duke University Press, 1997.

Kirihara, Donald. *Patterns of Time: Mizoguchi and the 1930s*. Madison: University of Wisconsin Press, 1992.

Kitahara Itoko. "'Kanjō' no media: Josei zasshi no Kantō Daishinsai tokushūgō o tegakari ni" / "Media History of Emotion: Analysis of Special Issues of Women's Magazines on the 1923 Great Kanto Earthquake." *Media shi kenkyū / Media History* 27 (March 2010): 14–31.

———, ed. *Shashinshū: Kantō Daishinsai* [Photo collection: The Great Kanto Earthquake]. Tokyo: Yoshikawa Kōbukan, 2010.

Komatsu Hiroshi. "The Foundation of Modernism: Japanese Cinema in the Year 1927." In "The Year 1927," special issue, *Film History* 17, no. 2/3 (2005): 363–75.

Kōno Kōhei. "Shinsai to kōkishin: Sanwa to bidan no sensēshonarizumu" [The earthquake and curiosity: Sensationalism in *sanwa* and *bidan*]. In *Kantō Daishinsai to kiroku eiga*, edited by Tōkyō Daigaku 21-seiki COE Puroguramu and Tōkyō Kokuritsu Kindai Bijutsukan Firumu Sentā, 113–20. Tokyo: Tōkyō Daigaku Daigakuin Jinbun Shakaikei Kenkyūka, 2004.

LaCapra, Dominick. *Writing History, Writing Trauma*. Baltimore, MD: Johns Hopkins University Press, 2001.

Lamarre, Thomas. *Shadows on the Screen: Tanizaki Jun'ichirō on Cinema and "Oriental" Aesthetics*. Ann Arbor: University of Michigan Press, 2005.

Lee, Laura. *Japanese Cinema between Frames*. Cham, Switzerland: Palgrave Macmillan, 2017.

Lewis, Diane Wei. "*Blood and Soul* (1923) and the Cultural Politics of Japanese Film Reform." *positions: asia critique* 26, no. 3 (August 2018): 450–82.

———. "From Manga to Film: Gender, Precarity, and the Textual Transformation of *Air Doll*." *Screen* 60, no. 1 (Spring 2019): 99–121.

———. "Kyoto—The 'Hollywood of Japan.'" In *A Companion to Japanese Cinema*, edited by David Desser. Malden, MA: Wiley-Blackwell, forthcoming.

———. "Media Fantasies: Women, Mobility, and Silent-Era Japanese Ballad Films." *Cinema Journal* 52, no. 3 (Spring 2013): 99–119.

———. "*Shiage* and Women's Flexible Labor in the Japanese Animation Industry." *Feminist Media Histories* 4, no. 1 (Winter 2018): 115–41.

Lippit, Seiji M. *Topographies of Japanese Modernism*. New York: Columbia University Press, 2002.

Lukács, Gabriella. *Scripted Affects, Branded Selves: Television, Subjectivity, and Capitalism in 1990s Japan*. Durham, NC: Duke University Press, 2010.

Lukács, Georg. "Reification and the Consciousness of the Proletariat." In *History and Class Consciousness: Studies in Marxist Dialectics*, translated by Rodney Livingstone, 83–222. Cambridge, MA: MIT Press, 1971.

Mack, Edward. *Manufacturing Modern Japanese Literature: Publishing, Prizes, and the Ascription of Literary Value*. Durham, NC: Duke University Press, 2010.

Mackie, Vera. *Creating Socialist Women in Japan: Gender, Labour and Activism, 1900–1937*. Cambridge: Cambridge University Press, 1997.

Maeda Ai. "The Development of Popular Fiction in the Late Taishō Era: Increasing Readership of Women's Magazines." Translated by Rebecca Copeland. *Text and the City: Essays on Japanese Modernity*, edited by James A. Fujii, 163–219. Durham, NC: Duke University Press, 2004.

Makino Mamoru. "Rethinking the Emergence of the Proletarian Film League of Japan (Prokino)." Translated by Markus Nornes. In *In Praise of Film Studies,* edited by Aaron Gerow and Markus Nornes, 15–45. Victoria, Canada: Kinema Club.

Marran, Christine L. *Poison Woman: Figuring Female Transgression in Modern Japanese Culture*. Minneapolis: University of Minnesota Press, 2007.

Masaki Yoshikatsu. "Tamashii no hōyō: *Geijutsuka no seikatsu* (1923) ni miru Murayama Tomoyoshi no engekikan" [Embrace of souls: Murayama Tomoyoshi's approach to theater, as seen in *Life of an Artist* (1923)]. In *Murayama Tomoyoshi: Gekiteki sentan*, edited by Iwamoto Kenji, 53–74. Tokyo: Shinwasha, 2012.

Massumi, Brian. "The Autonomy of Affect." *Cultural Critique* no. 31 (Autumn 1995): 83–109.

———. *Parables for the Virtual: Movement, Affect, Sensation*. Durham, NC: Duke University Press, 2002.

Matsuo Shōichi. *Kantō Daishinsai to kaigenrei* [The Great Kanto Earthquake and martial law]. Tokyo: Yoshikawa Kōbunkan, 2003.

Metz, Christian. *The Imaginary Signifier: Psychoanalysis and the Cinema*. Translated by Celia Britton, Annwyl Williams, Ben Brewster, and Alfred Guzzetti. Bloomington: Indiana University Press, 1986.

Miyao, Daisuke. *Aesthetics of Shadow: Lighting and Japanese Cinema*. Durham, NC: Duke University Press, 2013.

Morgan, Daniel. "Rethinking Bazin: Ontology and Realist Aesthetics." *Critical Inquiry* 32, no. 3 (Spring 2006): 443–81.

Mulvey, Laura. "Notes on Sirk and Melodrama." In *Home Is Where the Heart Is: Studies in Melodrama and the Women's Film*, edited by Christine Gledhill, 75–79. London: BFI Publishing, 1987.

———. "Visual Pleasure and Narrative Cinema." In *Narrative, Apparatus, Ideology: A Film Theory Reader*, edited by Philip Rosen, 198–209. New York: Columbia University Press, 1986.

Murayama Kyōichirō. "Mō hitotsu no Shōwa eiga-Monbushō eiga [Another Aspect of Showa-Era Cinema: A Short History of Ministry of Education (Monbusho) Films]." In *In Praise of Film Studies*, edited by Aaron Gerow and Markus Nornes, 176–83. Victoria, Canada: Kinema Club.

Murayama Tomoyoshi. *Engekiteki jijoden* [A dramatic autobiography]. 4 vols. Tokyo: Tōhō Shuppansha, 1970–1974.

———. *Kōseiha kenkyū* [Constructivist research]. Tokyo: Chūō Bijutsusha, 1926. Reprinted with *Genzai no geijutsu to mirai no geijutsu: ichimei, ishikiteki kōsei shugi e no michishirube* [The art of today and the art of tomorrow: Or, the road to conscious constructivism]. Tokyo: Honnoizumisha, 2002.

———. *Rensa shinzō kigeki, geijutsuka no seikatsu (aruiwa, operetta, geijutsuka no seikatsu to shinzō)* [A linked heart comedy, life of an artist (Or, an operetta, life and heart of an artist)]. In *Fukkokuban kindai bungei zasshi kishō jisshi* [Ten rare modern literary journal reprints]. Tokyo: Yūshōdō Shuppan, 2007.

———. "Rensageki" [The Chain Drama]. *Engeki/eiga* (1926).

Nakazawa Wataru. "Bunshin to hyōi: Ōizumi Kokuseki no *Chi to rei*" [Self and possession: Ōizumi Kokuseki's *Blood and Soul*]. *Shōnan Kokusai Joshi Tanki Daigaku kiyō* [Shōnan Women's Junior College bulletin] 6 (February 1999): 98–114.

Namiki Shinsaku. *Nihon Puroretaria Eiga Dōmei (Prokino) Zenshi* [A complete history of the Proletarian Film League of Japan (Prokino)]. Tokyo: Gōdō Shuppan, 1986.

Neale, Steve. "Melodrama and Tears." *Screen* 27, no. 6 (1986): 6–22.

Nihon eiga jigyō sōran Taishō jūgonen [Japan film trade review 1926]. Tokyo: Kokusai Eiga Tsūshinsha, 1926.

Nihon eiga nenkan Taishō jūsan-jūyonnen [Japan film yearbook 1924–25]. Tokyo: Tōkyō Asahi Shinbun Hakkōsho, 1925.

Nikkatsu gojūnenshi [Nikkatsu's fifty-year history]. Tokyo: Nikkatsu Kabushiki Kaisha, 1962.

Nikkatsu shijūnenshi [Nikkatsu's forty-year history]. Tokyo: Nikkatsu Kabushiki Kaisha, 1952.

Nishimoto Hajime. "Eiga to Monbushō (jō): Tōsei jidai no ichikōsatsu" / "Movie, Audiovisual Education and the Ministry of Education, Science and Culture (Part 1)." *Hokkaidō Daigaku Kyōiku Gakubu kiyō / The Annual Reports on Educational Science* 67 (1995): 259–92.

Noda Shinkichi. *Nihon dokyumentarī eiga zenshi* [A complete history of the Japanese documentary]. Tokyo: Shakai Shisōsha, 1984.

Nornes, Abé Mark. *Japanese Documentary Film: The Meiji Era through Hiroshima*. Minneapolis: University of Minnesota Press, 2003.

Omuka Toshiharu. *Nihon no avangyarudo geijutsu: "Mavo" to sono jidai* [Japan's avant-garde art: "Mavo" and its times]. Tokyo: Seidosha, 2001.

———, ed. *Taishōki shinkō bijutsu shiryō shūsei* [Collection of materials on Taishō-era avant-garde art]. Tokyo: Kokusho Kankōkai, 2006.

O'Rourke, Chris. "'On the First Rung of the Ladder of Fame': Would-Be Cinema Stars in Silent-Era Britain." *Film History* 26, no. 3 (2014): 84–105.

Ōsawa Jō, "Kantō Daishinsai kiroku eigagun no dōtei to bunseki—NFC shozoku firumu o chūshin to shite" / "Classification and Identification of the Documentary Films about the Great Kanto Earthquake—from the NFC Collection." *Kenkyū kiyō / Bulletin of the National Museum of Modern Art, Tokyo* no. 17 (2013): 48–62.

Ōya Atsuko. "Rensageki ni okeru eiga bamen no hyōka o megutte" [Regarding the reception of film scenes in *rensageki*]. *Āto risāchi* [Art research] 10 (2010): 51–60.

Parikka, Jussi. *What Is Media Archaeology?* Malden, MA: Polity Press, 2012.

Paul, William. *When Movies Were Theater: Architecture, Exhibition, and the Evolution of American Film*. New York: Columbia University Press, 2016.

Powell, Brian. "Japan's First Modern Theater: The Tsukiji Shōgekijō and Its Company, 1924–26." *Monumenta Nipponica* 30, no. 1 (Spring 1975): 69–85.

Rodowick, D. N. *The Virtual Life of Film*. Cambridge, MA: Harvard University Press, 2007.

Rosen, Philip, ed. *Narrative, Apparatus, Ideology: A Film Theory Reader*. New York: Columbia University Press, 1986.

Russell, Catherine. *The Cinema of Naruse Mikio: Women and Japanese Modernity*. Durham, NC: Duke University Press, 2008.

Ryang, Sonia. "The Great Kanto Earthquake and the Massacre of Koreans in 1923: Notes on Japan's Modern National Sovereignty." *Anthropological Quarterly* 76, no. 4 (2003): 691–708.

Saitō Tamaki. *Beautiful Fighting Girl.* Translated by J. Keith Vincent and Dawn Lawson. Minneapolis: University of Minnesota Press, 2011.

Salomon, Harald. "Movie Attendance of Japanese Children and Youth: The Ministry of Education's Policies and the Social Diffusion of Cinema, 1910–45." *Japonica Humboldtiana* 6 (2002): 141–66.

Sato, Barbara. *The New Japanese Woman: Modernity, Media, and Women in Interwar Japan.* Durham, NC: Duke University Press, 2003.

Satō Takumi. *"Kingu" no jidai: kokumin taishū zasshi no kōkyōsei* [The age of *King*: The public-ness of national mass magazines]. Tokyo: Iwanami Shoten, 2002.

Schencking, J. Charles. "Catastrophe, Opportunism, Contestation: The Fractured Politics of Reconstructing Tokyo following the Great Kantō Earthquake of 1923." *Modern Asian Studies* 40, no. 4 (2006): 833–73.

———. *The Great Kantō Earthquake and the Chimera of National Reconstruction in Japan.* New York: Columbia University Press, 2013.

———. "The Great Kanto Earthquake and the Culture of Catastrophe and Reconstruction in 1920s Japan." *Journal of Japanese Studies* 34, no. 2 (Summer 2008): 295–331.

———. "1923 Tokyo as a Devastated War and Occupation Zone: The Catastrophe One Confronted in Post Earthquake Japan." *Japanese Studies* 29, no. 1 (May 2009): 111–29.

Schinnerer, Otto P. "The History of Schnitzler's *Reigen*." *PMLA* 46, no. 3 (September 1931): 839–59.

Schivelbusch, Wolfgang. *The Railway Journey: The Industrialization of Time and Space in the 19th Century.* Berkeley: University of California Press, 1986.

Sedgwick, Eve Kosofsky. "Shame, Theatricality, and Queer Performativity: Henry James's *The Art of the Novel*." In Eve Kosofsky Sedgwick, *Touching Feeling: Affect, Pedagogy, Performativity*, 35–65. Durham, NC: Duke University Press, 2003.

———. *Touching Feeling: Affect, Pedagogy, Performativity.* Durham, NC: Duke University Press, 2003.

Shea, G. T. *Leftwing Literature in Japan: A Brief History of the Proletarian Literary Movement.* Tokyo: Hōsei University Press, 1964.

Silverberg, Miriam Rom. *Changing Song: The Marxist Manifestos of Nakano Shigeharu.* Princeton, NJ: Princeton University Press, 1990.

———. *Erotic Grotesque Nonsense: The Mass Culture of Japanese Modern Times.* Berkeley: University of California Press, 2006.

Stamp (Lindsey), Shelley. "'It's a Long Way to Filmland': Starlets, Screen Hopefuls, and Extras in Early Hollywood." In *American Cinema's Transitional Era: Audiences, Institutions, Practices*, edited by Charlie Keil and Shelley Stamp, 332–51. Berkeley: University of California Press, 2004.

———. *Movie-Struck Girls: Women and Motion Picture Culture after the Nickelodeon.* Princeton, NJ: Princeton University Press, 2000.

———. "Wages and Sin: *Traffic in Souls* and the White Slavery Scare." *Persistence of Vision* 9 (1991): 90–102.

Standish, Isolde. *A New History of Japanese Cinema: A Century of Narrative Film.* New York: Continuum, 2006.

Studlar, Gaylyn. "The Perils of Pleasure? Fan Magazine Discourse as Women's Commodified Culture in the 1920s." In *Silent Film*, edited by Richard Abel, 263–97. New Brunswick, NJ: Rutgers University Press, 1996.

———. "Visual Pleasure and the Masochistic Aesthetic." *Journal of Film and Video* 37, no. 2 (Spring 1985): 5–26.

Sugino Yōkichi. "Nakano Shigeharu to geijutsu taishūka ronsō: 'Tō' to no deai e no michi (jō)" / "Nakano Shigeharu and the Controversy on Popularization of Art." *Japanese Literature* 24, no. 4 (1975): 1–10.

———. "Nakano Shigeharu to geijutsu taishūka ronsō: 'Tō' to no deai e no michi (ge)" / "Nakano Shigeharu and the Controversy on Popularization of Art (Continued)." *Japanese Literature* 24, no. 7 (1975): 46–59.

Taishō Shinsaishi shashinchō [Token of the Taishō Earthquake photo collection]. Edited by the Naimushō Shakaikyoku [Home Ministry, Bureau of Social Affairs]. Tokyo: Naimushō Shakaikyoku, 1926.

Takemura Tamio. *Taishō bunka* [Taishō culture]. Tokyo: Kodansha, 1980.

Takizawa Kyōji. "Avangyarudo no 'seikatsu' to 'sakuhin': Murayama Tomoyoshi, 1922–1927" [Avant-garde "life" and "works": Murayama Tomoyoshi, 1922–1927]. In *Murayama Tomoyoshi: Gekiteki sentan* [Murayama Tomoyoshi: The theatrical cutting edge], edited by Iwamoto Kenji, 75–118. Tokyo: Shinwasha, 2012.

Tochigi Akira and Tsuneishi Fumiko. "Jōei eiga kaisetsu" [Notes on films screened]. In *Kantō Daishinsai to kiroku eiga*, edited by Tōkyō Daigaku 21-seiki COE Puroguramu and Tōkyō Kokuritsu Kindai Bijutsukan Firumu Sentā, 11–15. Tokyo: Tōkyō Daigaku Daigakuin Jinbun Shakaikei Kenkyūka, 2004.

Tōkyō Shinsairoku [Record of the Tokyo Earthquake]. Tokyo: Tōkyō Shinyakusho, 1926.

Tomita Mika. "Eiga toshi Kyōto ni okeru eiga bunka no seisei to juyō ni tsuite" [Regarding the formation and reception of film culture in film city Kyoto]. *Kyōto āto entateinmento sōsei kenkyū* [Research on the beginnings of Kyoto art and entertainment] (2003): 41–44.

Tomkins, Silvan. *Shame and Its Sisters: A Silvan Tomkins Reader.* Edited by Eve Kosofsky Sedgwick and Adam Frank. Durham, NC: Duke University Press, 1995.

Tsuneishi Fumiko. "1923-nen no 'gekishin': Kantō Daishinsai no dokyumento" [The "Severe Earthquake" of 1923: Documents on the Great Kanto Earthquake]. In *Eiga to shashin wa toshi o dō egaita ka* [How was the city depicted in film and photography?], edited by Takahashi Seori. Tokyo: Wejji, 2007.

Ueda Manabu. "Eiga jōsetsukan no shutsugen to henyō: 1900-nendai no Denkikan to sono kankyaku kara" [The appearance and transformation of purpose-built film theaters: The Denkikan and its patrons in the 1900s]. *Āto risāchi* [Art research] 9 (March 2009): 49–59.

———. *Nihon eiga sōsōki no kōgyō to kankyaku: Tōkyō to Kyōto o chūshin ni* [Entertainment and audiences in the early period of Japanese cinema: Focus on Tokyo and Kyoto]. Tokyo: Waseda Daigaku Shuppanbu, 2012.

Wang Jing. "Kantō Daishinsai to kōkū shashin" [The Great Kanto Earthquake and aerial photography]. In *Kankyō ni kokuinsareta ningen katsudō oyobi saigai no konseki kaidoku / Interpretation of the Traces of Human Activity and Natural Disasters Inscribed into the Environments*, 147–79. Yokohama: Kanagawa Daigaku 21-seiki COE Puroguramu "Jinrui Bunka Kenkyū No Tame No Himoji Shiryō No Taikeika" Kenkyū Suishin Kaigi, 2007.

Wanzo, Rebecca. *The Suffering Will Not Be Televised: African American Women and Sentimental Political Storytelling*. Albany: State University of New York Press, 2009.

Weisenfeld, Gennifer. *Imaging Disaster: Tokyo and the Visual Culture of Japan's Great Earthquake of 1923*. Berkeley: University of California Press, 2012.

———. *Mavo: Japanese Artists and the Avant-Garde, 1905–1931*. Berkeley: University of California Press, 2002.

Yamada Shōji. "Kantō Daishinsai to gendai: Shinsaiji no chōsenjin satsugai jiken to kokka sekinin / minshū sekinin" [The Great Kanto Earthquake and contemporary times: The earthquake's Korean massacres and state responsibility / the people's responsibility]. In *Sekaishi to shite no Kantō Daishinsai: Ajia, kokka, minshū* [The Great Kanto Earthquake as social history: Asia, nation, people]. Tokyo: Nihon Keizai Hyōronsha, 1994.

Yamamoto Kajirō. *Katsudōya suiro* [Waterways of a movie-maker]. Tokyo: Chikuma Shobō, 1965.

Yoshimi Shun'ya. *Media jidai no bunka shakaigaku* [A cultural sociology of the age of media]. Tokyo: Shin'yōsha, 1994.

———. *Toshi no doramaturugī: Tōkyō sakariba no shakaishi* [Urban dramaturgy: A social history of Tokyo's entertainment centers]. Tokyo: Kōbundō, 1987.

Yoshimoto Mitsuhiro. "Melodrama, Postmodernism, and Japanese Cinema." In *Melodrama and Asian Cinema*, edited by Wimal Dissanayake, 101–26. New York: Cambridge University Press, 1993.

Zhang, Lin. "Fashioning the Feminine Self in 'Prosumer Capitalism': Women's Work and the Transnational Reselling of Western Luxury Online." *Journal of Consumer Culture* 17, no. 2 (February 2015): 184–204.

Index

Page numbers for figures are in italics.

Harvard East Asian Monographs
(most recent titles)

400. Miya Elise Mizuta Lippit, *Aesthetic Life: Beauty and Art in Modern Japan*
401. Brian Steininger, *Chinese Literary Form in Heian Japan: Poetics and Practice*
402. Lisa Yoshikawa, *Making History Matter: Kuroita Katsumi and the Construction of Imperial Japan*
403. Michael P. Cronin, *Osaka Modern: The City in the Japanese Imaginary*
404. Soyoung Suh, *Naming the Local: Medicine, Language, and Identity in Korea since the 15th Century*
405. Yoon Sun Yang, *From Domestic Women to Sensitive Young Men: Translating the Individual in Early Colonial Korea*
406. Michal Daliot-Bul and Nissim Otmazgin, *The Anime Boom in the United States: Lessons for Global Creative Industries*
407. Nathan Hopson, *Ennobling the Savage Northeast: Tōhoku as Japanese Postwar Thought, 1945–2011*
408. Michael Fuller, *An Introduction to Chinese Poetry: From the Canon of Poetry to the Lyrics of the Song Dynasty*
409. Tie Xiao, *Revolutionary Waves: The Crowd in Modern China*
410. Anne Reinhardt, *Navigating Semi-Colonialism: Shipping, Sovereignty, and Nation-Building in China, 1860–1937*
411. Jennifer E. Altehenger, *Legal Lessons: Popularizing Laws in the People's Republic of China, 1949–1989*
412. Halle O'Neal, *Word Embodied: The Jeweled Pagoda Mandalas in Japanese Buddhist Art*
413. Maren A. Ehlers, *Give and Take: Poverty and the Status Order in Early Modern Japan*
414. Chieko Nakajima, *Body, Society, and Nation: The Creation of Public Health and Urban Culture in Shanghai*
415. Pu Wang, *The Translatability of Revolution: Guo Moruo and Twentieth-Century Chinese Culture*
416. Hwansoo Kim, *The Korean Buddhist Empire: A Transnational History (1910–1945)*
417. Joshua Hill, *Voting as a Rite: A History of Elections in Modern China*
418. Kirsten L. Ziomek, *Lost Histories: Recovering the Lives of Japan's Colonial Peoples*
419. Claudine Ang, *Poetic Transformations: Eighteenth-Century Cultural Projects on the Mekong Plains*
420. Evan N. Dawley, *Becoming Taiwanese: Ethnogenesis in a Colonial City, 1880s–1950s*
421. James McMullen, *The Worship of Confucius in Japan*
422. Nobuko Toyosawa, *Imaginative Mapping: Landscape and Japanese Identity in the Tokugawa and Meiji Eras*
423. Pierre Fuller, *Famine Relief in Warlord China*
424. Diane Wei Lewis, *Powers of the Real: Cinema, Gender, and Emotion in Interwar Japan*